"With his characteristic clarity and literary insight, Joel Green helps us attune our ears to the Letter of James and its message concerning the embodied life of faith. Not only is Green's commentary a welcome addition to the renowned New Testament Library series, but it also provides an indispensable guide to the wisdom of the eminently practical theologian known as James."

—Brittany E. Wilson, Associate Professor of New Testament,
Duke University Divinity School

"Joel Green's commentary on the book of James is a masterful blend of clarity and depth. He presents James as a practical theologian, deeply attuned to the pressing realities of his time. By illuminating the social struggles of Jews in the diaspora and drawing meaningful connections to contemporary challenges, Green offers a fresh and compelling perspective on the enduring relevance of James's call to justice, faith, and action. This commentary is an indispensable resource for scholars, pastors, and anyone seeking a profound engagement with this transformative epistle."

—Ekaputra Tupamahu, Associate Professor
of New Testament, Portland Seminary

"Green's commentary demonstrates that he has taken his own advice: he has read and reread the letter of James such that he sounds very similar to his muse. His prose is elegant and clear-sighted, and the commentary is dense in its richness without being loquacious. In addition to exposition of the grand themes that provide insight into the letter itself, like single-mindedness and the deep influence of Jesus's teaching, nuggets of wisdom appear throughout the volume, instructing readers on the virtues of faithful New Testament interpretation. This is commentary writing at the master level: not a string of obvious restatements of the scriptural text, whose lack of ingenuity barely qualify for the moniker 'comment,' but a wise invitation that sets the reader before the biblical text 'for the sake of having our dispositions and reflexes shaped by James-as-Scripture.' Green prepares me and compels me to *want* to read James; there is no higher praise for a commentary."

—Amy Peeler, Kenneth T. Wessner Professor
of New Testament, Wheaton College

"In this thoroughly engaging and deeply insightful commentary on the Epistle of James, Joel B. Green masterfully explores the first-century contexts of the epistle and illuminates modern contexts. James emerges as a practical theologian who speaks powerfully to two of the troubling issues of our time—growing poverty amid scandalous wealth and incendiary rhetoric in public discourse. A must-read for pastors and academics who care about these issues."
—Raj Nadella, Samuel A. Cartledge Associate Professor of New Testament, Columbia Theological Seminary

"Professor Green has crafted a coherent and carefully argued ethical reading of what can appear to be disjointed exhortations in a Jewish Christian writing of little interest to twenty-first-century believers. Providing a user-friendly translation, helpful charts, and careful attention to the resources James drew on from the Old Testament and Jesus tradition, Green finds contemporary challenges for readers to act according to God's vision of the world. In today's media environment, the detailed presentation of a Christian 'speech ethic' and the significance of metaphors for strengthening communal bonds is particularly illuminating."
—Pheme Perkins, Professor of New Testament and Joseph Professor of Catholic Spirituality, Boston College

"Preachers and teachers in the church often avoid James. Joel Green's commentary will change that, showing once and for all that James never was and certainly is not now an 'epistle of straw.' With historical and rhetorical insight, Green demonstrates how James is a powerful practical theology that shapes the vocation of Christian individuals and communities over against ancient and contemporary societal values that do harm to the vulnerable."
—O. Wesley Allen, Jr., Lois Craddock Perkins Professor of Homiletics, Perkins School of Theology, Southern Methodist University

JAMES

THE NEW TESTAMENT LIBRARY

Editorial Advisory Board

Joel B. Green

James

A Commentary

WESTMINSTER
JOHN KNOX PRESS
LOUISVILLE · KENTUCKY

© 2025 Joel B. Green

First edition
Published by Westminster John Knox Press
Louisville, Kentucky

25 26 27 28 29 30 31 32 33 34—10 9 8 7 6 5 4 3 2 1

Unless otherwise indicated, translations from the Letter of James are by the author.

Scripture quotations marked NRSV are from the New Revised Standard Version of the Bible, copyright © 1989 by the Division of Christian Education of the National Council of the Churches of Christ in the U.S.A. Used by permission.

Scripture quotations marked NRSVue are from the New Revised Standard Version Updated Edition. Copyright © 2021 National Council of the Churches of Christ in the United States of America. Used by permission. All rights reserved worldwide.

Scripture quotations marked CEB are from the *Common English Bible*, © 2011 Common English Bible. All rights reserved. Used by permission.

Scripture quotations marked NETS are taken from *A New English Translation of the Septuagint*, © 2007 by the International Organization for Septuagint and Cognate Studies, Inc. Used by permission of Oxford University Press. All rights reserved.

Scripture quotations marked NIV are from The Holy Bible, New International Version. Copyright © 1973, 1978, 1984, 2011 by Biblica, Inc.® Used by permission. All rights reserved worldwide.

See pp. 12–13, "Translations and Acknowledgments," for other permission information.

Book design by Jennifer K. Cox

Library of Congress Cataloging-in-Publication Data is on file
at the Library of Congress, Washington, D.C.

ISBN: 9780664221393

Most Westminster John Knox Press books are available at special quantity discounts when purchased in bulk by corporations, organizations, and special-interest groups. For more information, please email SpecialSales@wjkbooks.com.

To
Pamela
"Make it plain!"

CONTENTS

ABBREVIATIONS

General

&	and
/	or
§(§)	paragraph(s) or section(s)
×	times
AT	author's translation
BCE	before the Common Era
ca.	circa
CE	Common Era
cf.	*confer*, confer, compare
ch(s).	chapter(s)
ed(s).	edition, editor(s), edited by
e.g.	*exempli gratia*, for example
esp.	especially
ET	English Translation
et al.	*et alia*, and others
etc.	*et cetera*, and so forth, and the rest
Gk.	Greek
Heb.	Hebrew
i.e.	*id est*, that is
κτλ	καὶ τὰ λοιπά (= and the rest; etc.)
Lat.	Latin
LXX	Septuagint
ms(s).	manuscript(s)
n(n).	note(s)
NT	New Testament
OT	Old Testament
p(p).	page(s)
pl.	plural
rev.	revised
sg.	singular

trans.	translated by
US$	U.S. dollar(s)
v(v).	verse(s)
vol(s).	volume(s)

Biblical and Other Ancient Texts

Old Testament

Gen	Genesis
Exod	Exodus
Lev	Leviticus
Num	Numbers
Deut	Deuteronomy
Josh	Joshua
Judg	Judges
1 Sam	1 Samuel
2 Sam	2 Samuel
1 Kgs	1 Kings
2 Kgs	2 Kings
1 Chr	1 Chronicles
2 Chr	2 Chronicles
Neh	Nehemiah
Ps(s)	Psalm(s)
Prov	Proverbs
Eccl	Ecclesiastes
Isa	Isaiah
Jer	Jeremiah
Lam	Lamentations
Ezek	Ezekiel
Hos	Hosea
Hab	Habakkuk
Zech	Zechariah
Mal	Malachi

New Testament

Matt	Matthew
Rom	Romans
1 Cor	1 Corinthians
2 Cor	2 Corinthians
Gal	Galatians

Eph	Ephesians
Phil	Philippians
Col	Colossians
1 Thess	1 Thessalonians
1 Tim	1 Timothy
2 Tim	2 Timothy
Phlm	Philemon
Heb	Hebrews
Jas	James
1 Pet	1 Peter
2 Pet	2 Peter
Rev	Revelation

Apocrypha/Deuterocanonicals

2 Esd	2 Esdras
4 Macc	4 Maccabees
Sir	Sirach, Wisdom of
Tob	Tobit
Wis	Wisdom

Pseudepigrapha

Apoc. Ab.	Apocalypse of Abraham
2 Bar.	2 Baruch (Syriac Apocalypse)
1 En.	1 Enoch
3 En.	3 Enoch
Jub.	Jubilees
Let. Aris.	Letter of Aristeas
Pss. Sol.	Psalms of Solomon
T. Ab.	Testament of Abraham
T. Iss.	Testament of Issachar
T. Jac.	Testament of Jacob
T. Job	Testament of Job
T. Sim.	Testament of Simeon

Dead Sea Scrolls

| CD | Cairo Genizah copy of the Damascus Document |
| 1QS | Rule of the Community |

Apostolic Fathers

Barn.	Barnabas (Epistle of)
1 Clem.	1 Clement
2 Clem.	2 Clement
Did.	Didache

Other Ancient Writings

Cicero

    Amic.   *De amicitia*

Josephus

    Ant.   *Antiquities of the Jews*

Origen

    Hom. Luc.   *Homiliae in Lucam*

Philo

    Abraham   *On the Life of Abraham*
    Sobriety   *On Sobriety*
    Spec. Laws   *On the Special Laws*

Seneca

    Ira   *De ira*

Modern Literature

AB	Anchor Bible
ABD	*The Anchor Bible Dictionary.* 6 vols. Edited by David Noel Freedman. New York: Doubleday, 1992.
AGJU	Arbeiten zur Geschichte des antiken Judentums und des Urchristentums
ASV	American Standard Version
AV	Authorized (King James) Version
BDAG	Bauer, Walter, et al. *A Greek-English Lexicon of the New Testament and Other Early Christian Literature.* 3rd ed. Revised and edited by Frederick William Danker. Chicago: University of Chicago Press, 2000.
BDF	Blass, F., and A. Debrunner. *A Greek Grammar of the New Testament and Other Early Christian Literature.* Revised and edited by Robert W. Funk. Chicago: University of Chicago Press, 1961.
BECNT	Baker Exegetical Commentary on the New Testament
BHGNT	Baylor Handbook on the Greek New Testament
BibAnn	*The Biblical Annals*

BibInt	Biblical Interpretation Series
BZNW	Beihefte zur Zeitschrift für die neutestamentliche Wissenschaft
CBQ	*Catholic Biblical Quarterly*
CBR	*Currents in Biblical Research*
CEB	Common English Bible
CGL	*The Cambridge Greek Lexicon.* Edited by J. Diggle, B. L. Fraser, P. James, O. B. Simkin, A. A. Thompson, and S. J. Westripp. 2 vols. Cambridge: Cambridge University Press, 2021.
CSS	Cistercian Studies Series
DPL[2]	*Dictionary of Paul and His Letters.* 2nd ed. Edited by Scot McKnight. Downers Grove, IL: IVP Academic, 2023.
DSE	*Dictionary of Scripture and Ethics.* Edited by Joel B. Green. Grand Rapids: Baker Academic, 2011.
EDNT	*Exegetical Dictionary of the New Testament.* Edited by Horst Balz and Gerhard Schneider. 3 vols. Grand Rapids: Eerdmans, 1990–1993.
ESEC	Emory Studies in Early Christianity
EvQ	*Evangelical Quarterly*
FC	Fathers of the Church
HNTC	Harper's New Testament Commentaries
HTR	*Harvard Theological Review*
HvTSt	*Hervormde teologiese studies*
ICC	International Critical Commentary
Int	*Interpretation: A Journal of Bible and Theology*
Int	Interpretation: Resources for the Use of Scripture in the Church
JSNT	*Journal for the Study of the New Testament*
JSNTSup	Journal for the Study of the New Testament Supplement Series
L&N	*Greek-English Lexicon of the New Testament: Based on Semantic Domains.* 2 vols. Edited by Johannes P. Louw and Eugene A. Nida. New York: United Bible Societies, 1988.
LCL	Loeb Classical Library
LENT	Linguistic Exegesis of the New Testament
LNTS	Library of New Testament Studies
LSJ	Liddel, H. G., R. Scott, and H. S. Jones. *A Greek-English Lexicon.* 9th ed. With revised supplement. New York: Oxford University Press, 1996.

MGS	Montanari, Franco. *The Brill Dictionary of Ancient Greek*. Edited by Madeleine Goh and Chad Schroeder. Leiden: Brill, 2015.
MNTS	McMaster New Testament Studies
ModT	*Modern Theology*
NA[28]	*Novum Testamentum Graece*, Nestle-Aland, 28th ed.
NETS	New English Translation of the Septuagint
NICNT	New International Commentary on the New Testament
NIDB	*New Interpreter's Dictionary of the Bible*. Edited by Katharine Doob Sakenfeld. 5 vols. Nashville: Abingdon, 2006–2009.
NIGTC	New International Greek Testament Commentary
NIV	New International Version (2011)
NovT	*Novum Testamentum*
NovTSup	Supplements to Novum Testament
NRSV	New Revised Standard Version
NTOA	Novum Testamentum et Orbis Antiquus
NTR	New Testament Readings
NTS	*New Testament Studies*
OBO	Orbis Biblicus et Orientalis
OCD[3]	*Oxford Classical Dictionary*. Edited by Simon Hornblower and Antony Spawforth. 3rd ed. Oxford: Oxford University Press, 1996.
OTP	James H. Charlesworth, ed. *The Old Testament Pseudepigrapha*. 2 vols. Garden City, NY: Doubleday, 1983–1985.
PBTM	Paternoster Biblical and Theological Monographs
PiNTC	Pillar New Testament Commentary
RB	*Revue biblique*
RBL	*Review of Biblical Literature*
SBLDS	Society of Biblical Literature Dissertation Series
SJT	*Scottish Journal of Theology*
SNTW	Studies of the New Testament and Its World
STT	Studia Traditionis Theologiae: Explorations in Early and Medieval Theology
SUNT	Studien zur Umwelt des Neuen Testaments
SymS	Symposium Series
TDNT	*Theological Dictionary of the New Testament*. Edited by Gerhard Kittel and Gerhard Friedrich. Translated by Geoffrey W. Bromiley. 10 vols. Grand Rapids: Eerdmans, 1964–76.

TLNT	*Theological Lexicon of the New Testament.* Ceslas Spicq. Translated and edited by James D. Ernest. 3 vols. Peabody, MA: Hendrickson, 1994.
TLZ	*Theologische Literaturzeitung*
TynBul	*Tyndale Bulletin*
VCSup	Supplements to Vigiliae Christianae
WBC	Word Biblical Commentary
WTJ	*Westminster Theological Journal*
WUNT	Wissenschaftliche Untersuchungen zum Neuen Testament
ZSNT	Zacchaeus Studies: New Testament

BIBLIOGRAPHY

Commentaries

Adamson, James B. 1976. *The Epistle of James*. NICNT. Grand Rapids: Eerdmans.

Adewuya, J. Ayodeji. 2023. *An African Commentary on the Letter of James*. Global Readings. Eugene, OR: Cascade.

Albl, Martin C. 2017. "Hebrews and the Catholic Letters." Pages 427–57 in *The Bible and Disability: A Commentary*. Edited by Sarah J. Melcher, Mikeal C. Parsons, and Amos Yong. Waco, TX: Baylor University Press.

Allison, Dale C., Jr. 2013. *A Critical and Exegetical Commentary on the Epistle of James*. ICC. New York: Bloomsbury T&T Clark.

Andria, Solomon. 2006. "James." Pages 1509–16 in *Africa Bible Commentary*. Edited by Tokunboh Adeyemo. Nairobi: WordAlive; Grand Rapids: Zondervan.

Bede the Venerable. 1985. *Commentary on the Seven Catholic Letters*. Translated by David Hurst. CSS 82. Kalamazoo, MI: Cistercian.

Davids, Peter H. 1982. *The Epistle of James: A Commentary on the Greek Text*. NIGTC. Grand Rapids: Eerdmans.

Dibelius, Martin. 1976. *James*. Revised by Heinrich Greeven. Translated by Michael W. Williams. Hermeneia. Philadelphia: Fortress.

Gowler, David B. 2014. *James through the Centuries*. Wiley Blackwell Bible Commentaries. Malden, MA: Wiley Blackwell.

Johnson, Luke Timothy. 1995. *The Letter of James: A New Translation with Introduction and Commentary*. AB 37A. New York: Doubleday.

Laws, Sophie. 1980. *A Commentary on the Epistle of James*. HNTC. San Francisco: Harper & Row.

Martin, Ralph P. 1988. *James*. WBC 48. Waco, TX: Word.

McCartney, Dan G. 2009. *James*. BECNT. Grand Rapids: Baker Academic.

McKnight, Scot. 2011. *The Letter of James*. NICNT. Grand Rapids: Eerdmans.

Moo, Douglas J. 2000. *The Letter of James*. PiNTC. Grand Rapids: Eerdmans.

Other Secondary Sources

Aasgaard, Reider. 1997. "Brotherhood in Plutarch and Paul: Its Role and Character." Pages 166–82 in *Constructing Early Christian Families: Family as Social Reality and Metaphor.* Edited by Halvor Moxnes. London: Routledge.

———. 2005. "Brothers and Sisters in the Faith: Christian Siblingship as an Ecclesiological Mirror in the First Two Centuries." Pages 285–316 in *The Formation of the Early Church.* Edited by Jostein Ådna. WUNT 183. Tübingen: Mohr Siebeck.

Achtemeier, Paul J. 1996. *1 Peter: A Commentary on 1 Peter.* Hermeneia. Minneapolis: Fortress.

Adam, A. K. M. 2013. *James: A Handbook on the Greek Text.* BHGNT. Waco, TX: Baylor University Press.

Akiyama, Kengo. 2018. *The Love of Neighbor in Ancient Judaism: The Reception of Leviticus 19:18 in the Hebrew Bible, the Septuagint, the Book of Jubilees, the Dead Sea Scrolls, and the New Testament.* AGJU 105. Leiden: Brill.

Albl, Martin C. 2002. "'Are Any among You Sick?': The Health Care System in the Letter of James." *Journal of Biblical Literature* 121, no. 1:123–43.

Allison, Dale C., Jr. 2001. "The Fiction of James and Its *Sitz im Leben.*" *RB* 108, no. 4:529–70.

Anderson, Gary A. 2009. *Sin: A History.* New Haven: Yale University Press.

Aymer, Margaret P. 2007. *First Pure, Then Peaceable: Frederick Douglass Reads James.* LNTS 379. London: T&T Clark.

Baker, William R. 1995. *Personal Speech-Ethics in the Epistle of James.* WUNT 2/68. Tübingen: Mohr Siebeck.

———. 2002. "Christology in the Epistle of James." *EvQ* 74, no. 1:47–57.

Barclay, John M. G. 1996. *Jews in the Mediterranean Diaspora: From Alexander to Trajan (323 BCE–117 CE).* Berkeley: University of California Press.

———. 2015. *Paul and the Gift.* Grand Rapids: Eerdmans.

Barton, Stephen C. 1999. "New Testament Interpretation as Performance." *SJT* 52:179–208.

Bates, Matthew W. 2017. *Salvation by Allegiance Alone: Rethinking Faith, Works, and the Gospel of Jesus the King.* Grand Rapids: Baker Academic.

Batten, Alicia J. 2004. "God in the Letter of James: Patron or Benefactor?" *NTS* 50:257–72.

———. 2008. "The Degraded Poor and the Greedy Rich: Exploring the Language of Poverty and Wealth in James." Pages 65–77 in *The Social Sciences and Bible Translation.* Edited by Dietmar Neufeld. SymS 41. Atlanta: SBL Press.

———. 2017. *Friendship and Benefaction in James.* ESEC 15. Atlanta: SBL Press.

Bauckham, Richard J. 1992. "Hades, Hell." *ABD* 3:14–15.

———. 1998. "The Tongue Set on Fire by Hell (James 3:6)." Pages 119–31 in *The Fate of the Dead: Studies on the Jewish and Christian Apocalypses.* NovTSup 93. Leiden: Brill.

———. 1999. *James: Wisdom of James, Disciple of Jesus the Sage.* NTR. London: Routledge.

———. 2004. "The Spirit of God in Us Loathes Envy." Pages 270–81 in *The Holy Spirit and Christian Origins: Essays in Honor of James D. G. Dunn.* Edited by Graham N. Stanton, Bruce W. Longenecker, and Stephen C. Barton. Grand Rapids: Eerdmans.

———. 2021. "Messianic Jewish Identity in James." Pages 85–98 in *The Catholic Epistles: Critical Readings.* Edited by Darian R. Lockett. Critical Readings in Biblical Studies. London: T&T Clark.

Becker, Eve-Marie. *Paul on Humility.* 2020. Translated by Wayne Coppins. Baylor-Mohr Siebeck Studies in Early Christianity. Waco, TX: Baylor University Press.

Bellah, Robert N., Richard Madsen, William M. Sullivan, Ann Swidler, and Steven M. Tipton. 1985. *Habits of the Heart: Individualism and Commitment in American Life.* Berkeley: University of California Press.

Bennett, Thomas Andrew. 2017. *Labor of God: The Agony of the Cross as the Birth of the Church.* Waco, TX: Baylor University Press.

Berger, Klaus. 1993. "προσωπολημψία." *EDNT* 3:179–80.

———. 2003. *Identity and Experience in the New Testament.* Translated by Charles Muenchow. Minneapolis: Fortress.

Berridge, Kent C., and Morten L. Kringelbach. 2008. "Affective Neuroscience of Pleasure: Reward in Humans and Animals." *Psychopharmacology* 199, no. 3:457–80.

Berthelot, Katell. 2021. *Jews and Their Roman Rivals: Pagan Rome's Challenge to Israel.* Princeton: Princeton University Press.

Blidstein, Moshe. 2022. "Impure Mouths and Defiled Hearts: The Development of Deceit Impurity in Second Temple Judaism." *Religions* 13:678. https://doi.org/10.3390/rel13080678.

Boas, Evert van Ende, Albert Rijksbaron, Luuk Huitink, and Mathieu de Bakker. 2019. *The Cambridge Grammar of Classical Greek.* Cambridge: Cambridge University Press.

Borne, Étienne. 1961. *Atheism.* Translated by S. J. Tester. New York: Hawthorn.

Bouteneff, Peter C. 2008. *Beginnings: Ancient Christian Readings of the Biblical Creation Narratives.* Grand Rapids: Baker Academic.

Bowden, Andrew M. 2014. "An Overview of Interpretive Approaches to James 5.13–18." *CBR* 13, no. 1:67–81.

Briggs, Richard. 2010. *The Virtuous Reader: Old Testament Narrative and Interpretive Virtue.* Studies in Theological Interpretation. Grand Rapids: Baker Academic.

Broom, Timothy W., Robert S. Chavez, and Dylan D. Wagner. 2021. "Becoming the King in the North: Identification with Fictional Characters Is Associated with Greater Self–Other Neural Overlap." *Social Cognitive and Affective Neuroscience*. https://doi.org/10.1093/scan/nsab021.

Brueggemann, Walter. 2018. *Money and Possessions*. Int. Louisville: Westminster John Knox.

Campbell, R. Alastair. 1993. "The Elders: Seniority in Earliest Christianity." *TynBul* 44, no. 1:183–87.

———. 1994. *The Elders: Seniority within Earliest Christianity*. SNTW. Edinburgh: T&T Clark.

Cargal, Timothy B. 1993. *Restoring the Diaspora: Discursive Structure and Purpose in the Epistle of James*. SBLDS 144. Atlanta: Scholars Press.

Carpenter, Craig B. 2000. "James 4.5 Reconsidered." *NTS* 46:189–205.

Carter, Stephen L. 1993. *The Culture of Disbelief: How American Law and Politics Trivialize Religious Devotion*. New York: Basic Books.

Casson, Lionel. 1971. *Ships and Seamanship in the Ancient World*. Princeton: Princeton University Press.

Chatman, Seymour. 1978. *Story and Discourse: Narrative Structure in Fiction and Film*. Ithaca, NY: Cornell University Press.

Cheung, Luke L. 2003. *The Genre, Composition, and Hermeneutics of James*. PBTM. Carlisle: Paternoster.

Clarke, Andrew D. 2004. "Equality or Mutuality? Paul's Use of 'Brother' Language." Pages 151–64 in *The New Testament in Its First Century Setting: Essays on Context and Background in Honour of B. W. Winter on His 65th Birthday*. Grand Rapids: Eerdmans.

Cohick, Lynn H. 2009. *Women in the World of the Earliest Christians: Illuminating Ancient Ways of Life*. Grand Rapids: Baker Academic.

Craigo-Snell, Shannon. 2000. "Command Performance: Rethinking Performance Interpretation in the Context of Divine Discourse." *ModT* 16:475–94.

Damasio, Antonio R. 1994. *Descartes' Error: Emotion, Reason, and the Human Brain*. New York: Avon Books.

Dehghani, Morteza, Kate Johnson, Joe Hoover, Eyal Sagi, Justin Garten, Niki Jitendra Parmar, Stephen Vaisey, Rumen Iliev, and Jesse Graham. 2016. "Purity Homophily in Social Networks." *Journal of Experimental Psychology: General* 145, no. 3:366–75. https://doi.org/10.1037/xge0000139.

Derrida, Jacques. 1992. *Given Time 1: Counterfeit Money*. Translated by Peggy Kamuf. Carpenter Lectures. Chicago: University of Chicago Press.

DeSilva, David A. 2012. *The Jewish Teachers of Jesus, James, and Jude: What Early Christianity Learned from the Apocrypha and Pseudepigrapha*. Oxford: Oxford University Press.

de Tocqueville, Alexis. *Democracy in America*. 2000. French, 1835. Translated, edited, and introduced by Harvey C. Mansfield and Delba Winthrop. Chicago: University of Chicago Press.

Downs, David J. 2011. "Vices and Virtues, Lists of." *DSE* 808–9.

Dupriez, Bernard. 1991. *A Dictionary of Literary Devices*. Translated and adapted by Albert W. Halsall. New York: Harvester Wheatsheaf.

Edgar, David Hutchinson. 2001. *Has God Not Chosen the Poor? The Social Setting of the Epistle of James*. JSNTSup 206. Sheffield: Sheffield Academic.

Ellis, Nicholas J. 2019. "A Theology of Evil in the Epistle of James: Cosmic Trials and the *Dramatis Personae* of Evil." Pages 262–81 in *Evil in Second Temple Judaism and Early Christianity*. Edited by Chris Keith and Loren T. Stuckenbruck. WUNT 2/417. Tübingen: Mohr Siebeck.

Eng, Daniel Kong. 2020. "Eschatological Approval in the Epistle of James." PhD diss. University of Cambridge.

Evans, Vyvyan, and Melanie Green. 2006. *Cognitive Linguistics: An Introduction*. Edinburgh: Edinburgh University Press.

Faber, Riemer A. 1995. "The Juridical Nuance in the NT Use of Προσωπολημψία." *WTJ* 57:299–309.

Feldman, Jerome A. 2006. *From Molecule to Metaphor: A Neural Theory of Language*. Cambridge, MA: MIT Press.

Feldman, Louis H. 1993. *Jew and Gentile in the Ancient World: Attitudes and Interactions from Alexander to Justinian*. Princeton: Princeton University Press.

Feldmeier, Reinhard. 2014. *Power, Service, and Humility: A New Testament Ethic*. Waco, TX: Baylor University Press.

Foster, Robert J. 2014. *The Significance of Exemplars for the Interpretation of the Letter of James*. WUNT 2/376. Tübingen: Mohr Siebeck.

Friesen, Steven J. 2004. "Poverty in Pauline Studies beyond the So-Called New Consensus." *JSNT* 26, no. 3:323–61 (esp. 340–47).

Gabriel, Shira, and Ariana F. Young. 2011. "Becoming a Vampire without Being Bitten: The Narrative Collective-Assimilation Hypothesis." *Psychological Science* 22, no. 8:990–94. https://doi.org/10.1177/0956797611415541.

Giardina, Andrea. 1993. "The Merchant." Pages 245–71 in *The Romans*. Edited by Andrea Giardina. Translated by Lydia G. Cochrane. Chicago: University of Chicago Press.

Goldingay, John. 2016. *Biblical Theology: The God of the Christian Scriptures*. Downers Grove, IL: IVP Academic.

Goldingay, John, and Joel B. Green. 2011. "Loans." *DSE* 488–90.

Gordon, Barry. 1989. *The Economic Problem in Biblical and Patristic Thought*. VCSup 9. Leiden: Brill.

Gray, Patrick. 2004. "Points and Lines: Thematic Parallelism in the Letter of James and the *Testament of Job*." *NTS* 50:406–24.

Green, Joel B. 1997. *The Gospel of Luke*. NICNT. Grand Rapids: Eerdmans.

———. 2002. Review of *Logos and Law in the Letter of James: The Law of Nature, the Law of Moses, and the Law of Freedom*, by Matt A. Jackson-McCabe. *RBL*. bookreviews.org.

————. 2007. *Seized by Truth: Reading the Bible as Scripture*. Nashville: Abingdon.

————. 2011. "Hypocrisy." *DSE* 390–91.

————. 2013. "Healing and Healthcare." Pages 330–41 in *The World of the New Testament: Cultural, Social, and Historical Contexts*. Edited by Joel B. Green and Lee Martin McDonald. Grand Rapids: Baker Academic.

————. 2016. "Reading James Missionally." Pages 194–212 in *Reading the Bible Missionally*. Edited by Michael W. Goheen. The Gospel and Our Culture Series. Grand Rapids: Eerdmans.

————. 2017. "'Adam, What Have You Done?': New Testament Voices on the Origins of Sin." Pages 98–116 in *Evolution and the Fall*. Edited by William T. Cavanaugh and James K. A. Smith. Grand Rapids: Eerdmans.

————. 2020a. "Good News to the Poor: A Lukan Leitmotif." Pages 211–19 in *Luke as Narrative Theologian: Texts and Topics*. WUNT 446. Tübingen: Mohr Siebeck.

————. 2020b. "'I'll Show You My Faith' (James 2:18): Inspiring Models for Exilic Life." *Int* 74, no. 4:344–52.

————. 2020c. "Original Sin: A Wesleyan View." Pages 55–77 in *Original Sin and the Fall: Five Views*. Edited by Jim Stump and Chad Meister. Spectrum Multiview Books. Downers Grove, IL: IVP Academic.

————. 2020d. "'We Had to Celebrate and Rejoice!': Happiness in the Topsy-Turvy World of Luke-Acts." Pages 233–47 in *Luke as Narrative Theologian: Texts and Topics*. WUNT 446. Tübingen: Mohr Siebeck.

————. 2022. "Betwixt and Between: The Letter of James and the Human Condition." *BibAnn* 12, no. 2:295–308.

————. 2023. "James, Theological Education, and Practical Wisdom." Pages 96–107 in *Now to God Who Is Able*. Edited by Neal D. Presa and Anne Zaki. Eugene, OR: Wipf & Stock.

Gruen, Erich S. 2002. *Diaspora: Jews amidst Greeks and Romans*. Cambridge, MA: Harvard University Press.

Grundmann, Walter. 1974. "ταπεινός κτλ." *TDNT* 8:1–26.

Gupta, Nijay K. 2020. *Paul and the Language of Faith*. Grand Rapids: Eerdmans.

Hahn, Robert A. 1995. *Sickness and Healing: An Anthropological Perspective*. New Haven: Yale University Press.

Hamel, Gildas. 1990. *Poverty and Charity in Roman Palestine, First Three Centuries C.E.* University of California Publications: Near Eastern Studies 23. Berkeley: University of California.

Hartin, Patrick J. 1999. *A Spirituality of Perfection: Faith in Action in the Letter of James*. Collegeville, MN: Glazier.

Hayes, Christine E. 2020. "Purification and Purity." Pages 641–44 of vol. 2 in *T&T Clark Encyclopedia of Second Temple Judaism*. Edited by Loren T. Stuckenbruck and Daniel M. Gurtner. 2 vols. London: T&T Clark.

Helmbold, W. C., ed. and trans. 1939. *Plutarch's Moralia*, vol. *VI*. LCL 337. Cambridge, MA: Harvard University Press.

Hengel, Martin. 1974. *Judaism and Hellenism: Studies in Their Encounter in Palestine during the Early Hellenistic Period.* 2 vols. Philadelphia: Fortress.

Hengel, Martin, in collaboration with Christoph Markshies. 1989. *The "Hellenization" of Judaea in the First Century after Christ.* London: SCM.

Hicks, Richard James. 2021. *Emotion Made Right: Hellenistic Moral Progress and the (Un)Emotional Jesus in Mark.* BZNW 250. Berlin: de Gruyter.

Hogan, Larry O. 1992. *Healing in the Second Tempel* [sic] *Period.* NTOA 21. Göttingen: Vandenhoeck & Ruprecht.

Hurtado, Larry W. 2005. *Lord Jesus Christ: Devotion to Jesus in Earliest Christianity.* Grand Rapids: Eerdmans.

Isaac, Ephraim. 1983. "1 (Ethiopic Apocalypse of) Enoch: A New Translation and Introduction." *OTP* 1:5–89.

Ivarsson, Fredrik. 2006. "Vice Lists and Deviant Masculinity: The Rhetorical Function of 1 Corinthians 5:10–11 and 6:9–10." Pages 163–84 in *Mapping Gender in Ancient Religious Discourses.* Edited by Todd Penner and Caroline Vander Stichele. BibInt 84. Leiden: Brill.

Jackson-McCabe, Matt A. 2001. *Logos and Law in the Letter of James: The Law of Nature, the Law of Moses, and the Law of Freedom.* NovTSup 100. Leiden: Brill.

Johnson, Luke Timothy. 2004a. "Friendship with the World and Friendship with God: A Study of Discipleship in James." Pages 202–20 in *Brother of Jesus, Friend of God: Studies in the Letter of James.* Grand Rapids: Eerdmans.

———. 2004b. "The Mirror of Remembrance: James 1:22–25." Pages 168–81 in *Brother of Jesus, Friend of God: Studies in the Letter of James.* Grand Rapids: Eerdmans.

———. 2004c. "Taciturnity and True Religion: James 1:26–27." Pages 155–67 in *Brother of Jesus, Friend of God: Studies in the Letter of James.* Grand Rapids: Eerdmans.

———. 2004d. "The Use of Leviticus 19 in the Letter of James." Pages 123–35 in *Brother of Jesus, Friend of God: Studies in the Letter of James.* Grand Rapids: Eerdmans.

Johnson, Samuel. 2021. *A Dictionary of the English Language.* 1755, 1773. Edited by Beth Rapp Young, Jack Lynch, William Dorner, Amy Larner Giroux, Carmen Faye Mathes, and Abigail Moreshead. https://johnsonsdictionaryonline.com.

Kaiser, Ursula Ulrike. 2019. "'Receive the innate word that is able to save you' (Jas 1:21b): Soteriology in the Epistle of James." Pages 460–75 in *Sōtēria: Salvation in Early Christianity and Antiquity: Festschrift in Honour of Cilliers Breytenbach on the Occasion of His 65th Birthday.* Edited by

David S. du Toit, Christine Gerber, and Christiane Zimmermann. NovTSup 175. Leiden: Brill.

Kärkkäinen, Veli-Matti. 2015. *Creation and Humanity*. Vol. 3 of *A Constructive Christian Theology for the Pluralistic World*. Grand Rapids: Eerdmans.

Kee, Howard Clark. 1983. "Testament of the Twelve Patriarchs: A New Translation and Introduction." *OTP* 1:775–828.

Kirk, J. A. 1969. "The Meaning of Wisdom in James: Examination of a Hypothesis." *NTS* 16, no. 1:24–38.

Klawans, Jonathan. 2000. *Impurity and Sin in Ancient Judaism*. Oxford: Oxford University Press.

Klijn, A. F. J. 1983. "2 (Syriac Apocalypse of) Baruch: A New Translation and Introduction." *OTP* 1:615–52.

Kloppenborg Verbin, John S. 1999. "Patronage Avoidance in James." *HvTSt* 55, no. 4:755–94.

Konradt, Matthias. 1998. *Christliche Existenz nach dem Jakobusbrief: Eine Studie zu seiner soteriologischen und ethischen Konzeption*. SUNT 22. Göttingen: Vandenhoeck & Ruprecht.

Konstan, David. 1997. *Friendship in the Classical World*. Key Themes in Ancient History. Cambridge: Cambridge University Press.

Kotva, Joseph J., Jr. 2011. "Oaths." *DSE* 556–57.

Kümmel, Werner Georg. 1975. *Introduction to the New Testament*. Rev. ed. Translated by Howard Clark Kee. Nashville: Abingdon.

Lakoff, George, and Mark Johnson. 1980. *Metaphors We Live By*. Chicago: University of Chicago Press.

Lakoff, George, and Mark Turner. 1989. *More Than Cool Reason: A Field Guide to Poetic Metaphor*. Chicago: University of Chicago Press.

Lateiner, Donald, and Dimos Spatharas, eds. 2016. *The Ancient Emotion of Disgust*. Oxford: Oxford University Press.

Lee, Spike W. S., and Norbeto Schwarz. 2011. "Wiping the Slate Clean: Psychological Consequences of Physical Cleansing." *Current Directions in Psychological Science* 20, no. 5:307–11.

Lee, Spike W. S., Honghong Tang, Jing Wan, Xiaoqin Mai, and Chao Liu. 2015. "A Cultural Look at Moral Purity: Wiping the Face Clean." *Frontiers in Psychology* 6, no. 577:1–6. https://doi.org/10.3389/fpsyg.2015.00577.

Le Guin, Ursula K. 2000. *The Telling*. New York: Harcourt.

Levison, John R. 1997. *The Spirit in First Century Judaism*. AGJU 29. Leiden: Brill.

Lockett, Darian. 2008. *Purity and Worldview in the Epistle of James*. LNTS 366. London: T&T Clark.

———. 2020. "The Use of Leviticus 19 in James and 1 Peter: A Neglected Parallel." *CBQ* 82:456–72.

Lohse, Eduard. 1968. "προσωπολημψία κτλ." *TDNT* 6:779–80.

Longenecker, Bruce W. 2010. *Remember the Poor: Paul, Poverty, and the Greco-Roman World*. Grand Rapids: Eerdmans.

Longenecker, Richard N. 1970. *The Christology of Early Jewish Christianity*. London: SCM.

Lowe, Bruce A. 2009. "James 2:1 in the Πίστις Χριστοῦ Debate: Irrelevant or Indispensable?" Pages 239–57 in *The Faith of Jesus Christ: Exegetical, Biblical, and Theological Studies*. Edited by Michael F. Bird and Preston M. Sprinkle. Milton Keynes: Paternoster; Peabody, MA: Hendrickson.

MacDonald, Nathan. 2013. "Monotheism." Pages 77–84 in *The World of the New Testament: Cultural, Social, and Historical Contexts*. Edited by Joel B. Green and Lee Martin McDonald. Grand Rapids: Baker Academic.

Marcus, Joel. 1982. "The Evil Inclination in the Epistle of James." *CBQ* 44, no. 4:606–21.

———. 2014. "'The Twelve Tribes in the Diaspora' (James 1:1)." *NTS* 60:433–47.

Martin, Dale B. 1990. *Slavery as Salvation: The Metaphor of Slavery in Pauline Christianity*. New Haven: Yale University Press.

———. 1995. *The Corinthian Body*. New Haven: Yale University Press.

Matthews, Victor H. 2009. "Oil." *NIDB* 4:322–23.

McConville, J. Gordon. 2016. *Being Human in God's World: An Old Testament Theology of Humanity*. Grand Rapids: Baker Academic.

McKnight, Scot. 1990. "James 2:18a: The Unidentifiable Interlocutor." *WTJ* 52:355–64.

———. 2023. "James and Paul." *DPL*[2] 539–42.

Michaels, J. Ramsey. 2005. "Catholic Christologies in the Catholic Epistles." Pages 268–91 in *Contours of Christology in the New Testament*. Edited by Richard N. Longenecker. MNTS. Grand Rapids: Eerdmans.

Milkason, Jon D. 1996. "Oaths." *OCD*[3] 1057.

Moberly, R. W. L. 2000. *The Bible, Theology, and Faith: A Study of Abraham and Jesus*. Cambridge: Cambridge University Press.

Mongstad-Kvammen, Ingeborg. 2013. *Toward a Postcolonial Reading of the Epistle of James: James 2:1–13 in Its Roman Imperial Context*. BibInt 119. Leiden: Brill.

Morgan, Teresa. 2015. *Roman Faith and Christian Faith: Pistis and Fides in the Early Roman Empire and Early Churches*. Oxford: Oxford University Press.

Morson, Gary Saul. 1994. *Narrative and Freedom: The Shadows of Time*. New Haven: Yale University Press.

Mott, Lawrence W. 1997. *The Development of the Rudder: A Technological Tale*. Studies in Nautical Archaeology 3. College Station: Texas A&M University Press.

Moule, C. F. D. 1959. *An Idiom Book of New Testament Greek*. 2nd ed. Cambridge: Cambridge University Press.

Moxnes, Halvor. 1988. *The Economy of the Kingdom: Social Conflict and Economic Relations in Luke's Gospel*. Minneapolis: Fortress.

Niebuhr, Karl-Wilhelm. 2004. "A New Perspective on James? Neuere Forschungen zum Jakobusbrief." *TLZ* 129, no. 10:1019–44. http://www.thlz.com/artikel/5299/?inhalt=heft%3D2004%23r412.

———. 2013. "Ethics and Anthropology in the Letter of James: An Outline." Pages 223–42 in *Early Christian Ethics in Interaction with Jewish and Greco-Roman Contexts*. Edited by Jan Willem van Heten and Joseph Verheyden. Studies in Theology and Religion 17. Leiden: Brill.

———. 2016."Jakobus und Paulus über das Innere des Menschen und den Ursprung seiner ethischen Entscheidungen." *NTS* 62, no. 1:1–30.

———. 2020. "One God, One Lord in the Epistle of James." Pages 172–88 in *Monotheism and Christology in Greco-Roman Antiquity*. Edited by Matthew V. Novenson. NovTSup 180. Leiden: Brill.

———. 2021. "The Epistle of James in Light of Early Jewish Diaspora Letters." Pages 67–83 in *The Catholic Letters: Critical Readings*. Edited by Darian R. Lockett. Critical Readings in Biblical Studies. London: T&T Clark.

Niebuhr, Reinhold. 1941–1943. *The Nature and Destiny of Man: A Christian Interpretation*. 2 vols. New York: Scribner's Sons.

Nutton, Vivian. 2004. *Ancient Medicine*. Sciences of Antiquity. London: Routledge.

Origen. *Homilies on Luke*. 1996. Translated by Joseph T. Lienhard. FC. Washington, DC: Catholic University of America Press.

Penner, Todd C. 1996. *The Epistle of James and Eschatology: Re-reading an Ancient Greek Letter*. JSNTSup 121. Sheffield: Sheffield Academic.

Radl, Walter. 1993. "ὑπομονή." *EDNT* 3:405–6.

Richards, E. Randolph. 1991. *The Secretary in the Letters of Paul*. WUNT 2/42. Tübingen: Mohr Siebeck.

Ryan, Richard M., and Edward L. Deci. 2001. "On Happiness and Human Potentials: A Review of Research on Hedonic and Eudaimonic Well-Being." *Annual Review of Psychology* 52:141–66.

Sahlins, Marshall. 1972. *Stone Age Economics*. London: Routledge.

———. 1995. *How "Natives" Think: About Captain Cook, for Example*. Chicago: University of Chicago Press.

———. 2013. *What Kinship Is—And Is Not*. Chicago: University of Chicago Press.

Sanders, E. P. 1983. "Testament of Abraham: A New Translation and Introduction." *OTP* 1:871–902.

Sandnes, Karl Olav. 1997. "Equality within Patriarchal Structures: Some New Testament Perspectives on the Christian Fellowship as a Brother- or Sisterhood and a Family." Pages 150–65 in *Constructing Early Christian Families:*

Family as Social Reality and Metaphor. Edited by Halvor Moxnes. London: Routledge.

Scacewater, Todd. 2017. "The Dynamic and Righteous Use of Wealth in James 5:1–6." *Journal of Markets and Morality* 20, no. 2:227–42.

Schäfer, Peter. 1997. *Judeophobia: Attitudes toward the Jews in the Ancient World.* Cambridge, MA: Harvard University Press.

Schiffman, Lawrence H. 2009. "Shema." *NIDB* 5:224–25.

Schottroff, Luise. 1993. "The Woman Who Loved Much and the Pharisee Simon (Luke 7:36–50)." Pages 138–57 in *Let the Oppressed Go Free: Feminist Perspectives on the New Testament.* Louisville: Westminster John Knox.

Schweizer, Eduard. 1993."σῶμα." *EDNT* 3:321–25.

Seitz, Christopher R. 1993. "The Patience of Job in the Epistle of James." Pages 373–82 in *Konsequente Traditiongeschichte: Festschrift für Klaus Baltzer.* Edited by Rüdiger Bartelmus, Thomas Krüger, and Helmut Utzschneider. OBO 126. Freiburg: Universitätsverlag; Göttingen: Vandenhoeck & Ruprecht.

Sevenster, J. N. 1968. *Do You Know Greek? How Much Greek Could the First Jewish Christians Have Known?* NovTSup 19. Leiden: Brill.

Shiavone, Aldo. 1993. "The Jurist." Pages 55–84 in *The Romans.* Edited by Andrea Giardina. Translated by Lydia G. Cochrane. Chicago: University of Chicago Press.

Slingerland, Edward G. 2005. "Conceptual Blending, Somatic Marking, and Normativity: A Case Example from Ancient Chinese." *Cognitive Linguistics* 16:557–84.

Spitaler, Peter. 2007. "Διακρίνεσθαι in Mt. 21:21, Mk. 11:23, Acts 10:20, Rom. 4:20, 14:23, Jas. 1:6, and Jude 22—The 'Semantic Shift' That Went Unnoticed by Patristic Authors." *NovT* 49:1–39.

Spittler, Russell P. 1983. "Testament of Job: A New Translation and Introduction." *OTP* 1:829–68.

Stetka, Bret. 2014. "Why Everyone Should Read Harry Potter." *Scientific American.* September 9. https://www.scientificamerican.com/article/why-everyone-should-read-harry-potter/.

Stinespring, W. F. 1983. "Testament of Jacob: A New Translation and Introduction." *OTP* 1:913–18.

Strauss, Mark L. 2010. *Distorting Scripture? The Challenge of Bible Translation and Gender Accuracy.* Eugene, OR: Wipf & Stock.

Talbert, Charles H. 1991. *Learning through Suffering: The Educational Value of Suffering in the New Testament and in Its Milieu.* ZSNT. Collegeville, MN: Liturgical Press.

Tamez, Elsa. 1990. *The Scandalous Message of James: Faith without Works Is Dead.* Translated by John Eagleson. Rev. ed. New York: Crossroad.

Taylor, Charles. 1989. *Sources of the Self: The Making of the Modern Identity.* Cambridge, MA: Harvard University Press.

Taylor, Mark E. 2006. *A Text-Linguistic Investigation into the Discourse Structure of James.* LNTS 311. London: T&T Clark.

Taylor, Mark E., and George H. Guthrie. 2006. "The Structure of James." *CBQ* 68, no. 4:681–705.

Thiselton, Anthony C. 2009. "Oath." *NIDB* 4:309–12.

Timothy, William, Treal Taylor, Tumurbaatar Tuvschinjargal, and Jamsranjav Bayarsaikhan. 2016. "Reconstructing Equine Bridles from the Mongolian Bronze Age." *Journal of Ethnobiology* 36, no. 3:554–70.

Toews, John E. 2013. *The Story of Original Sin.* Eugene, OR: Pickwick.

Turner, Mark. 1991. *Reading Minds: The Study of English in the Age of Cognitive Science.* Princeton: Princeton University Press.

Vermes, Géza. 1997. *The Complete Dead Sea Scrolls in English.* New York: Penguin.

Verseput, Donald J. 1997. "Reworking the Puzzle of Faith and Deeds in James 2.14–26." *NTS* 43:97–115.

Veyne, Paul. 1987. *The Roman Empire.* Cambridge, MA: Harvard University Press.

von Siebenthal, Heinrich. 2019. *Ancient Greek Grammar for the Study of the New Testament.* Oxford: Peter Lang.

von Staden, Heinrich. 2000. "Body, Soul, and Nerves: Epicurus, Herophilus, Erasistratus, the Stoics, and Galen." Pages 79–116 in *Psyche and Soma: Physicians and Metaphysicians on the Mind-Body Problem from Antiquity to Enlightenment.* Edited by John P. Wright and Paul Potter. Oxford: Oxford University Press.

Wachob, Wesley Hiram. 2000. *The Voice of Jesus in the Social Rhetoric of James.* Society for New Testament Studies Monograph Series 106. Cambridge: Cambridge University Press.

Wall, Robert W. 2001. "The Intertextuality of Scripture: The Example of Rahab (James 2:25)." Pages 217–36 in *Bible at Qumran: Text, Shape, and Interpretation.* Edited by Peter W. Flint. Studies in the Dead Sea Scrolls and Related Literature. Grand Rapids: Eerdmans.

Ward, Roy Bowen. 1968. "The *Works of Abraham*: James 2:14–26." *HTR* 61:283–90.

———. 1969. "Partiality in the Assembly: James 2:2–4." *HTR* 62:87–97.

Warrington, Keith. 2004. "James 5:14–18: Healing Then and Now." *International Review of Mission* 93, nos. 370–71:346–67.

Watson, Duane F. 1992. "Gehenna." *ABD* 2:926–28.

———. 1993a. "James 2 in Light of Greco-Roman Schemes of Argumentation." *NTS* 39:94–121.

————. 1993b. "The Rhetoric of James 3:1–12 and a Classical Pattern of Argumentation." *NovT* 35, no. 1:48–64.

————. 2016. "Paul and Boasting." Pages 90–112 in *Paul in the Greco-Roman World: A Handbook*. Vol. 1. Rev. ed. London: Bloomsbury T&T Clark.

————. 2021. "An Assessment of the Rhetoric and Rhetorical Analysis of the Letter of James." Pages 415–32 in *The Catholic Letters: Critical Readings*. Edited by Darian R. Lockett. Critical Readings in Biblical Studies. London: T&T Clark.

Wesley, John. 1976 (1754). *Explanatory Notes upon the New Testament*. London: Epworth.

Westfall, Cynthia Long. 2019. "Mapping the Text: How Discourse Analysis Helps Reveal the Way through James." Pages 11–44 in *The Epistle of James: Linguistic Exegesis of an Early Christian Letter*. Edited by James D. Dvorak and Zachary K. Dawson. LENT 1. Eugene, OR: Pickwick.

Wheeler, Sondra Ely. 1995. *Wealth as Peril and Obligation: The New Testament on Possessions*. Grand Rapids: Eerdmans.

Whitlark, Jason A. 2010. "Ἔμφυτος Λόγος: A New Covenant Motif in the Letter of James." *Horizons in Biblical Theology* 32:144–65.

Whittaker, C. R. 1993. "The Poor." Pages 272–99 in *The Romans*. Edited by Andrea Giardina. Translated by Lydia G. Cochrane. Chicago: University of Chicago Press.

Williams, Craig W. 2012. *Reading Roman Friendship*. Cambridge: Cambridge University Press.

Wilson, Brittany E. 2015. *Unmanly Men: Refigurations of Masculinity in Luke-Acts*. New York: Oxford University Press.

Wilson, Jonathan R. 2011. "Virtue(s)." *DSE* 811–14.

Wolfe, Tom. 1987. *The Bonfire of the Vanities*. New York: Farrar, Straus & Giroux.

Wolff, Hans Walter. 1974. *Anthropology of the Old Testament*. London: SCM.

Wright, R. B. 1985. "Psalms of Solomon: A New Translation and Introduction." *OTP* 2:639–70.

Yu, Chun Ling. 2018. *Bonds and Boundaries among the Early Churches: Community Maintenance in the Letter of James and the Didache*. STT 29. Turnhout: Brepols.

INTRODUCTION

Reading and Hearing the Letter of James

The prospect of commenting on the Letter of James ought to raise a collective eyebrow. After all, doing so is not without its existential challenges. On the one hand, James himself warns that "teachers will be judged more stringently" (3:1)—and what are commentators if not women and men engaged at some level in the craft of teaching? Happily, those cautionary words of James focus on the fiery, venomous tongue rather than on getting the letter's message right at every turn. Even so, the concern James documents, not only in Jas 3 but also throughout the letter, for nurturing the faithful life of those people and communities who hear and read his words is enough to give one pause.

On the other hand, those of us who consider James as the church's Scripture can hardly entertain his message about listening to the word versus doing it without recognizing the need for some reflection and introspection with regard to both ourselves and our churches. "You must be doers of the word and not only listeners who mislead themselves. This is because those who listen to the word and are not doers—they are like those who look closely at their natural selves in a mirror, for they look at themselves, walk away, and immediately forget what they were like" (1:22–24). A more penetrating call to shift our focus from reading a text like James's letter for *information* to reading it for *reformation* or *transformation* is difficult to imagine.

The fantasy novelist Ursula Le Guin wrote, "*To learn a belief without belief is to sing a song without the tune.*" She goes on: "A yielding, an obedience, a willingness to accept these notes as the right notes, this pattern as the true pattern, is the essential gesture of performance, translation, and understanding."[1] Learning from James requires such gestures and postures as this, and more. Simply put, it is not enough to get James's message right if all that is meant by the exercise is concluding that we have drawn some conclusions about what he has to say. For James, hearing well goes much deeper. His practical wisdom is aimed at fashioning faithful life patterns by which to conceptualize, experience,

---

1. Le Guin 2000, 97–98 (emphasis original). See further, Green 2007, 1–23.

and respond to a world that is not so friendly to those who have declared and seek to live out their allegiance to the Lord Jesus Christ. Undoubtedly, if one wanted to expound on the importance of readerly virtue in interpretation of Scripture, the Letter of James would have a major role to play.[2]

We need more James, we who live in the first half of the twenty-first century. His letter speaks prophetically and pastorally about a range of issues that plague us. Two jump off the page, requiring not so much that we recognize them but that we recognize their address to us. The first comprises a host of issues related to wealth and poverty, and the second is our apparent incapacity to control our tongues. The contemporary evidence for both is clear enough, whether we are talking about life locally or globally. For the first, we need only consider the seemingly ever-growing distance between the annual salary of almost any celebrated chief executive officer and the yearly sum of wages for those in the same company but on the lower end of the pay scale; or the global rise in the number of billionaires versus the billions of people who live at or below the poverty line set by the World Bank or the World Health Organization; or the surprising, perplexing existence of people with at least one full-time job who, despite their working full-time, cannot afford any place to lay their heads at night other than their own cars. For the second, one need only review how people speak to each other on social media or in the "comments" section of articles posted in traditional media, or point to the general loss of restraint in the public square or within our households. Unfortunately, vexing speech habits characterize those who claim to be Christ-followers, too, and not only so-called secular folk. We sometimes act as though our words are powerless, allowing us to use them in dismissive, slanderous, ostracizing ways. Too many of us have turned a deaf ear or blind eye to the personal and relational work that words actually perform, whether constructive or deconstructive.

Less obvious points of contact with James's letter proliferate. It is one thing to recognize the disparity between rich and poor, for example, but quite another to recognize, say, the effects of that disparity on health care or average lifespan—both of which concern James, too.[3] And what about the world system against which James's letter sets itself, a system too easily embraced by both the powerful and the weak, both the wealthy and the needy, that unselfconsciously accords privilege to those with wealth and power? Is this not the very favoritism—in the courtroom, for example, or in the assembly of Christ-followers— against which James rails?[4] What of the "masters of the universe," wizards of times and seasons and commerce whose arrogance leads them to plan and

---

2. Indeed, someone ought to take up the concern with NT texts that Briggs brought to OT narrative (2010).

3. See below, on Jas 1 and 4.

4. See below, on Jas 2.

live as they please, quite apart from any consideration of what God is up to in the world?[5] Consider well, too, the baseline vocation that James everywhere promotes among his readers and hearers: consistency and integrity of heart and life in devotion to God (in opposition to double-mindedness or practices that can only be described as double-faced and double-tongued).

No one would accuse James of being "the church's first great theologian." This popular way of describing Paul would not make much sense of James and his contribution. Clearly, though, James is an exemplary theologian of the Jesus movement, a practical theologian, we might say, who has devoured Jesus's message and ruminated on it in relation to Israel's Scriptures. He articulates for his audience practical wisdom, wise habits of perception and practice.

Of course, knowing James's letter includes coming to terms with its "stuff," its arguments, its appeals, its perspectives, its interpretation of Jesus's message, its engagement with Israel's Scriptures, its grasp of contemporary Jewish and Greco-Roman thought, and so on. But James cultivates the kind of *knowing* that calls for his readers and hearers to envisage the world as God does and act accordingly, personally and communally. How might twenty-first-century audiences thus receive his words? Let me recommend three paths, none of which excludes the others and, indeed, each of which crisscrosses the others.

First, read and interact with James for no good reason. By this I mean to urge that we do not come to James in order to mine wise nuggets of wisdom or to formulate ideas for modern-day application. We can trace a sharp line between utilitarian approaches that treat scriptural texts like James as a how-to manual or a database for addressing our questions, on the one hand; and, on the other hand, the formation of James-patterned minds that stand ready to receive the Lord's wisdom. The latter requires patient, deliberate reading (and rereading)—reading, as it were, for no good reason but for the sake of having our dispositions and reflexes shaped by James-as-Scripture.

Second, enter as fully into James's world as humanly possible, recognizing that the primary challenge we face is not that we transform James's message into a relevant word for today but that we are transformed by James's message to have renewed minds and hearts and ever-renewing lives in our contexts. This is really a corollary of the first recommendation, since research has demonstrated how significantly reading influences readers. For example, empirical studies have shown that those who read Harry Potter books generate increased empathy. Textually, this is associated with the company Harry Potter keeps with stigmatized out-groups. Functional neuroimaging (fMRI) of fans of *Game of Thrones* has demonstrated that identifying with this or that character transforms one's sensibilities so that fans become more similar to the character with whom they identify. And, strange as it may seem, reading vampire novels stimulates

5. On "masters of the universe," see below, on 4:13–16.

readers' psychological transformation into vampires.[6] What might James's readers and hearers become if they (or we) were to find their (our) homes in this letter? How would they (we) come to hear and internalize his words about perfection, moral purity, humans made in God's likeness, and prayer for the sick and disabled? How might their (our) lives be shaped by James's central concern with double love: love for God and love for neighbor?

Third, if we think of James's letter as a script or a score, we can also reflect on how we "perform" James in our own contexts. Performance is not play-acting. Rather, it assumes the gravity of embodying and giving expression to James's letter. Whether one is thinking of an analogy with a musical or a theatric performance, a script or score stands complete on its own, but it also invites greater fulfillment, or activation, in the event of performance. In this respect, performance speaks to creative fidelity: *fidelity* in the sense that the notes on the score or words in the playscript set the contours of performance, *creative* in the sense that our differing contexts invite and call for different expressions of the same score or script. Combating favoritism in our lives and gatherings as God's people may look different in West Texas versus in West Africa, yet we can agree that favoritism (showing special favor) has no place among our personal and communal dispositions. Practices of humility may take different forms in Albany, New York, versus in Albany, New Zealand, but we can still receive James's instruction: "Humble yourselves before the Lord, and he will lift you up" (4:10). (Some therefore prefer the metaphor of *improvisation* over *performance*.)[7] In some or perhaps many instances, we will discern that our contemporary situation is much like the situation James envisions in his time. Other parts of the letter will require more by way of reflection and imagination. Either way, the challenge is to learn from James both how he has drawn on his theological sources and norms, Jesus's message and Israel's Scriptures chief among them, and the contours of the script or score he has crafted, as he challenges and encourages those who read and hear his letter.

Matters of Introduction

When we first pick up a book, we predictably ask—or perhaps we assume some answers to—a few basic questions that prepare us for what we are about to read: Who wrote it? When was it written? What kind of book is it? And so on. In biblical studies, we group such questions under the heading of "introduction."

Despite three hundred years of scholarly inquiry into such matters of introduction, these preliminary questions sometimes continue to perplex readers of biblical texts. Many of us have come to imagine that tying down reliable

---

6. See Stetka 2014; Gabriel and Young 2011; Broom, Chavez, and Wagner 2021.
7. See Barton 1999; Craigo-Snell 2000.

James and the Jesus Tradition

Although the Letter of James never quotes the words of Jesus, or claims to be drawing on them, we find numerous instances of James's creative appropriation of Jesus's teaching. These encourage the view that the letter's author was more than familiar with Jesus's sayings, that he was deeply influenced by them in the formulation of the letter's practical wisdom. The following verses represent only a small sampling of the parallels.

James*	Jesus's Teaching
"Anyone among you who lacks wisdom should ask God, who gives to everyone without a second thought, without reservation, and it will be given to you." (1:5)	"Ask, and you will receive. Search, and you will find. Knock, and the door will be opened to you. For everyone who asks, receives." (Matt 7:7–8 CEB)
"Whoever asks should ask in faith, without doubting." (1:6)	"If you have faith, you will receive whatever you pray for." (Matt 21:22 CEB)
"Truly happy are those who endure testing for, having proven themselves, they will receive the garland of life God has promised to those who love him." (1:12)	"But whoever stands firm until the end will be saved." (Matt 10:22 CEB)
"You must be doers of the word and not only listeners who mislead themselves." (1:22)	"But those who don't put into practice what they hear are like a person who built a house without a foundation." (Luke 6:49 CEB; cf. 8:15; 11:28)
"Has God not chosen the poor according to worldly standards to be rich in terms of faith, and to be heirs of the kingdom he has promised to those who love him?" (2:5)	"Happy are you who are poor, because God's kingdom is yours." (Luke 6:20 CEB)
"After all, judgment will be merciless for anyone who has not shown mercy. Mercy triumphs over judgment." (2:13)	"Happy are people who show mercy, because they will receive mercy." (Matt 5:7 CEB)
"Your wealth has rotted. Moths have ruined your clothes. Your gold and silver have become corroded. Their corrosion will be evidence against you. It will eat your flesh like fire. You have laid up treasure for the last days." (5:2–3)	"Do not store up for yourselves treasures on earth, where moth and rust consume and where thieves break in and steal; but store up for yourselves treasures in heaven, where neither moth nor rust consumes and where thieves do not break in and steal. For where your treasure is, there your heart will be also." (Matt 6:19–21 NRSV)

"Above all, my brothers and sisters, do not utter an oath—neither by heaven nor by earth, nor by anything else. But let your 'Yes' be yes and your 'No' be no, so that you may not fall under judgment." (5:12)	"But I say to you, Do not swear at all, either by heaven, for it is the throne of God, or by the earth, for it is his footstool, or by Jerusalem, for it is the city of the great King. And do not swear by your head, for you cannot make one hair white or black. Let your word be 'Yes, Yes' or 'No, No'; anything more than this comes from the evil one." (Matt 5:34–37 NRSV)

* Translations of James are my own (AT).

answers to these questions is necessary before we can make sense of the book. As it turns out, though, our interests are not always aligned well with the interests of the ancients: thus we find that the evidence before us does not always allow for the certainty we seek. In the mid-twentieth century, scholars often gave us their "assured results" on such matters, but subsequent study has recognized how tenuous those results often were, built as they were on the shifting sands of unconfirmed assumptions and problematic models of apostolic and postapostolic developments. In many cases, comments on introductory matters now come (or ought to come) with a healthy dose of humility regarding what we actually know.

In most but not all respects, our approach to introductory questions begins with the same options formulated fifty years ago, among an earlier generation of students of James's letter.[8] If the shape of those arguments has largely remained static, though, the general direction of scholarly opinion on some of them has shifted. My purpose here is to locate on the map my working assumptions and, briefly, to comment on why I have reached my conclusions. Our entry point is Jas 1:1:

> James, a servant of God and of the Lord Jesus Christ, to the twelve tribes who are in the diaspora, greetings.

As we will see, what might seem like a straightforward orientation to questions of introduction has served more to focus the terms of the debate than to resolve it.

---

8. Fifty years ago, the standard, critical introduction to the NT was by Kümmel (German in 1973, English in 1975). With respect to James, he lays out the issues well, though the intervening years have witnessed some different conclusions.

Who Is James?

Who is this James whom the letter identifies as its author? Although many first-century Christ-followers might have carried the name *James* (Gk: *Iakōbos*), the NT refers to only five:

1. James, brother of John and son of Zebedee, a Galilean fisherman, one of the Twelve;[9]
2. James, brother of Jesus, leader of the Jesus movement in Jerusalem;[10]
3. James, son of Alphaeus, one of the Twelve;[11]
4. James (or James the younger), brother of Joseph and son of (a) Mary;[12] and
5. James, father of one of the Twelve: Judas (not Iscariot).[13]

Given his status among the Twelve, James (1 above) might have been a candidate, but he was beheaded under King Herod Agrippa (Acts 12:1–2), thus before Agrippa's death in 44 CE. We know next to nothing about three of these Jameses (3, 4, and 5), so it is highly unlikely that one of them could refer to himself simply as "James, a servant of God and of the Lord Jesus Christ," without further markers of identification. Accordingly, that Jas 1:1 refers to James (2), Jesus's brother, is universally acknowledged.

What is not universally recognized, though, is that James, Jesus's brother, actually wrote the letter that bears his name. Before taking up this question, we should recognize that identifying the actual author of James's letter as we turn to study it may carry only secondary importance. This is because, irrespective of our decisions concerning its actual authorship, we ought to recognize that those early Christ-followers who heard or read this letter would have believed that they were actually hearing the voice of James, the Lord's brother. At the very least, this James is the letter's implied author, and they would have had no reason to imagine they were receiving a communique written by someone else in James's name.[14]

---

9. Matt 4:21; 10:2; 17:1; Mark 1:19, 29; 3:17; 5:37; 9:2; 10:35, 41; 13:3; 14:33; Luke 5:10; 6:14; 8:51; 9:28, 54; Acts 1:13; 12:2.

10. Matt 13:55; Mark 6:3; Acts 12:17; 15:13; 21:18; 1 Cor 15:7; Gal 1:19; 2:9, 12; Jude 1; cf. Acts 1:14.

11. Matt 10:3; Mark 3:18; Luke 6:15; Acts 1:13.

12. Matt 27:56; Mark 15:40; 16:1; Luke 24:10.

13. Luke 6:16; Acts 1:13.

14. This point is articulated well by K.-W. Niebuhr: "In the light of the knowledge we have of the reception milieu of early Christianity, it seems inconceivable to me that the receivers of the letter could assume someone other than the Lord's brother James to be the sender" (2013, 226; cf. K.-W. Niebuhr 2004).

Did James, Jesus's Brother, Author the Letter of James?

Can we take the self-attribution of James as the letter's author at face value? This question has two parts. First, what does it mean in antiquity *to author* a letter? This query turns on the ease with which we read modern, Western sensibilities back into the world of the ancient Mediterranean. Our concerns with individualism and originality, and thus with ownership of intellectual property and plagiarism, typically lead us to imagine first-century authors retreating alone to their desks, taking writing instruments in hand, and committing their thoughts to "paper" (that is, to a papyrus roll). However, ancient practices differed from our own in rather marked ways. Professional scribes (whom we may call "secretaries" or "amanuenses") often wrote on behalf of others, with the nature of their contributions appearing along a continuum. For example, they might serve as recorders, composers, editors, or even in a role like today's ghost writers. Their contributions might go named or unnamed. "Authors" of letters, then, might *authorize* documents that carry their names even when they did not dictate or write them from start to finish. Simply put, individual originality was not valued or mandated among the ancients in the way it is today. If James used an amanuensis, therefore, this would not detract from his authorial status.[15]

Second, can we credit James, Jesus's brother, with writing this letter, even after considering this somewhat less restrictive notion of "writing" or "authoring"? Primary among the objections raised is whether the son of a Galilean craftsperson would be capable of writing with competence in the Greek language and with the literary flair sometimes demonstrated in this letter. Three considerations mitigate this now-outdated objection. First, as is now well-known, the use of the Greek language was far more pervasive in the region we call Palestine than scholars once assumed.[16] Second, also well-known, this was especially the case in Jerusalem, where James would have spent the twenty-plus years of his life after Jesus's death and resurrection and before writing his letter.[17] Given James's emerging significance and leadership role in the Jerusalem church, we can only assume his heightened ability to traffic in Greek. This

15. For an example of an uncritical adherence to contemporary, Western assumptions about authorship, we need look no further than Kümmel 1975, 412–13. First, he notes that we have no evidence to support James's dependence on a secretary. Although true, this is unremarkable, given widespread practice. Second, he observes that James's use of a secretary would leave unanswered the question of "which part of the whole comes from the real author and which part comes from the 'secretary.'" Cf. Richards 1991.

16. This was demonstrated in Sevenster 1968.

17. The cultural intermixing following the Gk. conquest of Palestine in the late 4th century BCE eventuated in its hellenization, including facility in the Gk. language generally and, in a city like Jerusalem, significant facility. See Hengel 1974 (his basic argument continues to hold, with later nuance); Hengel with Markshies 1989.

includes his ability to blend Jewish and Greco-Roman traditions.[18] Third, as I have already hinted, there is no reason to doubt that James, like authors more generally, drew on the professional expertise of a scribe in the preparation of this letter. None of this proves that James, Jesus's brother, was the author of the letter that bears his name. However, these considerations rule out of court any claim that the letter's Greek is cause for rejecting James's authorship.[19]

Other standard objections are less compelling, too. For example, one might wonder whether a conservative on issues of Torah like James could be responsible for the approach to Torah taken in the letter. In this scenario, James's attitude toward Torah is evaluated on the basis of Luke's presentation of James in the Acts of the Apostles, particularly in those instances where James addresses Jew-gentile relations (cf. Gal 2:12). These present no real parallel with this letter, however, since issues specific to the status of gentiles among Jewish messianists are never mentioned in the letter. Instead, James presses forward his argument with the Shema and love command (love of God, love of neighbor) (1) in continuity with Israel's Scriptures and scriptural traditions, (2) having been schooled by Jesus's instruction regarding love of God and love of neighbor (e.g., Matt 22:35–39; Mark 12:28–31; cf. Luke 10:25–27), so as (3) to address directly those concerns he has discerned among the Jewish messianists he addresses.[20]

Alternatively, questions might be raised about the range of matters James addresses, and particularly whether those issues belong to the early Jesus movement (i.e., before James's death in 62 CE) or later. This approach is problematic in two respects. First, the older, evolutionary models that posited a stage-one church followed by stage two, and so on, have been rejected as having no purchase in the evidence. Accordingly, the presumption that some topics were alive early on but others much later no longer convinces readers. Second, this letter reveals that the author reflects and instructs on an array of concerns at home already in the Jesus tradition (i.e., in the early decades of the Jesus movement): wealth and poverty, for example, or arrogance, purity, neighbor love, speech habits, confession, prayer, and so on. In the commentary itself, we will see how, on point after point, James's message is both deeply embedded in the Jesus tradition and aware of corresponding concerns in earlier Second Temple Jewish literature.

The primary question regarding the authorship of this letter, then, is why we would not take its self-attribution at face value. This would recommend

---

18. See Watson 2021. Note Watson's (2021, 432) assessment that James, Jesus's brother, wrote the letter in the 50s CE, "trying to give voice to the gospel with lots of tools at hand, but no conventional blueprint as to how to proceed."

19. Cf. Penner 1996, 35–47.

20. By *Jewish Messianists*, I refer to Torah-observant Jews whose allegiance is to God and the Lord Jesus Christ. See below: "What Has James Written? To Whom Is It Addressed?"

a date of composition in the 50s CE.[21] Although we cannot prove that James, Jesus's brother, authored the letter, we have no grounds for rejecting this working assumption.

What Has James Written? To Whom Is It Addressed?

These two questions—genre and authorial audience—are intertwined. This is because most regard the Letter of James as, indeed, a letter, though lacking some of the trappings of a letter. (For example, it has no initial word of greeting nor an epistolary closing.) Given that genre forms allow for significant plasticity, this is not altogether surprising, and surely 1:1 establishes audience expectations that they are about to hear or read a letter addressed to them from James, Jesus's brother and leader of the church in Jerusalem. More to the point, most regard this document as an encyclical letter providing moral instruction (or concerned with moral formation) from James in Jerusalem to the diaspora.[22] In fact, the Letter of James compares favorably with similar early Jewish diaspora letters in terms of its aim, composition, and major motifs—for example, the Epistle of Jeremiah (Jer 29; 36 LXX), two letters reproduced (and a third referenced) at the beginning of 2 Maccabees (1:1–9; 1:10–2:18; cf. 1:7–8), an epistle that concludes 2 Baruch (chs. 78–86), and a letter from Baruch reproduced in 4 Baruch (6.19–25).[23]

If we find a broad consensus on genre, the contested question concerns the audience to whom James's letter is addressed: "the twelve tribes who are in the diaspora." Three options have their champions, though one of them, the third, garners by far the most support in scholarship today.

1. James writes to all Christ-followers, both Jewish and gentile, as the new Israel.[24] Although there is no reason to think the communities that would have received James's letter were entirely devoid of gentiles, this option falters on the complete absence in James's letter of instruction relative to the moral vices typical of gentiles (cf. 1 Pet 4:1–6) and the letter's thoroughgoing assumption that its audience is Torah-observant.

---

21. An earlier date would be difficult to square with the time required for James to achieve his status as central leader of the Jerusalem church. A slightly later date is possible, but only slightly, given James's death in 62 CE. The letter itself provides nothing on which to hang a chronological reference that might satisfy further curiosity about the letter's date. Attempts to pin down a date based on the relationship of James and Paul, on James's knowledge of Paul's letters, or on how best to square James's and Paul's instruction on faith and deeds—such efforts can do no more than construct hypotheses on top of theories. See the excursus "James and Paul."

22. See Bauckham 1999, 11–28.

23. See K.-W. Niebuhr 2021.

24. See, e.g., Kümmel 1975, 407–8; Marcus 2014.

2. James writes to Jews, including those who follow Jesus and those who do not. According to this viewpoint, apart from 1:1, the Letter of James is entirely explicable without reference to the Lord Jesus Christ.[25] On the one hand, it is true that the Letter of James does little to distinguish itself as "Christian." This is not surprising, though, given that this historical moment knew no distinct religion called Christianity. Instead, Christ-followers comprised a renewal movement within Israel. On the other hand, just beneath the surface of the entire letter flows the strong currents of the Jesus tradition. James never quotes Jesus, but the parallels with material in the Synoptic Gospels are inescapable (as the commentary will show). James's instruction flows from Israel's scriptural traditions through the Jesus tradition. The result is a collection of theological and ethical ruminations aimed at the ongoing formation of Christ-followers. Additionally, James refers to "the faith of our glorious Lord Jesus Christ" (2:1). Also, he uses the term *Lord* (*kyrios*) of both God and Jesus (sometimes in ambiguous ways that could refer to either), and includes references to the *Lord* that almost certainly refer to Jesus (5:7–8, 14–15).

3. James writes to Jewish Christ-followers, or Jewish messianists, outside the borders of Israel's historic land. Taken on its own, "the twelve tribes" could refer metaphorically to Israel, though here it more likely signifies "restored Israel." That is, James's reference to Jesus as Lord and Christ presses in the direction of a Jewish renewal movement comprising Torah-observant Jews whose allegiance, like James's, is to God and the Lord Jesus Christ (1:1).[26]

James as Practical Theologian

Among the roles James played in the early Jesus movement is the one most on display in the Letter of James, which is James the practical theologian. This is not because he concerns himself with "practical matters" instead of "theological issues"—a dichotomy alien to James's place in history. Nor is he trying to demonstrate the "practical application" of the gospel for daily life or seeking to bridge the chasm between "theory" and "practice"—again, dualisms more at home in the modern era than in his. Rather, in James's hands, theology is critical reflection on the personal and corporate practices among communities of Christ-followers. Accordingly, we see James analyzing the lived experiences

25. See, e.g., Allison 2013, who regards the mention of Jesus in 2:1 as an interpolation, though no textual basis exists for excluding this reference to the "Lord Jesus Christ" in 2:1.
26. Cf., e.g., Bauckham 2021.

of Jewish messianists as a minority people in a world patterned after Roman social conventions and sensibilities. In James's perspective, their lives in the diaspora are set within the borders of the daily influence of a series of taken-for-granted values that work against Israel's confession to love God entirely and its corollary of neighbor love. These include such values as status-craving, economic security, bitter rivalry, and devious self-promotion, as well as forms of violence (including retaliation and violent speech) thought necessary to make something of oneself within this world system.

Diaspora life brings with it a steady diet of trials as a minoritized people, like these Jewish messianists, seek to thrive in their scattered settings while at the same time remaining faithful to their Lord. James invites his audience to step back from their day-to-day lives and review them from the perspective of God's wisdom. In doing so, he sets before them a practical wisdom that will guide their interpretation of their contexts and their lives within those contexts, challenge their assumptions about how to live out the true word by which God has chosen to give them new birth (1:18), furnish fresh insight into the possibilities of faithful life, and enable alternative responses to the trials that come their way.

His is not a theology seminar, but he is well aware that theological commitments—for example, about God, the Lord Jesus, the nature of humanity, and the end of time—are deeply embedded in the practices of his audience. We might say that he teases them out, exposes them, and redirects them. He is after a theological formation guided by, and guiding, practices aligned with this double love, love of God and love of neighbor.

James's efforts as a practical theologian are challenged by a divergent vision of life and faith, by people who apparently claim faith but whose practices reveal a divergent set of allegiances. This explains James's bodily metaphors: double-minded, double-tongued, and double-faced. It explains his call to purity and his concern with Christ-followers who are (or may be) contaminated by the world. And it explains the incredulity about their lives that he captures in down-to-earth language: "Both fresh water and salt water do not flow from the same spring, do they? My brothers and sisters, can a fig tree produce olives or a grapevine figs? Of course not, and neither does a saltwater spring yield fresh water" (3:11–12). He thus sets before his readers two ways: Are you friend of God or friend of the world? And he drives home the impossibility of having it both ways.

Translations and Acknowledgments

Unless otherwise indicated, all translations of material from the Letter of James are my own, from NA[28]. At times, my translation parallels the CEB; this is due to my work as one of the translators of James in the CEB.

I worked out some of my thinking on the Letter of James in other publications, including the following:

- "Betwixt and Between: The Letter of James and the Human Condition." *BibAnn* 12, no. 2 (2022): 295–308. Adapted with permission. https://doi.org/10.31743/biban.13477.
- "'I'll Show You My Faith' (James 2:18): Inspiring Models for Exilic Life." *Int* 74, no. 4 (2020): 344–52. Adapted with permission of SAGE Publications. https://doi.org/10.1177/0020964320936402.
- "James, Theological Education, and Practical Wisdom." Pages 96–107 in *Now to God Who Is Able*. Edited by Neal D. Presa and Anne Zaki. Eugene, OR: Wipf & Stock, 2023. Adapted with permission
- "Reading James Missionally." Pages 194–212 in *Reading the Bible Missionally*. Edited by Michael W. Goheen. The Gospel and Our Culture Series. Grand Rapids: Eerdmans, 2016. Adapted with permission.

COMMENTARY ON THE LETTER OF JAMES

James 1:1
Greetings

Although James otherwise lacks the expected features of a Hellenistic letter, the opening is typical of the letter form: identification of the sender, identification of the receiver, and greetings. In the NT, the letter opening in Acts 15:23 provides the closest analogy: "The apostles and elders, to the gentile believers in Antioch, Syria, and Cilicia, greetings."[1] Interestingly, the letter embedded in Luke's account shares similarities with the Letter of James: (1) each is a circular letter with a distributed audience, (2) both originate in Jerusalem, and (3) behind each stands James, the prominent leader of the community of Christ-followers in Jerusalem. We are accustomed to contemporary parallels, whether in formal ("Dear [name]," "Sincerely yours") or informal ("Hi, [name]," "Best") communiques. Accordingly, we may dismiss their significance: Are they really *dear*? Are those *best wishes* genuine? James's greeting may be highly stylized, but we should not pass over it too quickly. With coded language, James begins immediately to set the stage for the material that follows.[2]

1:1 James, a servant[a] of God and of the Lord Jesus Christ,[b] to the twelve tribes who are in the diaspora, greetings.

a. I have avoided translating the Gk. term *doulos* as "slave" in order to avoid the undeniably inhumane construction and practice of "slavery" in the Roman world (and elsewhere; see, too, Adewuya 2023, 9–10). That James can refer to human beings, all of them, as made in God's likeness (3:9; cf. Gen 1:26–27) demonstrates that Rome's slave society may inform but has not determined his understanding of *doulos*.

---

1. Cf. Acts 23:26: "Claudius Lysias, to the most noble Governor Felix, greetings."
2. By referring to James's "coded language," I do not mean to suggest that he uses mysterious or secretive words requiring esoteric knowledge or cryptography. Rather, his word choices trigger well-known associations for the population comprising his audience.

b. Because neither "God" nor "Lord Jesus Christ" has a definite article in the Gk. text, we could read this opening phrase as a reference to Jesus as both God and Lord— e.g., "servant of Jesus Christ, God and Lord" or "servant of God, that is, the Lord Jesus Christ" (the latter taking *kai* in an epexegetical sense, as explanatory). Even in the more traditional translation I have given (cf., e.g., AV, CEB, NIV, NRSV), James's grammar coordinates references to "God" and "Lord" in a way that speaks to their potential interchangeability. Cf. Michaels 2005, 270–72.

Apart from giving us his name, James provides little by which we might identify him. What he says of himself, that he serves God and the Lord Jesus Christ, presumably could be said of many Jameses who belonged to the larger messianic Jewish community. This alone directs our attention firmly to the one James whose renown was such that he needed no further titles or descriptors in order to speak authoritatively to brothers and sisters outside Palestine. James, John's brother and prominent among Jesus's twelve apostles, is already dead, martyred under Herod (Acts 12:1–2). James, Jesus's brother, heads the Jerusalem church (Acts 12:17; 15:13–21; 21:18; Gal 1:19; 2:7–10). This James, then, stands behind this circular letter from Jerusalem to the diaspora—"stands behind" since, according to letter-writing practices in Roman antiquity, secretaries were typically entrusted with the actual drafting and redrafting of such missives.

If James, Jesus's brother, authorized this letter, why does his letter opening not mention this relationship? First, throughout his letter James demonstrates his familiarity with Jesus's teaching, and this would include Jesus's definition of siblings. *Brother* and *sister*—these relations are not defined by shared parentage or genograms, but by obedience to God (Matt 12:50; Mark 3:35; Luke 8:21). Second, by referring to himself as *servant*, James associates himself with God and the Lord, as well as his audience, in two interrelated ways. On the one hand, drawing on scriptural usage, he thus presents himself in prophetic garb, as one who represents and speaks on behalf of God and the Lord Jesus.[3] Accordingly, his hearers and readers should receive this letter as divine speech. On the other hand, he portrays himself in terms of his unbending devotion to God and the Lord Jesus. Coupled with his reference to Jesus as *Lord*, his self-designation as *servant* activates a household schema. The importance of this schema (particularly for identifying the patterns of thinking, feeling, believing, and behaving appropriate to *this* household) will be developed in the letter as a whole, but here it already signifies the importance of single-minded allegiance (rather than the double-mindedness against which James warns: 1:7–8; 4:8). The status of servants was tied to the status of the household heads they served,

---

3. Cf., e.g., Jer 7:25; 25:4; Isa 20:3; Ezek 38:17; Amos 3:7. For similar usage in the NT, see Rom 1:1; Phil 1:1; 2 Pet 1:1. Jude 1. Cf. D. Martin 1990, 54–58.

so it is worth our reflecting on James's claim to serve God and the Lord Jesus— a claim that signifies *both* humility before God and the Lord *and* lofty status among God's people, because God gives grace to the humble and the Lord honors those who humble themselves (4:6, 10).

From the outset, James's self-reference establishes the letter's hermeneutical orientation, a theological and especially christological filter through which to read what follows. James mentions Jesus explicitly only twice in the letter— here and in 2:1: "the faith of our glorious Lord Jesus Christ." Additionally, James almost certainly speaks of Jesus when he later refers to "the coming of the Lord" (5:7–8). Otherwise, James reveals something of his theological commitments in the ambiguity of his references to the Lord.[4] Does he refer to Israel's God (the Father—1:17, 27; 3:9) or to the Lord Jesus Christ? We are not always sure, and this notable interchangeability accentuates the high Christology at hand already in 1:1. Indeed, to refer to Jesus as *Lord* identifies Jesus with Israel's God in a way that draws on early affirmations of Jesus among Jews who follow Christ.[5] James's letter opening should not be reduced to christological acclamation, though. Situated at the beginning, James's phrasing frames the perspective from which to read the letter: in the light of Jesus's unveiling of God's agenda and the faithfulness for which it calls.

A few manuscripts designate James's letter as a "General" or "Catholic" Epistle (*katholikē epistolē*),[6] undoubtedly because the letter otherwise provides so little to help identify its audience. Taken on its own, "the twelve tribes" could refer metaphorically to Israel, though here it more likely signifies "restored Israel." Following James's acclamation of Jesus as Lord and Christ, the phrase presses in the direction of *Israel, whose hope has been restored in Jesus's coming*. In other words, James participates in and now addresses a Jewish restorationist movement. Their location is the diaspora, meaning outside the borders of Israel's historic land. For some, the image of *diaspora* might invoke images of betwixt and between, a people torn from their homeland, a vale (or trail) of tears for the displaced. Others recognize that, by the first century CE, the Jewish diaspora was a more established amalgamation of forced and voluntary migration, lacking for most the angst accompanying refugee status. Even if experiences of diaspora varied, even if few Jewish expatriates seemed compelled to return to the homeland, plentiful evidence still suggests koinonia with the homeland (esp. participation in the temple tax) and, outside the homeland, patterns of

4. E.g., Jas 1:7; 4:10, 15; 5:14.
5. See, e.g., 1 Cor 16:22; Rev 22:20; and especially Hurtado 2005; Baker 2002. K.-W. Niebuhr 2020, 187: "If we cannot sharply distinguish between God and Jesus Christ as recipients of the requests, prayers, and perhaps also complaints of the believers [in James], then every reference to such practices in the letter may testify to possible forms of Christ veneration as well." Cf. already R. Longenecker 1970, 120–36.
6. Cf. mss. ‭א‬ A B*.

Jewish resistance (and of anti-Jewish attitudes and behavior). Those patterns of resistance centered on such distinguishing commitments and practices as circumcision, diet, and Sabbath-keeping.[7] Even for those comfortably settled in their diasporic homes (and this is true of first-century Jewish or modern-day Korean and Chinese diasporas), questions of identity and life patterns remain.

The challenge lay in the character and maintenance of faithful life in settings lacking a Jewish majority. James himself describes "devotion that is pure and unsullied" in part as "keep[ing] ourselves from being contaminated by the world" (1:27). "Adulterers! Do you not know that friendship with the world means enmity with God?" (4:4). Thus James seems little concerned with external forces except insofar as external, worldly patterns of life might be internalized among Christ-followers. He never mentions circumcision, diet, and Sabbath-keeping, presumably because these could be taken for granted among his audience. Instead, he refers to a range of challenges among God's people: various trials (1:2–3, 12), distress among society's vulnerable (1:27), worldly contamination (1:27), conflicts and disputes (4:1), deceit (5:4), unjust verdicts (5:6), murder (5:6), and the potential of drifting away from the truth (5:19). James 1:1, then, imagines a distributed audience threatened by assimilation into patterns of life alien to the way of faithfulness toward God and the Lord Jesus Christ.

---

7. See Gruen 2002; on circumcision, diet, and Sabbath, see Barclay 1996, 428–42; L. Feldman 1993, 153–70.

James 1:2–27
Introduction: Divine Wisdom versus Self-deception amid Trials

On an initial reading, this opening section of James's letter might look like a hodgepodge of wisdom sayings cast as commands. Closer examination reveals word links drawing together what first appear to be isolated directives. For example, those who endure amid trials lack (*leipō*) nothing, but those who lack (*leipō*) wisdom should ask God (1:4–5). Additionally, important parallels and contrasts contribute to an overall sense of the coherence of James's introduction. For example, standing firm leads to the life God promised (1:2–4, 12), but allowing one's cravings to rule leads to sin and death (1:14–15). Similarly, consider James's admonition in 1:13–18: Make no mistake: every perfect gift comes from God, but temptations do not come from God. Even so, it remains easier to map these linguistic and thematic connections than to coordinate them into a compelling structure.[1]

My thinking about James's structure often takes its cues from his use of the direct address, "my (dear) brothers and sisters."[2] Generally speaking, address forms signal and promote either relations marked by power ("Your honor," "Hey, kid") or those marked by affinity, even mutuality ("Friends," "Sisters and brothers"). James's discourse moves in the latter direction, setting aside structured hierarchy in favor of belonging and egalitarianism. Triggering relationships marked by solidarity, James goes on to sketch the life patterns by which resemblance among these family members is measured: not hair color, height, or attached ear lobes, but endurance amid trials, humbly welcoming the implanted word, caring for orphans and widows in their difficulties, and so on. In James, references to his siblings tend also to mark shifts in the discourse, as in 1:2, 19: "My brothers and sisters, consider the various tests you

---

1. Cf., e.g., M. Taylor 2006, 1–34, surveying a range of proposals; M. Taylor and Guthrie 2006; Westfall 2019.

2. See Jas 1:2, 16, 19; 2:1, 5, 14; 3:1, 10, 12; 5:12, 19 (all as AT); cf. "brothers and sisters" in 4:11; 5:7, 9, 10.

encounter as occasions for the greatest happiness" and "understand, my dear brothers and sisters."[3]

James introduces his letter in two ways. First, like the prelude in a musical composition, this section announces motifs that will receive more complex development in what follows. The following chart is illustrative.

James 1:2–27 as "Introduction"		
James 1	**Motif**	**James 2–5**
1:2–4, 12–16	Testing and Endurance	5:7–12
1:5–8, 17–18	Wisdom	3:13–18
1:2, 6	Faith/Faithfulness	2:1–3, 14–26; 5:15
1:5–8	Prayer	4:3; 5:13–18
1:8	Double-mindedness	4:8
1:9–11	Wealth and Poverty	2:1–13; 4:13–5:6
1:19, 26	Speech Ethics	3:1–11
1:19–27	Putting Faith into Practice	2:14–26
1:21, 27	Purity	3:6, 17; 4:4–8

James pulls back the curtain on those aspects of diasporic life that motivate his letter and sets the theological terms for how he will approach them. Reading these paragraphs as relatively isolated commands allows us to move from one concern, such as trials and the need for wisdom (1:2–8), to another, such as the contrast between the poor and wealthy (1:9–11), as though they were unrelated. If we acknowledge coherence in James's presentation, however, the outcome is somewhat different. He begins with trials, yes, but insists that proper response to trials depends on God's wisdom, graciously given. And those who share God's wisdom uncouple their impoverishment from the lowly status that typically accompanies it. Likewise, from the perspective of God's wisdom, those with wealth are assessed negatively; they are wasting away. Although James will spell out additional concerns in his introduction, they often swirl around this basic polarity: impoverished brothers and sisters, on the one hand; and

---

3. The wording in 1:16, "Do not be deceived, my dear brothers and sisters," has the opposite effect, drawing James's audience in, urging them to consider the contrasting outcomes of God's desire or purpose (*boulomai*, 1:17–18) and the outcomes of human desire or craving (*epithymia*, 1:13–15): thriving versus death.

the wealthy, on the other. (Interestingly, only the poor are addressed as James's siblings, his kin; the wealthy are simply "the wealthy" [1:9–10].)[4]

Second, James lays out two paths—one associated with those who are poor but wise, the other associated with those who are wealthy and self-deceived.

Two Ways in James 1:2–27		
	Path A	**Path B**
Consequences	Maturity Garland of life Salvation Blessedness	Disappear like a flower Wither away Give birth to death Worthless devotion
Source	Generous God Creator God God's word, implanted	Doubt Double-mindedness Craving Self-deception

Activities	Consider trials as occasions for
	  happiness
	Praying in faith
	Satisfaction in lowliness
	Endure testing
	Set aside impurity and evil
	Welcome and do God's word
	Care for orphans and widows
	Avoid the world's
	  contamination
		Doubt
		Satisfaction in wealth
		Allow cravings to grow
		Refuse to set aside impurity
		  and evil
		Hearers, not doers
		Anger
		Lack of control over speech

The setting for both paths is the same: a dispersed people experiencing trials. James's thought participates in the pervasive scriptural motif that God's aim for humanity includes putting pressure on them so that they might flourish.[5] The term James uses can signify *trials* (a morally neutral term), but also *testing* (which promotes human development and flourishing) and *tempting* (which thwarts human growth and crushes life).[6] All experience *trials* in the diaspora;

---

4. James does not draw a hard line between the wealthy and the community of "brothers and sisters," however. For James, as we will see, "the wealthy" are not simply those with wealth; rather, they are those whose wealth-oriented sensibilities and behaviors (e.g., favoritism, disregarding God in their life planning, and unjust or even violent exercise of power) speak against their status as "brothers and sisters."

5. Goldingay 2016, 177; cf. Moberly 2000, esp. 238–42.

6. James uses *peirasmos* (1:2, 12); its verbal form, *peirazō* (1:13 [3×], 14); and, speaking of God, *apeirastos* (1:13). See Moberly 2000, 239–40.

trials morph into *temptation* when people respond poorly. James presses this point home when he claims that *temptations* have their root in human craving, not in God. Moral failure cannot be traced back to external pressures alone, nor can God be blamed. Rather, internal inclinations give rise to sin and death. Throughout his introduction, James's images contrast these two paths using images like maturity and completeness, high status, a garland of life, God's salvation, and blessedness—over against images of becoming unmoored, instability, perishing, death, and worthless devotion. These images recruit bodily experiences of security and danger, health and sickness, and stimulate intuitive responses—kneejerk reactions that, when activated, promote feelings that sway persons at a preconscious level toward this path instead of that one. Clearly, James biases his readers and hearers toward life—a life marked by flourishing and integrity, not double-mindedness (1:4, 7–8).

In the period of Second Temple Judaism, James has good company in his diagnosis of the human situation in terms of an inclination toward sin.[7] However, he presses harder in his recognition of the crushing influence of craving—so overwhelming that it requires more than closer adherence to God's instruction, an extra measure of self-control, or greater dependence on one's rational capacities. The human heart leans toward sin, so a powerful antidote is needed: God's "true word, . . . the implanted word that has the power to save you" (1:18, 21), which Christ-followers must receive with open arms and put into practice (1:22–27). This is none other than the wisdom God gives, the capacity both to understand and to act—to embody patterns of perception and performance that find their true north in God's ways.

1:2–18 Testing and the Way of Wisdom

1:2 My brothers and sisters, consider the various trials you encounter as occasions for the greatest happiness, 3 knowing that the testing of your faithfulness produces endurance. 4 Let endurance complete its work so that you may be mature, whole, lacking nothing.

5 Anyone among you who lacks wisdom should ask God, who gives to everyone without a second thought, without reservation, and it will be given to you. 6 Whoever asks should ask in faith, without doubting,[a] for whoever doubts is like the surf of the sea, driven and tossed by the wind. 7-8 Those people, double-minded and unstable in all their ways, must never expect they will receive anything from the Lord.

9 Brothers and sisters who are of low status should express confidence[b] concerning their high status. 10 The wealthy should express confidence

---

7. E.g., 2 Esd 3–4; Sir 5:2; 15:14–15; 19:28; 23:4–5; Philo, *Spec. Laws* 2.163; 4 Macc 1.1; CD 2.15. See Marcus 1982.

concerning their low status because they will fade away like wildflowers. 11 The sun rises with its scorching heat and bakes the grass so that its flowers fall, and it loses its beauty. Just like that, in the midst of their daily lives,[c] the wealthy will fade away.

12 Truly happy are those who endure testing for, having proven themselves, they will receive the garland of life that God[d] has promised to those who love him. 13 No one being tested should say, "God is tempting me!" This is because God cannot be tempted by evil, nor does he tempt anyone. 14 Everyone is tempted by their own cravings, lured away and seduced by them. 15 Once that craving conceives, it gives birth to sin— and sin, once it reaches adulthood, gives birth to death. 16 Do not be deceived, my dear brothers and sisters! 17 Every good gift, every perfect gift, is from above and comes down from the Father of Lights, in whose character there is no variation or shifting shadow.[e] 18 He chose to give us birth by means of his true word so that we might be a kind of foretaste[f] of what would become of everything he created.

a. How best to understand *diakrinō* in this cotext is disputed. (Cotext refers to the words surrounding a term, phrase, or longer passage. Attention to cotext provides important assistance in determining meaning.) If *pistis* has the sense of *confidence* in 1:6, then a reading of *diakrinō* as *filing a complaint against* or *arguing with* (cf. Adam 2013, 8; Spitaler 2007) is possible; on retaining the language of *doubting*, see Allison 2013, 178–81; cf. *CGL* 1:349–50.

b. For this rendering of *kauchaomai*, see L&N §33.368. The traditional translation, "I boast," generally understood today as an expression of arrogance, does not reflect the sense of James's directive.

c. *Poreia* signifies travel or journey (*CGL* 2:1165)—including, in Roman antiquity, especially travel in the service of a trade; by metaphoric extension, it can signify a life path. Its usage here may anticipate 4:13: "Today or tomorrow we will go [*poreuomai*] to this or that city and spend a year there, trading and making money."

d. Following the best witnesses ($\mathfrak{P}^{74}$, ℵ, A, B, et al.), NA[28] does not identify a subject for the verb *epēngeilato* (has promised). This likely represents the initial text, which later scribes regarded as inadequate; accordingly, they added either *kyrios* ("Lord"—P, 5, 307, 436, et al.) or *theos* ("God"—1175, 1243, 1735, et al.).

e. For this translation of *tropēs aposkiasma*, see L&N §14.61.

f. *Aparchē*, usually translated as *firstfruits* (a term that evokes a sacrificial context), has here the extended sense of *the first* or *an initial sampling of what is to come*—cf. Rom 16:5; 1 Cor 16:15.

The first unit of James's introduction is set off by matching references to his hearers and readers: "my [dear] brothers and sisters" (1:2, 19). It can be divided into four paragraphs that promote an inversion of conventional wisdom (regarding trials, 1:2–4; regarding lowly status and wealth, 1:9–11), implore

James's audience to endure today in the hope of present flourishing and future reward (1:2–4, 12–18), certify that temptations arise because of the human condition and not because God introduces them (1:12–18), and present God's hold-nothing-back graciousness as the means by which human cravings can be overcome and trials may be resisted (1:5–8, 12–18). Like a Celtic knot, James's strands of thought are so intricately interlaced that they are not easily disentangled.

As with so much of this letter, James concerns himself here with epistemology, what we know and how we know it. He shows his hand concerning the importance of *knowing* in his use of the terms "I know" (*ginōskō*, 1:3) and "practical wisdom" (*sophia*, 1:5). In truth, though, the entire opening section of the letter turns on the fresh insight James urges his audience to exercise. Who would guess that people mired in trials should understand them as occasions for the greatest happiness? Those of low status—are they not the down and out? Yet, James recalibrates conventional standards of valuation, declaring the lowly as exalted and the exalted as brought low. James grounds this conversion of the imagination in transformed patterns of thinking and believing that (1) reorient the self in the world, (2) are shaped within and shared by one's extended network (what James calls "brothers and sisters"), and so (3) generate and maintain coherence within the community and at the same time identify and animate responses of resistance toward life patterns that oppose God's wisdom, and (4) are on display in one's practices. In short, James calls for his readers and hearers to envisage the world as God does and act accordingly, and to do so together. Moreover, for James these transformed patterns of thinking and believing (5) are not the result of human mastery but comprise God's gift to those who ask with confidence in God (1:5).

Even if new ways of knowing come from God, James marks the way forward with words that draw deeply on Israel's Scriptures and Jesus's teaching. This is important in two ways. On the one hand, James pulls back the curtain on what he regards as his most important theological resource, namely, the divine voice on display in Israel's Scriptures and in Jesus's ministry. On the other hand, personal and community identities are *narratively constructed*—that is, identity is sculpted, propagated, and preserved by the stories we tell about ourselves, collectively and personally. Accordingly, transformation entails a reordering of life in terms of a fresh adaptation of the narrative shared among and told by the community.

For his part, James locates his brothers and sisters in an overarching narrative with four primary kernels:[8]

---

8. I borrow the term "kernel" from Chatman's classic work *Story and Discourse* (1978, 53): "nodes or hinges in the structure, branching points which force a narrative into one or two (or more) possible paths." I am adapting material first published in Green 2016.

Creation → Jesus's Advent → Present, Diasporic Life → Consummation

James's opening chapter alludes to all four—creation (1:17), Jesus's advent (1:1), diasporic life and its trials (1:1–2), and the consummation (1:12, 18)—but James's reflections on creation and, especially, on Gen 1–3 take center stage. This is noteworthy because stories about beginnings (cosmology) and endings (eschatology) play key roles in how we understand God's nature, God's engagement with the world, and relationships among God's creatures.

James's opening comment raises the question of the origin of trials, including the possible charge that God is their source. Israel's Scriptures say that God tests his people (e.g., Gen 22:1: "God tested Abraham"), which accentuates the problem. James takes up this concern by turning to the opening chapters of Genesis. He refers in 1:17 to "the Father of Lights," which recalls God's work in Gen 1:3–5, 14–18: the creation of light and of heavenly bodies that illumine the earth. James's claim that "every good gift" comes from God evokes God's affirmation of creation's goodness (Gen 1:4, 10, 12, 18, 21, 25, 31). He ends this section by referring to "everything God created" (1:18).[9] And the problem of testing has James reflecting on Gen 3, even if he does not mention Adam and Eve by name.

Working within the wider biblical tradition, he has only three choices for identifying temptation's cause: God, Satan, or human beings. James rejects the first: "No one being tested should say, 'God is tempting me!'" (1:13); does not mention the second;[10] and advocates for the third: "Everyone is tempted by their own cravings, lured away and seduced by them" (1:14). As John Wesley observes in his comments on James, "We are therefore to look for the cause of every sin, *in*, not *out of*, ourselves."[11] James's interest in the etiology of sin has an analogue in the Jewish text *Life of Adam and Eve* (late first century CE?). In it, Adam and Eve, expelled from Eden, try to explain suffering and pain; sin's roots, we learn, are nourished by the poison of insatiable craving. Similarly, in 2 Esdras (late first century CE), Adam was burdened with an evil inclination, a predisposition toward evil that continues to exercise overwhelming influence on all humanity.

If we read the two creation accounts in Gen 1–3 side by side rather than sequentially, we gain a stronger sense of James's portrait. This is because Genesis, on this reading, does not recount humanity's loss of God's image (and James certainly does not regard God's likeness as having been lost; cf. 3:9) but rather exposes the perplexing riddle of the human situation. Genesis 1:1–2:4a has God

---

9. Gk. *ktisma*: "what was created"—cf. Wis 9:2; 13:5; 14:11; 1 Tim 4:4; Rev 5:13; 8:9.

10. That is, James does not mention the second in this textual unit; cf., however, 2:19; 3:14–16; 4:7.

11. Wesley 1976, 857.

creating humanity in God's own image, so that human beings are "like God." Genesis 2:4b–3:24 has human beings seeking, misguidedly, to be "like God." "Genesis 1–3, therefore, depicts the human condition in its conflicted relation to good and evil, life and death," with "humans . . . entrusted with presencing God in the world yet . . . subject to a fatal misreading of what this means as subjective reality."[12] The life of human beings, from this vantage point, is deeply (and frustratingly) paradoxical. They are like God yet misconstrue the possibilities and limitations of godlikeness. James participates in that enigma: the optimism of happiness, confidence, faith, and life versus the overpowering burden of human craving. For James, human hearts bend toward double-mindedness, favoritism, wrong speaking, arrogance, selfish ambition, violence—all of which, we will learn, are tied to earthly dispositions and behavior (cf. 3:14–16). The solution— wisdom from above, the gift of God's "true word"—though external, must be internalized. It must be welcomed and practiced.

[1:2–4] James introduces his letter with a chain of effects that grounds the process from trials to endurance and from endurance to wholeness in "the greatest happiness." This formulation is not an invitation to masochism (finding pleasure in suffering) or escapism (rising above circumstances amid suffering). Rather, James's instruction turns on ancient (and sometimes contemporary) views of happiness, which he mentions twice in this larger subsection (1:2, 12): "Consider the various trials you encounter as occasions for the greatest happiness. . . . Truly happy are those who endure testing."[13] *Happiness* in these instances is not cheeriness or a smiley face. In fact, James's terminology does not denote any emotion, at least as this is usually understood in the modern West. James's world largely understood emotion as the outcome of irrational impulses that ought to be regulated by a rational person, whereas James concerns himself with inclinations and behaviors associated with human flourishing. Thus in contemporary terms, James's usage is more at home in today's research on happiness than in popular usage, which often reduces happiness to glib and fleeting responses to one's current circumstances. In contemporary study, happiness refers to growth, integrity, and well-being.[14] Always centered in a community and its way of life, happiness entails an integrated life that follows and embodies that way. Using ancient formulations, happiness for James is not the absence of suffering (as in Epicureanism) but is more akin to the Stoic notion of living in harmony with the way things really are. Note, however, that "the way things really are" is itself perspectival, grounded in specific

---

12. McConville 2016, 41, 43.

13. Among the terms associated with *happiness* (L&N §§25.116–34), James uses *chara* in 1:2; 4:9; *makarios* in 1:12, 25; and *makarizō* in 5:11. (The use of *chairō* in 1:1, "greetings," lies outside this semantic domain.)

14. See, e.g., Ryan and Deci 2001; Berridge and Kringelbach 2008.

communities and traditions. For the cultural anthropologist, "each people knows their own kind of happiness";[15] so we recognize instantly that, from the beginning of his letter, James seeks to form a people, to inspire in them a particular way of seeing things (and then presses them to respond accordingly). Their troubled, diasporic lives are formative. Trials foster human flourishing.[16]

James's world of thought is reminiscent of Jesus's Sermon on the Plain, in which Jesus identifies the happiness of those who are poor, hungry, weeping, and experiencing all sorts of harassment (Luke 6:20–26). In the Sermon on the Plain, as in James, happiness is not a momentary condition based on one's good fortune but a pronouncement over lives lived before God. Such lives may be distant from the colonnades and embellishments of power and privilege, and they may attract harassment from those who have not embraced this vision of faithful life, yet they are affirmed and celebrated in God's economy.

James's *trials* are unspecified, and his use of the adjective *various* advances further the apparently vague nature of his directive. The framing of his letter in a diasporic setting and in relation to God's messianic people ensures, though, that he is not so much concerned with life's mundane annoyances and irritants—but neither does he refer to persecution (a term we reserve for a more formally sanctioned, malevolent pursuit of people regarded as "other"). Given the status of this writing, a letter from Jerusalem to the diaspora, what he does not say is important too. He does not register the slightest inkling that these trials should be understood within an autobiographical narrative, as though past sins have led to present troubles.[17] Instead, he refers to unsought harassment crossing paths with his readers and hearers[18] as a consequence of their identification with the God of Israel and the Lord Jesus Christ. James makes this clear with his interpretation of "various trials" (1:2) as "(the means of) the testing *of your faith*" (1:3).[19]

References to *faith/faithfulness* congregate in James's letter, especially in chapters 1–2, but not always with the same nuance.[20] Here, the sense is *allegiance*: a relationship with God and the Lord Jesus Christ exemplified in James's own single-minded service (1:1), now broadened to include those whom James

15. Sahlins 1995, 12.

16. This identifies one among several ways Scripture addresses the problem of suffering. See Talbert 1991.

17. Cf. 2 Bar. 79.2: the scattering of God's people was God's response to their sin and nonobservance of God's Instructions (or Torah); Lam 1:5, concerning Jerusalem: "Certainly the LORD caused her grief because of her many wrong acts. Her children have gone away, captive before the enemy" (CEB).

18. For the sense conveyed by *peripiptō*, "I encounter," see Luke 10:30: A traveler from Jerusalem to Jericho "fell among" bandits.

19. For this rendering of *dokimion*, see MGS 546.

20. *Pistis* appears in Jas 1:3, 6; 2:1, 5, 14, 17, 18 [3×], 20, 22 [2×], 24, 26; 5:15.

regards as his siblings. This is a constancy of dedication and obedience subject to testing in the cauldron of harassment. For James, allegiance is personal, to be sure, but also communal, as signified by his use of the second-person plural (in Southern idiom, "y'all's" [*hymōn*] faithfulness).

For the faithful, the telos of trials is perfection or wholeness, a concept that lies at the intersection of the words James has chosen: mature, complete, lacking nothing. *Perfection* is not a mechanistic metaphor for James, as though it could be determined by using assembly-line standards set by a blueprint or patterned norm; nor is it a static state at which the faithful might arrive, nor the sinlessness sometimes associated with the term today. As happiness refers to embodying the values of one's community and growing in relation to one's life purpose, so here those perfected through trials sustain wholehearted, single-minded allegiance to God in the context of hounding tests of faithfulness, centering themselves in relation to God by allowing this orientation toward God to shape their (and the community's) life patterns.[21] Recall Jesus's words in the Sermon on the Mount, "Be perfect, just as your heavenly Father is perfect," set in the context of his instruction on love for neighbor and for enemy (Matt 5:48 AT); or his words to the wealthy young person later in the First Gospel: "If you want to be perfect, go, sell whatever you have, and give to the poor" (19:21 AT). In Matthew, as in James, perfection draws its meaning from God's character and agenda: it entails ongoing, uncompromising devotion to God and God's ways.

It should be clear enough that, for James, happiness and wholeness are not relegated to the eschatological future. Those who think James has in mind only or primarily an end-time reward seem perplexed that humans might be deemed as perfect or whole (or as having achieved perfection or wholeness) in this life, perhaps because they have not fully taken the measure of James's notion of perfection. As with Matthew's Gospel, so with James, perfection is not cast as a superhuman demand, but entails consistency and integrity of heart and life in devotion to God. It involves living into one's humanity, that is, reflecting God's image in one's engagement with God's people and all creation. Or perhaps they are overly influenced by parallels to James's chain of effects in Rom 5:3–5 (trials → endurance → character → hope) and 1 Pet 1:6–7 (trials → genuine faith → praise, glory, and honor at Jesus's appearance), which do share an end-time horizon.[22] James has an end-time perspective too (cf. 1:12, 18), but this is not his first concern. Here, he does not so much project happiness and wholeness into the future as he orients his audience to life before God in the present, in which happiness and perfection are potentialities.

---

21. See esp. Hartin 1999; Bauckham 1999.

22. For eschatological interpretations of James's notion of perfection, see, e.g., Bede 1985, 9; Davids 1982, 70; McCartney 2009, 87–88; otherwise, e.g., Laws 1980, 52; McKnight 2011, 81–82.

For James, humans are not automatons for whom trials reflexively cultivate human flourishing. How one responds is crucial, as is allowing the proper response to complete its work on one's (and the community's) character and behavior. If proper response to trials is pivotal for happiness and wholeness, though, the nature of that response is not easy to capture in English translation. The older AV and ASV refer to "patience," especially problematic today since *patience* often implies resignation and passivity.[23] Contemporary translations, which read "endurance" (CEB, NRSV) or "perseverance" (NIV), are better, but these too can leave the door open to thoughts of acquiescence or mere survival. James's term (*hypomonē*) connotes, instead, a courageous fidelity that emerges through stubborn trust in God—what one interpreter identifies as "a militant patience that arises from the roots of oppression."[24] Another recognizes it as an "unyielding, defiant perseverance in the face of aggressive misfortune."[25] Amid trials, we might say, James urges theological discernment and practices of resistance. When saying this, though, we must be quick to honor James's perspective that such resistance is nonviolent and refuses to cede God's authority and initiative to human beings caught in trials, even to brothers and sisters (see, e.g., 4:1–12). We would do well to take better inventory of the instruments of resistance available to those whose wholehearted devotion is to God, the chief of which include, for James, seeking wisdom from God (e.g., 1:5–8) and faith working itself out in neighborly love (e.g., 2:1–26).

[5–8] James defines the nature and practice of happiness and wholeness in relation to a particular conception and way of life before God, which James now identifies as "wisdom." Those who lack wisdom should ask God for it. This prayer is so tied to God's character that those whose lives are congruent with God's character receive what they request, but those whose lives are contrary to God's character receive nothing. In the former paragraph (1:2–4), nothing is lacking, a rather imprecise or universalizing claim that begs for and now receives clarification. The thing that could be lacking, the one thing needed, is wisdom, the capacity to understand and to act faithfully.

Two caveats need to be stated: (1) Contrary to our contemporary tendencies to separate knowing, being, and doing, James's instruction assumes an embodied psychology and spirituality in which these are indivisible. Lest modern notions of cognition cause us to stumble, we then with James should learn to think of "inner" and "outer," of "heart" and "life," of "mind" and "body" as fully integrated.[26] What is needed is *practical wisdom*: patterns of think-

23. However, S. Johnson's *Dictionary of the English Language* (1755) has "indurance" as the first meaning of "patience."
24. Tamez 1990, 44.
25. Radl 1993, 405. Cf. *TLNT* 3:414–20.
26. Cf. Berger 2003, 60–81.

ing, feeling, believing, *and behaving*—and, so, wise habits of perception and practice. (2) James recognizes wisdom and its counterfeit, with either available to those caught in trials, so he urges his audience to "ask God." Wisdom from above (which he will later describe as "first pure, then peaceable, gentle, leadable, full of mercy and good fruits, lacking partiality, not double-faced" [3:17]) is needed, not its antithesis (which is "earthly, worldly, and diabolic," realized in "bitter rivalry and devious self-promotion in your hearts," along with "disorder and every contemptible deed" [3:14–16]). James aims to shape people in relation to God's character and God's ways.

Asking God sets the horizons within which James's readers and hearers might interpret their lives. Faithful life for Christ-followers in the diaspora is more than a matter of human ingenuity or human measures and countermeasures. Rather, it is a life open to the God of Israel and thus open to having one's categories for making sense of and experiencing the world shaped by God. This first attempt to characterize God (1:5; the second, in 1:13, 17–18) speaks of God's reliability and capaciousness. From one vantage point, his portrait of God here recalls Jesus's words, "Ask and it will be given to you"—words that appear in Matthew's and Luke's Gospels in the context of imaginative words of encouragement to trust God's goodness (Matt 7:7–12; Luke 11:1–13). Framed differently, though, James suggests a certain naivete on God's part, at least from a human, and especially Roman, point of view. If, in the real world, even friends and household relations are marked by more-or-less carefully monitored reciprocity, debt, and obligation; and if, in the real world, the pledge of a "free gift" rings hollow;[27] then James's portrait is astonishing in its representation of the God who gives without first calculating risk and reward, and without keeping score concerning who owes whom. God freely and simply gives.

God gives freely, but not automatically. Those lacking wisdom should ask, and they should ask in faith. James has referred to *faith* in 1:3, there with the sense of testing one's (and the community's) allegiance to God and the Lord Jesus Christ. Here, faith has more the sense of *confidence* (1:6), in contrast to vacillating or allowing oneself to be pulled in different directions (1:6–8). This faith is an interior disposition, to be sure, but also entails certain relational commitments and manifestations.[28] Entrusting oneself to God's openhandedness implies a readiness to act in line with and on the basis of God's wisdom.

Those who are confident, who will receive God's wisdom, stand in contrast to those who will not receive, whose sensibilities are described with three overlapping terms: doubt (i.e., uncertainty or wavering loyalty,[29] addled by

27. Cf. Derrida 1992: Circles of exchange turn gifts into debts to be repaid. On reciprocity in traditional societies, see Sahlins 1972.
28. See Morgan 2015, 342, 470–71.
29. See Yu 2018, 122.

entertaining alternatives to God's wisdom), double-mindedness, and instability. These terms do not describe three different kinds of human beings, but one kind in three ways: the self at variance with itself, the self tugged in different directions. James's diagnosis reflects the human condition as this is represented in Gen 1–3: like God, yet inclined toward evil.[30] Israel's basic affirmation, the Shema, ties oneness of commitment to the oneness of God. God is one ("The LORD your God, the LORD is one" [AT]) and Israel shall love the one God singularly ("with all your heart, all your being, and all your strength," Deut 6:4–5 CEB). Jesus repeats these words in the first half of the double-love command: Love God wholly (and love your neighbor as yourself; Matt 22:35–39; Mark 12:28–31; cf. Luke 10:25–27). However, this singleness of commitment is compromised by the double-hearted, double-faced, double-tongued, or, as here, the double-minded.[31] James thus identifies people for whom trials lead them away from God. They are the opposite of those who ask for wisdom as an expression of confidence in God, but in this respect they are also the negative image of God. By nature, God gives single-heartedly, simply, to those who ask in faith. These people, though, are complex in their dueling compulsions. Accordingly, we are not surprised later to hear James liken them to (unimaginable) fountains from which pour both fresh and salty water as they both bless God and curse those made in God's likeness (3:9–12).

Identifying indecisive people in this way, James presses for disambiguation. Are they friends of the world or friends of God? Within the community of Christ-followers or outside it? Human flourishing, completeness, and integrity lie outside the reach of those with ambiguous loyalties.

[9–11] God's wisdom can turn conventional perspectives and practices upside down. This was the case with trials (1:2–4) and now is the case with the wealthy and the poor. The struggles of Christ-followers distributed outside Palestine now manifest as issues of status, which are inevitably enmeshed with economics. James declares a great reversal, not only in the eschatological future but also in the ecclesiological present (1:9–10a),[32] then details why the benefits of wealth are unstable and short-lived (1:10b–11). In this way, James recognizes and addresses the trials of the impoverished among his audience, but also speaks firmly (and bitingly) about the trials of those with wealth. These verses are cast in the third person, like wisdom sayings, affirming what simply is so from God's perspective. James's readers and hearers are thus invited to assess themselves according to the terms of this counterworldly formula.

---

30. See above, on 1:2–18.

31. Cf. Ps 12:2; 1 Chr 12:33. For related texts, see Cheung 2003, 197–201; Allison 2013, 186–91.

32. James's overall message clearly has an eschatological edge, but this is not front and center at this point. Instead, he provides a theological lens for assessing present life within communities of Christ-followers. Cf. Brueggemann 2018, 249–64.

James uses conventional metaphors in unconventional ways to articulate his topsy-turvy wisdom. First, to borrow the language of conceptual metaphor, humans commonly imagine that UP IS MORE and DOWN IS LESS. These metaphors speak to conceptual patterns that support a host of related value judgments as abstract ideas like *more or less*, or *better or worse*, map on to embodied, experiential concepts hardwired in our brains.[33] Accordingly, it almost goes without saying that greater honor comes with more wealth, and the scenario James paints works itself out in myriad ways every day. For example, an influential wealthy person and a poor person enter the room. To the wealthy person you say, "Sit in this excellent seat," while to the poor you say, "Stand over there," or, "Sit at my feet" (2:2–3). Cutting against the grain, though, James claims that lowly status tied to a paucity of economic resources is prized, while lofty status associated with wealth is disdained. Second, identifying those who are lowly as "brothers and sisters," James activates a relational schema concerning who is in and who is out, who belongs and who does not. Since, in traditional societies, wealth is not an end to itself but an instrument for accumulating power and privilege, we might expect wealth to have won status and belongingness for the wealthy insider. James's perspective moves against the current, however. Count the impoverished among our kin, not the wealthy. Mary's Song in Luke 1 exemplifies these two surprising patterns for mapping relationships:

Up–down:	[God] has pulled the powerful down from their thrones and lifted up the lowly.
In–out:	[God] has filled the hungry with good things and sent the rich away empty-handed.

> (Luke 1:52–53 CEB)

Jesus's teaching reflects this orientation, too:

> All who lift themselves up will be brought low.
> But all who make themselves low will be lifted up.
> (Matt 23:12 CEB; cf. Luke 14:11; 18:14)
> So the last will be first,
> and the first will be last.
> (Matt 20:16 NRSV; cf. Luke 13:30)

James's perspective, then, has a worthy lineage.

Although James knows the word *ptōchos*, usually translated as "poor" (Jas 2:2, 3, 5, 6) but also capable of signifying marginal status more generally, he does not use it here. Instead, he uses *tapeinos* (1:9), which typically connotes "lowly status" and belongs to a word group that signifies "humility" (cf. 4:6)

---

33. The use of capital letters for representing cognitive metaphors is conventional. For background, see J. Feldman 2006 (see 199–201 for the childhood development of this cognitive metaphor).

but can also refer to "lacking life's resources."[34] Since words are often known by the company they keep, it is obvious that James refers here to brothers and sisters with minimal resources. This is because the term is juxtaposed with *plousios*, "wealthy" (1:10–11; cf. 2:5, 6; 5:1). Even so, keeping the notion of *low status* in mind is important. First, Israel's Scriptures bear witness to the tradition of associating humility and poverty: the poor turn to God for help, and God comes to their aid.[35] Second, thinking in the social, relational, and moral terms of status cautions against our essentializing either "poor" or "wealthy," as though the meaning attached to significant economic holdings is something other than a social construction, and as though members of either group are naturally characterized by such and such approved (or disapproved), stereotypical properties: "That is just the way they are." Moreover, whether one is regarded as wealthy or poor depends on one's location or community of reference,[36] just as the identification of one's social status depends on one's community of reference.

Structural poverty was the norm for most people in the Roman world, with some 90 percent of the population living at, near, or below subsistence level.[37] In such a world, it makes no sense to speak of a middle class. Instead, the remaining population would have been wealthy by any comparison, with 1 or 2 percent having what would be, for almost everyone else, inconceivable wealth. Even if this category of people would have been very much a minority, "the wealthy" label is important for our reading of this text in two ways. First, the wealthy generally have access to life experiences unavailable to the impoverished, and this explains the direction James will take in his prophetic critique. It is too much to say that the wealthy lived care-free lives, but they were able to avoid physical labor, they could afford the range of health-care interventions available in the first-century Mediterranean world, they dwelled in large villas or compounds separate from society's riffraff, and they could otherwise buffer themselves from threats to life and limb. The wealthy might easily imagine (or the impoverished might easily imagine of the wealthy) that wealth allowed them to circumvent life's limitations. Second, *wealth* describes not only the resources held by society's top 10 percent, but also, and especially, a way of comporting oneself in the world. Luke describes the Pharisees as "lovers of

34. *Tapeinos* also appears in Mary's Song: God has lifted up "the lowly" (Luke 1:52).

35. E.g., Pss 9:18; 10:17–18; 12:5; 14:6; 68:10; 69:33; Isa 10:2; cf. Gal 2:10. See Grundmann 1974, 8:6, 9–10.

36. To illustrate: Today, some 50 percent of the world's population live on US$2 a day. From this perspective, the vast majority of the populations of minority-world countries are wealthy. In their own communities, however, such "wealthy" people may be impoverished—lacking access to basic health care, unable to afford basic necessities, etc.

37. Friesen 2004. B. Longenecker's (2010) more optimistic assessment still identifies over 80 percent of the population as living at, near, or below subsistence level.

money" (16:14) not because they have considerable financial resources but because they relish the status that wealth invites (including, e.g., prominent seats in the synagogue and at the banquet table—cf. 11:39–44; 14:7–14).[38] For James, the way of wealth expresses itself in favoritism, extravagant clothing and jewelry, privileged seating arrangements, disdain for the impoverished, harassment of the impoverished, use of the court system against the impoverished, insulting the Lord's name, carrying on without consideration of God's agenda, swindling the working poor, lives of luxury and pleasure, and condemning and murdering the righteous (2:2–7; 4:13–5:6). How wealth is made and how it is used—both come under James's scrutiny. At the same time, James acknowledges that wealth need not lead down this road. Thus, he names two wealthy people, Abraham and Job, as exemplars of practical wisdom (2:21–24; 5:11), and he underscores the importance of putting wealth in the service of hospitality toward and care of the needy (2:8–17; cf. 1:27). Nevertheless he discerns, in the most penetrating way, the lure of wealth—for the impoverished, who either live life by its rules or yearn for the status, power, privilege, and self-satisfaction it might bring, or both; and for the wealthy, for whom wealth commands godlike devotion and whom wealth recruits for its evil ends.

Are the wealthy to be counted within the communities of Christ-followers to whom James addresses his letter? Although this question is much debated,[39] it is actually wrongheaded, depending as it does on the absolutizing or essentializing of wealth. The real question is whether wealth has its way in cultivating a lifeworld contrary to God's wisdom; if the answer is yes, then how could those who thus claim to be Christ-followers be numbered among the "brothers and sisters"? God's wisdom is practical wisdom, after all, and faith is relationally embodied. Accordingly, James counters the way of wealth in his simple contrast: the impoverished have high status; the wealthy have low status. Both must see the world and live their lives differently, now according to God's wisdom. James's message does not expect the impoverished to take the place of the wealthy, as though towering over others is the precondition of human flourishing. Rather, happiness for the impoverished and for the wealthy requires a recalibration of everyone's place in God's world over against the standards of evaluation common in the wider world. In his characterization of the wealthy (vv. 10b–11), James will draw on Isa 40, which includes a metaphorical portrait that befits James's position here. Just as "every valley will be raised up, and every mountain and hill will be flattened" so that "uneven ground will become level, and rough terrain a valley plain" (Isa 40:4 CEB), so the lowly are raised up and the lofty are flattened.

Psalm 73 provides a remarkable window into common views of the wealthy:

38. Cf. Moxnes 1988.
39. See the helpful summary in Batten 2017, 114–16.

> For they have no pain;
> > their bodies are sound and sleek.
> They are not in trouble as others are;
> > they are not plagued like other people.
> . . . .
> always at ease,
> > they increase in riches. (Ps 73:3–12 NRSV)

For the psalmist, though, this is only part of the story. The wealthy are arrogant, cruel, and wicked; for the psalmist, the wicked wealthy are destined for ruin. This is the way of wealth.

James's analysis is similar. Indeed, let us set this psalmic description side by side with the twin realities that the wealthy of the Roman world enjoyed passive forms of income, with wealth attracting more wealth, and that they lived on average about twice as long as the impoverished. It thus comes as no surprise that James's prophetic words undo the way of wealth by unmasking its illusory façade, pulling back the curtain on its deceptive promise. With scriptural resonances, he drives home the fact that the wealthy are no different from the impoverished. It is almost as if he were to write, "Just like everyone else, the wealthy, too, will fade away like wildflowers." This is the lot of all humans. As Isaiah has it,

> All people are grass,
> > their constancy is like the flower of the field.
> The grass withers, the flower fades,
> > when the breath of the LORD blows upon it;
> > surely the people are grass.
> The grass withers, the flower fades;
> > but the word of our God will stand forever.
> > (Isa 40:6–8 NRSV; cf. Pss 90:3–6; 103:15–16)

Echoing these words, James counters any hope that wealth defeats the limitations of human life.

[12–18] James revisits his introductory interest in the way his readers and auditors respond to trials (1:2–4); likewise, he tackles a problem lingering in the background or, perhaps, moved into the foreground by some to whom he writes. This is the question: What is the source of these trials? God is tempting me, right? Reflecting on God's character and on the human condition, James slams the door on the idea that God stands behind temptation, claiming instead that God has provided the means for winning the tug-of-war humans have with themselves, with their own bent toward evil. Although James speaks of the devil later in his letter,[40] diabolic influence is not featured here.

---

40. See 3:14–16; 4:7.

First (v. 12), James recapitulates his opening directive on enduring trials (1:2–4). The connection between these two texts is unmistakable, given the considerable linguistic and conceptual parallels:

- Greatest/true happiness (1:2, 12)
- Trials/testing (1:2, 12)
- Endurance (1:3, 12)
- Means of testing/proven through testing (1:3, 12)

Amid these notable similarities, we find what appears to be a key difference. In the earlier text, James follows a chain of effects from trials to endurance and from endurance to maturity and wholeness. Here, though, endurance is tied less to moral formation, leading instead to receiving "the garland of life God has promised to those who love him" (1:12). We should not exaggerate this distinction, however. Rather, this change of language allows James to identify love as the disposition out of which endurance is practiced. In the same way, faith-as-allegiance and faith-as-confidence (1:3, 6) are integral to love. When the Shema, Israel's daily profession of faith and covenantal allegiance, is introduced in Deuteronomy, loving God wholly is set firmly within the framework of learning, teaching, and obeying God's commands (Deut 6:1–9). Drawing on Torah, Jesus glosses this perfect love for God by issuing the double-love command: love of God and love of neighbor (Matt 22:35–39; Mark 12:28–31; cf. Luke 10:25–27; Lev 19:18). The enmeshment of double-love and obedience continues elsewhere in the NT, too—for example, in 1 John 5:2: "This is how we know we love God's children, when we love God and keep his commandments" (AT). This shift from the language of endurance and faith to the vocabulary of love opens the path for and anticipates James's development of the royal law, the law of freedom, where he binds the Shema together with neighborly love (2:8–18). Of course, by identifying his audience as "dear" or "beloved" (*agapētos*) brothers and sisters (1:16, 19; 2:5), James has already pointed the way toward coupling love of God and communal love.

The term James uses to introduce this paragraph is typically translated as "blessed" and is associated with macarisms (pronouncements of *blessedness*) in both the OT and NT. Among these, the most famous may be the heading of the psalter: "Blessed is the one who does not follow the counsel of the ungodly" (Ps 1:1 AT); and the Beatitudes of Jesus (Matt 5:3–12; Luke 6:20–23): "Blessed are . . . " My translation of the term in question as "truly happy" takes advantage of the recovery of the word *happiness*,[41] not as a fleeting reaction to congenial life events but as the condition of human flourishing for those whose working

---

41. Cf. some contemporary translations of Ps 1:1: "Happy are those . . ." (NRSV); "The truly happy person . . ." (CEB); "Happy the man . . ." (NETS).

assumptions, dispositions, and practices are calibrated with reference to day-to-day life before God.[42] To be sure, this is an implicit indictment of those who look as if they are living the happy life. They are wealthy or benefit from the backing of those with plenty, they have good reputations and command public deference, and so on. However, those people measure the goodness of their lives according to an erroneous order of things, their mistake revealed in their failure to receive "the garland of life." Like the Beatitudes of Jesus, James's pronouncement does not so much identify what should or will be the case, but how things in fact are. In other words, his words are not prescriptive but ascriptive—not a vision of life that must await the eschaton, but one grounded in the present disclosure of God's agenda. As such, they constitute an invitation to embrace the valuation of things characteristic of God's agenda, which ties together the present and the eschaton. Loving God, manifest in enduring trials—this is James's invitation to a vocation of faithful life that participates in God's life.

As earlier in the letter, so here the prescribed response to trials is *endurance*, by which those who are tested demonstrate that they are "tried and true" (1:12 CEB). This is not silent acquiescence, but the bold determination modeled in Jesus's story of the widow who, denied justice, refuses the docile script given her by society and repeatedly takes her case to the judge (Luke 18:1–8). In the Lukan narrative, as here, courageous persistence finds its ground in one's trust in God[43]—who, in Luke, will not delay in granting justice; and who, in James, has promised a garland of life to those whose love for him is on display amid trials. "Crown" (1:12 NRSV) refers to a "wreath" or "garland," often of flowers or leaves, used in a variety of contexts in the ancient world to recognize someone with great honor.[44] "Life" designates the nature of the wreath given those who endure (cf. Rev 2:10)—not a garland woven from fresh vegetation that, in a few days, will shrivel and die, but life with God, today and in the eschaton.

More talk about testing presses the difficult theological question of its etiology. James first speaks of God's character as a way to trace temptation's origins not to God but to the human condition (1:13–15). As he moves through this discussion, James demonstrates the importance of the range of connotations activated by the term *peirasmos*—used neutrally to identify *trials*, positively for *testing* that stimulates human development and flourishing, and negatively for *tempting* that impedes human development and stifles life.[45] For James, *trials* function like a "Y" in the road, with one fork (*testing*) leading to flourishing,

---

42. Here I depend on Green 2020d, 245–46; see above, on 1:2–4.

43. Luke (18:8) refers to the petitioning woman as an exemplar of *faithfulness*.

44. *CGL* 2:1287 (*stephanos*): "a mark of honour" given to victorious athletes or bestowed on persons for extraordinary service, or worn by royalty.

45. *Peirasmos* is used in 1:12; its negation, *apeirastos*, is used in 1:13; and its verbal form, *peirazō*, is used in 1:13 (3×), 14. See above, on 1:2–27.

happiness, life; and the other fork (*tempting*) leading to stunted growth, decline, death. Although this underscores the weighty significance of proper response amid trials, James's gloomy portrait of the human condition seems to allow no room for optimism around human flourishing. He speaks of God's character, second, in order to introduce welcome words concerning God's medicant for healing the human condition (1:16–18).

We turn first, then, to the origins of temptation.[46] James's notion of divine providence does not stretch to the point of making God responsible either for human choices or even for the evil inclination that characterizes all human beings. Instead, James insists that God is untemptable and is not the cause of temptation. Although Christian theology would eventually develop various theologies of *original sin*, this terminology is absent from Israel's Scriptures. Moreover, the common Protestant understanding of Gen 3 as the story of humanity's *fall,* and therefore the introduction of inherited sin and guilt, is missing from Israel's Scriptures as well as, in the post-apostolic era, from the writings of early church theologian-exegetes through the first three centuries of the Common Era.[47] Jewish texts roughly contemporary with James's letter may be of more interest, even though they do not speak of original sin either. This is because a few display an interest in sin's cause and relate it to the story of Adam and Eve. In Life of Adam and Eve, for example, the serpent gives Eve—and apparently the human family—a heart inclined toward evil. Second Esdras portrays humans as possessing an evil inclination though without plainly identifying its origins. In a notable contrast with James, these other Jewish texts do not locate human agency under the control of this bent toward evil; for them, humans can follow God's Instructions (or Torah), if only they would.

Recall that James opened his letter with a chain of effects (1:2–4):

trials → endurance → wholeness in "the greatest happiness"

This is closely paralleled in the present paragraph (1:12):

trials → endurance as an expression of love → life

Both contrast sharply with the chain of effects by which James now unveils the human condition (1:14–15):

cravings → temptation → sin → death

---

46. For this discussion, I am dependent on Green 2020c.

47. Cf., e.g., Toews 2013, 48–72; Bouteneff 2008. Significantly, Anderson (2009) discusses the development of the concept of *sin* without a single reference to Gen 3.

James uses a two-part metaphor to expand his picture of *craving*: a tempting fishing lure with which to attract a fish and draw it from the water (1:14).[48] In this way, James gets at the source of his audience's real difficulties: the potency of their internal inclinations. The term I have translated as *craving* can have the more neutral sense of *desire*, but in moral discourse it generally carries the negative sense of *evil desire*.[49] Here its role vis-à-vis sin and death qualifies it as negative and places it in the company of the wider notion of the evil inclination. James introduces the modifier "one's own" to underscore personal culpability: "by *their own* cravings" (1:14).[50] Given this state of affairs, genuine happiness and a garland of life seem forever out of reach. We can almost hear the words of 2 Esdras:

> What benefit is it to us that we are promised an immortal time, but we have done works that bring death? What good is it to us that everlasting hope has been predicted for us, but we have utterly failed? What good is it that safe and healthy dwelling places are reserved, but we have behaved badly? (2 Esd 7:119–121 CEB)

What James sketches is even more damning, however, since he proceeds as though "what we have done" was practically inevitable, given our servitude to our own overpowering cravings. With good reason, later Christian thought about "original sin" might be recast in terms of "human misery."[51]

Typically, when James names his addressees "brothers and sisters," this signals a shift in his letter. His warning, "Do not be deceived, my dear brothers and sisters!" (1:16), marks an exception, however, since the message of this paragraph (1:12–18) pivots on this warning against self-deception. The problem of deception centers on the source of temptation, so James furthers his claim that temptations cannot be traced back to God—first, by expanding on his portrait of God (1:17; see 1:13); and second, by urging that, far from tempting human beings, God is the one who provides the wherewithal for setting aside the overwhelming influence of internal, evil desires.

We might imagine that James's denial would be stronger if he were to claim not only that *every* good gift comes from above (that is, from God), but also that *only* good gifts come from God. He does make a parallel point, though. Unlike the old gods of the Greek and Roman pantheons, Israel's God cannot be regarded as capricious (fickle, erratic). Nor is God like the unstable, double-minded person (1:8). This is a statement less concerning God's essence and more about the constancy and dependability of God's character. From sunup

---

48. Cargal 1993, 81–82.

49. *Epithymia* (1:14, 15). For related language, cf. *hēdonē* (pleasure) in 4:1, 3; *epithymeō* (I desire/crave) in 4:2; and *epipotheō* (I long for) in 4:5. See L. Johnson 1995, 193–94.

50. Together with the fact that Jas 1:14 does not mention diabolic influence, his use of *tēs idias*, "one's own," accentuates his narrow focus on the human condition and human culpability.

51. Kärkkäinen 2015, 387–425.

to sundown, we follow the shadows as they shorten through the morning, vanish (or nearly so) at midday, and lengthen into the evening (and this would be true even if one thinks, as many ancients did, that the sun revolves around the earth). Rooting his reference to shifting shadows in his portrait of God as Creator, "the Father of Lights" (see Gen 1:3–5, 14–19), James urges that God's character is fixed; if we detect shifting shadows, this is because God's creatures have moved in relation to God's character, not because God's character has wavered. God's inclination to give good gifts never fluctuates.

The evil inclination that plagues all humans is indeed powerful, but it need not be all-powerful. We can follow the logic of James's counterproposal by setting side by side two genealogies:[52]

James 1:15	James 1:18
Human desire (or craving)	God's desire (or choice)
"conceives" and "gives birth to sin"	"to give us birth by means of his true word"
"sin, once it reaches adulthood, gives birth to death"	"so that we might be a kind of foretaste of what would become of everything he created"

Birthing language dots the landscape of James's prose—most obviously in his references to *conceiving* (1:15) and *giving birth* (using two terms, *tiktō* in 1:15, *apokeuō* in 1:15, 18), but also in his references to the *implanted* word (1:21) and to *natural selves* (1:23).[53] Drawing on the conceptual metaphor CAUSATION IS PROGENERATION,[54] James artfully portrays God's agency in the birthing activity that results in the identification of these Christ-followers as the first of God's restored people. Although the Letter of James never mentions Jesus's crucifixion, it is nonetheless interesting that, here, he uses an image with significance for atonement theology: atonement as God's labor in the birthing of God's people.[55] Note, too, the profundity of James's claim, that these lowly, mostly Jewish Christ-followers, migrants living outside Israel's ancestral lands, are honored as "a kind of foretaste" of God's purpose for all creation. To change the metaphor, James regards them—that is, those who have been given birth by God's true word, who love God, who demonstrate their

---

52. Cf. Cargal 1993, 85.

53. See Kaiser 2019, 464–65. Her translation of *emphytos* as "innate" highlights the term's relation to the birthing scheme, but "implanted" reminds us that God's true word interrupts the conception-birthing-maturing-birthing work of human craving from outside the human.

54. Cf. Turner 1991, 166–67.

55. Cf. Bennett 2017.

allegiance to God through courageous endurance amid trials—as a kind of out-post pointing to the consummation of God's plan. By way of contrast, through a series of births, human craving has as its consequence no life at all, but death. That is, though both lineages employ the metaphor of giving birth, one is a monstrous parody of the other.

Much about this lengthy paragraph (1:12–18) points in the direction of "last things." Those who endure will receive life with God (1:12). The end toward which evil desire presses is death (1:15). God's purpose for all creation rounds out James's discourse (1:18). Set within these markers of future orientation is the present life of James's readers and hearers. The future, we might say, casts its shadow backward on the present, to indicate what is genuinely true; to bind together in God's singular purpose the past, present, and future; and to call—and enable—Christ-followers to live accordingly.

Drawing on Isa 40, James earlier noted the temporary character of human life and drew attention especially to the loss of beauty and vitality among the wealthy (Jas 1:10–11). The Isaian text contrasts the transitory nature of human existence with God's word, which endures forever (Isa 40:8). Unsurprisingly, then, James concludes his discussion of God's remedy for the human situation with reference to God's true word—the means by which God's people are enabled to share in God's life and to emulate God's fidelity. James does not specify the content of this "true word," but his use of creation motifs suggests a meaningful parallel between God's word in creation (Gen 1: "God said . . .") and God's word in the birth that leads to embodying and signifying new creation. "Birth" and "true word"—this is the language of the good news that opens the way to the transformation that overpowers the human proclivity to sin.[56]

1:19–27 Purity and the Implanted Word

1:19 Understand, my dear brothers and sisters, and[a] let everyone be quick to listen, slow to speak, slow to anger. 20 This is because a person's anger does not produce God's righteousness. 21 Therefore, in humility,[b] removing all filth and ubiquitous wickedness, welcome the implanted word that has the power to save you.[c] 22 You must be doers of the word and not only listeners who mislead themselves. 23 This is because those who listen to

---

56. See Davids 1982, 89–90; Konradt 1998, 41–100; Cheung 2003, 86–87. For "true word," cf. Eph 1:13; Col 1:5; 2 Tim 2:15. On the conversionary image of "(new) birth," see John 3:3, 7; 1 Pet 1:3, 23; 2:2; Titus 3:5 (for a parallel to Jas 1:10–11 in its use of Isa 40, see esp. 1 Pet 1:23–25: "having been given new birth not from perishable seed but imperishable, through the living and enduring word of God—since 'all humanity is like grass and all human glory like the flower of grass. The grass withers and the flower falls off, but the word of the Lord endures forever.' This is the word that was proclaimed to you as good news" (AT). On the view that "word" refers instead to universal reason, as in Stoicism, see below on 1:21.

the word and are not doers—they are like those who look closely at their natural selves[d] in a mirror, 24 for they look at themselves, walk away, and immediately forget what they were like. 25 Contrast those who observe the perfect law, the law of freedom, and keep at it: they are not listeners who forget but active doers. They will be genuinely happy in their doing. 26 If those who think they are devout do not control what they say, then they deceive their own hearts; their devotion is a sham. 27 Devotion that is pure and unsullied in God the Father's eyes is this: to come to the aid of orphans and widows in their trouble and suffering,[e] and to keep ourselves from being contaminated by the world.

a. I read the particle *de* (and) with a continuative sense. Accordingly, the first imperative, "understand," directs James's audience to grasp what he has been developing in 1:2–18; the second imperative, "be quick to listen," begins to draw out the implications of his earlier instruction.

b. The prepositional phrase "in humility" could modify "removing" or "welcome," or both. I have chosen the last option.

c. The NRSV reads "to save your souls" (*sōsai tas psychas hymōn*). Since the term *psychē* does not signify a metaphysical entity separate from the body, the translation here refers simply to human selves.

d. James's phrase, *to prosōpon tēs geneseōs autou*, is difficult—e.g., "the face of his genesis" (Adam 2013, 22) or "the face of begetting"—that is, "natural appearance" (L. Johnson 2004b, 170).

e. For this translation of *thlipsis*, see L&N §22.2.

James's opening concern with trials and the nature of his audience's responses to them (1:2–4) led him to reflect on the situation of the lowly and impoverished (the "degraded poor") and the elevated and wealthy (the "greedy rich,"[57] 1:9–11). There, his primary conceptual metaphors were spatial as he overturned conventional standards for identifying who is up or down (MORE IS UP, LESS IS DOWN) and who is in or out (CLOSENESS IS BELONGING). It is tempting to generalize from this early introduction of the problem of wealth and impoverishment, and so to imagine that this is James's overarching concern throughout the letter.[58] Indeed, in the textual unit now before us, how one comports oneself vis-à-vis the vulnerable (widows and orphans) serves as a test of genuine devotion to God. However, this unit takes up additional matters—especially speech ethics (1:19–20, 26)[59] and integrity (as opposed to an apparently all-too-common breakdown between hearing and doing)—that do not fit comfortably

57. Batten 2008.
58. This impulse is supported by the range of economic concerns that appear throughout the letter (e.g., 2:1–17; 4:13–5:6).
59. Cf. Baker 1995, 84–104.

within the categories of poverty and wealth. Moreover, all these interests (speech ethics, integrity, and care for the defenseless) are developed under the umbrella of another conceptual metaphor: MORALITY IS PURITY. Overall, James's word choices suggest a broader concern with inter-relationality—that is, with nurturing the faithful life of the communities to which he addresses his letter.

Importantly, the use of these metaphors is not merely descriptive or conceptual but also generative.[60] Hearing James well is more than simply a matter of figuring out what his word choices signify. It also entails recognizing how his metaphors create and strengthen relational bonds. With these metaphors, James fashions a community. He does this, certainly, by drawing on Israel's Scriptures, especially as they are understood in relation to the Lord Jesus Christ; in his hands, Scripture and the Jesus tradition help to shape the patterns by which his audience conceptualizes, experiences, and responds to the world. But his metaphors also expose his concern with the internal life of these communities. He thus participates in a kind of public theology, since faithfulness must be worked out in relation to a world whose patterns and conventions are out of step with God's mission; after all, these communities of God's people serve as outposts in that world. In the present unit (1:19–27), James's central metaphor is MORALITY IS PURITY. This means that the abstract notion of morality is mapped onto (or conceived in terms of) the concrete experience of bodily cleanliness. Although his message gains texture and depth when understood within Jewish traditions of purity, his categories are available, too, to those whose lives are not steeped in that tradition.[61] As a matter of course, humans are not drawn to, but reflexively recoil from, filth, pollution, and contamination. James's language thus biases his readers and hearers toward moral purity—with purity determined from God's perspective, not the world's. This is especially important for his community-sculpting enterprise because research has shown that humans display a high correlation between shared moral commitments and close social networks.[62]

Excursus: Purity in Ancient Judaism

Israel's corporate life was structured around two binaries: holy versus ordinary (or common) and pure versus impure (Lev 10:10).[63] The purity binary could be further divided, generally, between ritual purity and moral purity. *Ordinary* does not signify *sinful*, nor

60. I refer to "metaphor" not as a figure of speech, but, following conceptual metaphor theory more generally, as a way of conceiving and ordering human experience. See Evans and Green 2006, 286–327.

61. Lee, Tang, Wan, Mai, and Liu (2015) note that the link between morality and purity exists across cultures even though that link manifests itself in different ways. Cf. Lateiner and Spatharas 2016.

62. E.g., Dehghani, K. Johnson, Hoover, Sagi, Garten, Parmar, Vaisey, Iliev, and Graham 2016.

63. For this summary, I am indebted to Hayes 2020; more fully, see Klawans 2000. On purity and James, see esp. Lockett 2008.

do instances of *ritual impurity* reduce to the idea of *sin*; these pertain to everyday life, and God's Instructions (or Torah) outline how to respond in ways that guard and steward loci of God's presence: the tabernacle or temple, the Sabbath, and God's own people. Concerns with purity have to do with embodied faith, or embodied spirituality, though in different ways. Ritual purity relates to external contaminants (what comes into or what touches the body), moral purity to internal contaminants. For example, Jesus, as Matthew recounts, observes that moral impurity arises in the human heart (i.e., the seat of understanding, volition, and emotion, according to ancient psychology) and proceeds out of the mouth: "evil thoughts, murders, adulteries, sexual sins, thefts, false testimonies, and slanders" (Matt 15:19 AT). These willful, sinful behaviors serve as examples of moral impurity. In Israel's Scriptures, moral impurity results from idolatry, bloodshed, and sexual offences (e.g., Lev 18, 20). Accordingly, when James speaks of being contaminated by the world (1:27), he is not concerned with a person's or a community's mere presence in the world but with their internalization of the action-guiding ways of the world.

We can think of moral purity and moral impurity as nonoverlapping spheres and the line between them as a boundary, separating life-giving sensibilities and behaviors from those sensibilities and behaviors that work against life. In short, moral impurity expresses itself as an embodied force that frustrates human flourishing and community. Unlike ritual impurity, moral impurity is avoidable and willful: it is noncontagious, it invites divine discipline, and it calls for repentance.

James frames this textual unit with purity language: *filth* and *evil* in 1:21; *pure*, *unsullied*, and *contaminated* in 1:27. He thus casts the whole within a concern to draw boundaries with regard both to certain behaviors that characterize the moral versus the immoral life and to the overall, divine perspective from which that boundary is drawn. James's language is conversionary—not in the sense of moving from one religion to another, but in the sense of embracing more fully, embodying more integrally, and putting into practice more faithfully the way of life to which one has committed oneself (or the faith one has professed). By conversionary, then, I refer to transformed patterns of human life—of thinking, feeling, believing, and behaving—with certain practices (1:27) but not others (1:19–20, 26) serving as the embodiment of those commitments and as the window through which one's deepest commitments are on display. James uses purity language in the service of his call to integrity, to counter double-mindedness by fusing together *is* and *does*.

Powerful metaphors are demanded by the circumstances James describes. After all, we construe and order the world through metaphors;[64] accordingly, behavioral change is woven together with a makeover of the patterns by which we make sense of the world. With his language choices, James leverages a transformation of perspective that reorients his readers and hearers. Earlier, he

64. Cf. Lakoff and M. Johnson 1980.

warned his beloved siblings not to be deceived (1:16). In that context, the focus was on misconceptions of God, as though God were the tempter rather than the uncalculating, unwavering giver of good gifts. Using overlapping terms,[65] James expands his concern with deception by noting, first, that his audience is in danger of self-trickery, as though they were lying to themselves, reaching conclusions based on false assumptions, false memories, or patently false information (1:22). Second, he warns that self-induced deception penetrates to the core of a person's inner life, the heart, thus emphasizing the viral nature of false beliefs (1:26). At stake is the difference between competing ways of construing faithful life: the wrong way, whereby people delude themselves as they adopt worldly life patterns, choosing to believe that these patterns provide the measure and means of human thriving; the right way, congruent with God's perspective on and enabling of human wholeness.

Is human flourishing marked by moral purity or filth? What provides the appropriate basis for self-examination and self-improvement, mirror reflections of our natural selves or the mirror provided by the perfect law? Which qualifies the truly happy person, hearing alone or hearing that leads to doing? These questions practically answer themselves, and this is what makes James's message so piercing, so forceful.

This final unit of James's introduction points the way to what will follow: care for the vulnerable (ch. 2), speech ethics (ch. 3), the danger of the world's moral pollutants (chs. 4–5), and, everywhere, an emphasis on integrity and wholeness (chs. 2–5). The dispersal of God's people throughout the larger world brings with it external pressures for the faithful, pressures that now manifest themselves in internal discord. The internal life of the communities to whom James addresses his letter are in the spotlight, but these cannot be addressed apart from the attractiveness of life patterns offered by the larger world.

[1:19–21] If James's siblings were to embrace the topsy-turvy vision he has set before them, what consequences would follow? By opening this paragraph with his reference to "my dear brothers and sisters," he both draws his audience into his circle of kin and furthers his efforts at shaping a familial ethos. First, he calls on them "to understand"—clearly not in the sense of their ability to regurgitate his words but in the sense of internalized, tacit insight actualized in beliefs and behaviors. This directive is backward looking and pertains to grasping (and being grasped by) his instruction on genuine happiness, status reversal, God's character, the evil inclination, and the problem of double-mindedness. Second, he exemplifies the behavioral patterns this internalized insight manifests: "Be quick to listen, slow to speak, slow to anger." Third, he instructs them on how they might gain freedom from their sinful proclivities.

---

65. Jas 1:16, *planaō* (I deceive); 1:22, *paralogizomai* (I deceive); 1:26, *apataō* (I deceive).

We find nothing novel in James's proverbial instruction on controlled speech. Similar instruction is well-known in the Greco-Roman world, including within Second Temple Judaism.[66] However, this does not keep him from making speech a telling test case for divulging whether a person or community is exercising courageous endurance amid external pressures. More remarkable is the way James frames these pithy directives theologically. Here, anger is rendered problematic in relation to God, not in an abstract sense. Irrespective of how anger might be appraised in the wider world, within the lifeworld James imagines, anger belongs to the category of moral toxins. Anger does not produce God's righteousness. We might say that human anger is incongruent with God's righteousness; it does not put God's justice on display; the exercise of human anger is not how God sets things right.

We might imagine that James's critique of *anger* is carte blanche, as though anger in all its forms runs counter to divine righteousness. Two considerations militate against such a reading. First, Stoic psychology of the first century should not be confused with psychology in a post-Freudian world. In Greco-Roman moral philosophy, "feeling" the onset of an emotion like anger is not the emotion itself. Feeling angry becomes problematic when that feeling gives way to angry behavior.[67] Seneca (ca. 4 BCE–65 CE) summarizes: "Emotion . . . does not consist in being moved by the impressions presented to the mind, but in surrendering to them" (*Ira* 2.3.1 AT). In Mark 3:5, for example, Jesus "looked around at [those in the synagogue] with anger," but this leads to healing, not to inflamed behavior. Second, although this is James's only use of the term (1:19–20), he nonetheless targets elsewhere the kind of behavior we might associate with feelings that manifest themselves in virulent or embittered conduct. This includes the work of the untamed tongue ("a restless evil, full of deadly poison," 3:8), gloating and other expressions of rivalry and self-promotion (3:14–16), lashing out against each other in the community (4:1–2), vilifying and damning those within the community (4:11–12), and even murder (4:2; cf. 5:6). This is the anger against which James sets himself: becoming so inflamed by what we might call *angry feelings* that we are delivered over to them so that they move us to malevolent behavior. This is the anger that counters James's interest in the faithful, flourishing life of the communities who name Jesus as Lord.

Humility (1:21), not anger, is the necessary precondition for setting aside morally offensive pollutants (like anger!) and welcoming the "implanted word."

66. E.g., Prov 16:32 LXX: "Those who are slow to anger are better than a warrior, and those who control their anger are better than one who captures a city" (AT); 29:20 LXX; Sir 5:11 LXX: "Be quick in your hearing, and patiently give your response" (AT); 20:7 LXX. For Greco-Roman literature, see L. Johnson 2004c, 157–64. More generally, see Baker 1995, 23–83.

67. My purpose here is not to adjudicate competing approaches to emotion, but simply to urge that we take seriously what James is targeting when he speaks of anger. On Greco-Roman "emotion," see Hicks 2021.

Clearly, for James, the character of interpersonal, communal interactions provides a key barometer of one's allegiance to God and God's ways.

James provides three commands: (1) Understand! (2) Let everyone be quick to listen! (1:19). The second leads to a sidenote on the trouble with anger (1:20). (3) "Welcome the implanted word!" (1:21). This last directive recalls James's earlier reference to the true word by which God birthed James and his siblings (1:18), contrasts lives shaped by anger and those shaped by humility, and frames his instruction in conversionary terms (i.e., in relation to conforming more genuinely to one's professed commitments and allegiances). This remove-and-welcome combination signals repentance (1:21); it speaks of human reformation. The term James uses, *remove*, evokes images of the dressing room: taking off (and putting on) one's clothes. *Filth* fills out the image, since this term is found in references to smutty attire (as in 2:2). If we think of clothing simply in utilitarian terms or as an external covering or decoration, James's point is easy to miss. Once we grasp the ancient view that clothing and personal identity, clothing and character, clothing and status, clothing and interpersonal relationships, are intertwined, his message is more pressing.[68] Here, then, undressing signals the first step of a deep change in one's personhood-in-relation-to-one's-community; the image of disrobing oneself of (and no longer outfitting oneself in) pervasive moral impurity and wickedness paves the way for extending hospitality to the implanted word. And this movement from moral filth to welcoming the word is marked by a deep-seated shift—from angry dispositions and behavior (which involve taking matters into one's violent hands and so opposing God's royal rule) to dispositions and behavior marked by humility (not passivity, but a gentleness or warmheartedness atypical of the arrogant or brazen).

References to theological or moral disrobing often pair *taking off* with *putting on*, as in Rom 13:12: "Let us remove the works of darkness and put on the weapons of light" (AT; cf. Eph 4:20–24; Col 3:8–10). But James completes the sequence by substituting open-armed hospitality toward the implanted word for actions that people might undertake on their own power to practice faithful living. For James, then, repentance, "taking off," is yoked with receiving from outside oneself what is needed for faithful response amid trials. In this respect, James is more like what we find in 1 Peter: "Therefore, having removed every evil and every deceit, and pretenses and jealousies and all slander, like newborn babies you are to yearn for the pure milk of the word so that in it you may grow up into salvation" (1 Pet 2:1–2 AT). As 1 Peter pairs the removal of filthy clothing with new birth, so James couples the removal of filthy clothing with welcoming the implanted word. And as 1 Peter speaks of God's word

---

68. See Berger 2003, 40–43. The significance granted one's attire continues to the modern era in the West. Recall Shakespeare (*Hamlet*, 1.3.78): "For the apparel oft proclaims the man."

that enables newborns to "grow up into salvation," so James characterizes the implanted word by its "power to save."

Apart from its local cotext, one might imagine that the phrase *implanted word* refers to innate cognitive capacities (reason) shared among members of the human family. Here, though, such a reading would be problematic,[69] first, because of James's pessimistic assessment of the human condition. Simply put, left to their own devices, humans lack the resources to master their own cravings, which lead to sin and death; natural capabilities are insufficient for following God's will (1:12–16). Instead, those who actualize their divine vocation (i.e., those whose thriving lives portend the consummation of God's purpose for all creatures) are enabled to do so by God's true word (1:17–18). Reading *implanted word* as a reference to innate human capacities is problematic, second, because for James this word has a soteriological purpose: "the implanted word . . . has the power to save you." Salvation, in this cotext, can have an eschatological sense (given the end-time allusions in James's introduction— e.g., 1:12, 15, 18), but it can have this meaning only because it first entails that people are liberated from enslavement to their own evil inclinations. *Implanted word*, then, refers not to innate human faculties but to God's good news planted and taking root in the lives of James's brothers and sisters.[70]

[22–25] James's comparison of two kinds of people is reminiscent of Jesus's words at the close of the Sermon on the Mount (Matt 7:24–27) and the Sermon on the Plain (Luke 6:46–49). The opening of this final paragraph in Luke's version is especially noteworthy: "Why do you call me 'Lord, Lord,' and do not do what I say?" (v. 46 AT). Those who only hear are like those who build a house without a foundation (Luke) or build on sand (Matthew). Those who hear and put what they hear into practice build on solid rock. The latter withstands the onslaught while the former is totally destroyed. More sharply, Jesus elsewhere proclaims in Luke's Gospel, "Truly happy . . . are those who hear God's word and put it into practice!" (Luke 11:28 AT). James's words sound a similar note. Where Matthew and Luke distinguish between the wise and the foolish, though, James juxtaposes those who are genuinely happy and those who, in their self-deception, play a terrible trick on themselves. The latter have adopted life patterns they trust are oriented toward faithfulness to God, but their conceptions of God are erroneous, their life patterns misguided (and so, the lifeworld they share is delusional). They listen but do not practice what they are told. The common verb for "hearing" in the NT, *akouō*, often connotes "hear and

---

69. *Pace* Jackson-McCabe (2001), who argues that *emphytos logos* (implanted word) refers to natural reason embodied in God's Instructions (or Torah); cf. Green 2002. See Whitlark 2010; Konradt 1998, 85–90.

70. It is difficult not to think of a scriptural text like Jer 31:31–35, which anticipates a time when God will engrave his Instructions (or Torah) on the hearts of his people (cf. Ezek 11:17–21; 36:23–32).

understand" or even "hear and obey." But James uses a different term, *akroatēs*, to signify "one who merely listens." Mere listening—this is the problem with the self-deluded. By way of comparison, "active doers" align themselves with the truth and act accordingly. They are "genuinely happy": amid trials, in their lowliness, in their humility, empowered by the gospel, reflecting God's upside-down, right-side-up reckoning, they flourish both now and in the eschaton.[71]

The contrast between mere listeners and active doers frames this paragraph (1:22–23a, 25bc). At the center we find a twofold simile: listeners are like this; doers are like that. Even though James's use of the mirror as an object lesson has challenges, its force is easy to grasp: With one group, but not the other, gazing into the mirror has no effect. What James teaches is the same whether we think of today's highly reflective mirrors made from applying a thin layer of silver to one side of a sheet of glass (already available in rudimentary form in the first century) or the murkier mirrors of antiquity, made from polished brass or bronze (cf. 1 Cor 13:12 AT: "For now we see obliquely, in a mirror"). Though mirrors might be associated with vanity (Isa 3:22–24), first-century moral instruction turned to them as instruments for self-improvement.[72] Looking in the mirror, whether at oneself or at an exemplar to emulate, ought to make a positive difference.

The self-deceived see their "natural selves" in the mirror. This could refer to the human condition as James has articulated it, with people enslaved to their own cravings, their hearts bent toward evil and moral filth. Now that they have seen their natural condition, we might expect them to take self-corrective steps. It could also refer to the words spoken over the first humans (made in God's image, Gen 1:26), the promise of fulfilling the human vocation of presencing God in their interactions with God's creation. Now that they have seen what they are created and called to be, we might expect that they would undertake measures to actualize the vocation given them collectively by God. Either way, the futility of the exercise is the same—not because they fail to see but because they quickly forget and fail to act on what they have seen.

Others, however, have as their mirror "the perfect law, the law of freedom." While the self-deceived scrutinize themselves in the mirror, they instantly forget what they have seen; the exercise leads nowhere. This second group glances at the mirror, then perseveres; the implication is that they internalize what they see with the result that their hearing metamorphoses into doing. What is this law they see in the mirror, the law that leads from listening to doing? On the one hand, it is the "perfect" law, with James using terminology he has earlier associated with human wholeness and integrity, with human flourishing (1:4). On the other hand, it is the law "of freedom"—which, in this context, must

---

71. On "happiness," see above, on 1:2–18 and on 1:19–27.
72. L. Johnson 2004b, 173–76.

signify the liberating effect it has vis-à-vis a person's bondage, their inclination toward evil. Accordingly, the law of which James speaks refers to God's "true word" (1:18), the "implanted word" (1:21)—that is, the good news through which James and his siblings are enabled to live conversionary lives, to thrive, even amid trials as God's messianic people scattered throughout the world.

[26–27] We would be badly mistaken to imagine that James has just referred to speech ethics (1:19–20, 22) as a thought experiment or theoretical test case. His return to it here confirms speech as a genuine and pressing concern for James as he contemplates the internal life of the scattered communities to whom he writes. His approach is simple: to contrast two behavioral patterns: one cannot be confused with genuine devotion to God; the other puts genuine devotion to God on display. *Devotion* (sometimes translated as "religion") in this case refers to the practice of obligations associated with worshiping God, and particularly the need for palpable correspondence between moral life and worship.[73] Consider the words of Isaiah, who rails against sacrificial offerings, feasts, and other religious celebrations in the absence of moral purity. Instead, he demands: "Wash! Be clean! Remove your ugly deeds from my sight. Put an end to such evil; learn to do good. Seek justice: help the oppressed; defend the orphan; plead for the widow" (Isa 1:16–17 CEB; see 1:11–17). Or consider the perhaps more prosaic but equally demanding words of Jesus in the Sermon on the Mount: First, be reconciled to your brother or sister, and only then make your gift at the altar (Matt 5:23–24). Anything else, for James, is worthless, unproductive, a sham, like idol worship.[74]

On the negative side of the ledger, James focuses narrowly on one's ability to control what they say, a topic to which he will return at length in chapter 3. The immediate reference, though, would be back to his caution concerning angry speech in 1:20. Clearly, those for whom the mirror of God's perfect law has been effective do not lash out against each other in anger; they hear and do: thus they do not deceive themselves (1:22–25). The relational character of James's concern is front and center. Life amid trials has Christ-followers turning against each other, abusing each other with their words in ways that evidently reflect the opposition they encounter from those outside their messianic communities. James depicts the depth of the problem when he refers to them as deceiving their hearts. Understanding the significance of his portrait depends on our recalling the ancient view that the heart is the center of one's emotional, intellectual, and volitional life. Their self-deception reaches the core of their inner life, we might say, and exhibits itself in mercurial speech. James's wording recalls Job's judgment that, if his heart were to be deceived, he would be an idolater

---

73. Cf. Verseput 1997, 101–4; *TLNT* 1:200–204.

74. James's term, *mataios* (1:26), is used of idol worship in, e.g., Jer 2:5 LXX; Acts 14:15; see Lockett 2008, 114.

(Job 31:24–28)[75]—an allusion made all the more serious when James names Job as a model of courageous endurance (5:11).

Working again with the conceptual metaphor MORALITY IS PURITY,[76] James is careful to identify the perspective from which purity is determined. This is pure and unsullied devotion *in God the Father's eyes* (and for James, of course, God's perspective is traced in Scripture and refracted through Jesus's message). This reference to "the Father" may reflect Ps 68:5, in which God is portrayed as the Father of orphans and defender of widows. If so, James clarifies that those whose devotion to God is genuine put feet and hands to God's compassion for society's vulnerable.[77] If the lives of these scattered messianic communities are set amid trials, how much more would those systemically devoid of resources and support find trouble that leads to suffering? Courageous endurance amid trials is now explained in terms not of withdrawing into an enclave or protecting one's own assets but of modeling God's own behavior in coming to the aid of those experiencing even more misery.

The NT refers to the *world* in a variety of ways; depending on the definition used, *world* might be assessed positively, negatively, or neutrally. Here and throughout his letter, James is unrelentingly negative in his portrayal of the world, even pitting friendship with the world as the opposite of friendship with God (1:27; 2:5; 3:6; 4:4 [2×]). It is important to recognize, then, that *world* (*kosmos*) does not refer simply to God's creation, the human family, or to the planet Earth. In the case of James, we might think more accurately of "lifeworld"—that is, the world as a given society understands and experiences it, with its common values and practices shaped and transmitted through successive generations, typically at a preconscious level. James's concern, then, is that Christ-followers might internalize an understanding of the way the world works by setting their moral and relational compasses with reference to a lifeworld that does not honor or serve God; this cannot do other than give rise to moral impurity. Genuine devotion, devotion that is morally pure, has its compass set instead in relation to God the Father. Accordingly, avoiding the world's pollutants refers far less to withdrawing from the world into an insulated colony of "people like us" and much more to ensuring that God's word is planted deep inside (1:21), God's word—and not the lifeworld propagated, in this case, by Rome—which permeates life and generates patterns of thinking, feeling, believing, and behaving.

---

75. The term *apataō* is in Job 31:27 (Göttingen LXX, critical ed.): "If my heart was secretly *deceived*."

76. See above on 1:19–27.

77. Israel's Scriptures are rife with references to the orphan and the widow (or the orphan, the widow, and the immigrant) as emblematic of society's unprotected and impoverished, who are therefore to receive special care—e.g., Exod 22:21–22; Lev 19:33–34; Deut 24:17; Pss 10:18; 82:3; Isa 1:17; Jer 7:6.

James 2:1–26
Demonstrating Faithfulness

From the introduction to this letter (ch. 1), we see James's overall concern that his readers and hearers, predominately Jewish Christ-followers distributed outside Israel's ancestral lands, exercise practical wisdom. The wisdom he promotes is both conceptual (a way of making sense of the world in relation to God) and practice-oriented (entailing patterns of behavior congruent with this way of making sense of the world in relation to God). As he moves from the letter's introduction to this first short essay, he continues this overarching theme by focusing on a specific, obviously central, set of circumstances in which practical wisdom is needed. This has to do with community relations vis-à-vis the poor—that is, needy, powerless people of low status. Apparently for James, the regard with which the community holds the poor, especially as its regard for the poor is on display in its behavior toward the poor, serves as a key barometer of the genuineness of its faith.

Chapter 2 is set off by its opening address, "my brothers and sisters" (2:1), followed by an announcement of topic (favoritism). This linguistic pattern is repeated at the beginning of chapter 3, "my brothers and sisters," plus a warning to teachers (3:1). This first section of the body of the letter identifies the character of diasporic testing realized in issues of power and privilege, themselves rooted in judgments concerning status honor. Distributed outside the land of the Jews, these Christ-followers experience perhaps all the more strongly the realities of their hybrid existence—their identities and life patterns tugged both in the direction of Roman conventions and in a counterdirection, namely, toward service of the Lord Jesus Christ.[1] Motifs raised in Jas 1 continue. James's concern with practical wisdom surfaced in 1:5, 22–27; the proper appraisal of the poor and rich in 1:9–11; care for the vulnerable in 1:27; and, especially, double-mindedness as a possible manifestation of a problematic cultural hybridity in 1:6–8.

The first major section of James's letter (1:2–27) orients his audience to the sensibilities and practices comprising faithful, diasporic life. Now James

---

1. Although "hybridity" often entails the combination of previous, discrete cultural influences into fresh cultural expressions, the conventions that concern James here are incompatible with following Christ.

pulls back the curtain on evil-minded, Torah-breaking sensibilities and practices that display favoritism toward the elite of this world. He contrasts this
favoritism with faithful patterns of life inspired by Jesus's own faith—patterns
that account for their status as siblings, God's choice of the poor, Scripture's
royal law: "Love your neighbor as yourself" (2:8, citing Lev 19:18), and the
priority of mercy (2:1–13). James follows his critique of favoritism toward the
elite with four exhibits concerning faith and wealth, and faith and deeds, more
generally (2:14–26).

Faith is important to James's theology, and the term congregates especially
in chapter 2 (vv. 1, 5, 14 [2×], 17, 18 [3×], 20, 22 [2×], 24, 26).[2] The verb *to
believe* appears in James only in chapter 2 (vv. 19 [2×], 23). We might say,
then, that James devotes this present section to his articulation of the nature
of genuine faith. This faith cannot be reduced to an interior disposition, nor to
one's acceptance of a set of beliefs. Faith entails relational commitments and
manifestations,[3] and these are demonstrated by the Lord Jesus Christ. The faith
that James seeks is living and active, involving patterns of thinking and believing, yes, but also of feeling and behaving. Borrowing an image that James has
used (1:22–25), we might say that James now summons his readers and hearers
to study themselves in the mirror of faith represented by good exemplars (Abraham and Rahab) and bad (inhospitable well-wishers and demons)—to learn and
act accordingly (2:14–26). Moreover, he grounds those faithful patterns of life
in Jesus's own faith, in God's choice of the poor, and in Scripture (2:1–13). The
result is a masterpiece of persuasion, with James's appeal leaving no room for
double-mindedness. The life of faith for Jews in the Greco-Roman era might
be correlated especially with circumcision, dietary laws, and Sabbath-keeping
(see above, on 1:1), but James presses his audience of messianists further. For
them, faith is realized, too, in care for the poor: those who occupy society's
fringe, the powerless, the dishonored.

2:1–13 Neighbor Love versus Favoritism

2:1 My brothers and sisters, do not hold the faith of our glorious Lord Jesus
Christ together with acts of favoritism.[a] **2** After all,[b] if[c] a man[d] wearing
a gold ring and fine clothes enters your gathering, and a poor person
dressed in filthy rags also enters, **3** and you take special notice of the one
wearing fine clothes, saying, "Sit in this excellent seat," while saying to
the poor person, "Stand over there" or "Sit at my feet," **4** have you not
made distinctions among yourselves and become evil-minded judges?

---

2. Outside of ch. 2, *pistis* appears in 1:3, 6; 5:15.
3. See Morgan 2015.

5 My dear brothers and sisters, listen! Has God not chosen the poor according to worldly standards to be rich in terms of faith,^{e} and to be heirs of the kingdom he has promised to those who love him? 6 But you have dishonored the poor. Is it not the wealthy who tyrannize you and drag you into court? 7 Are they not the ones who insult the good name invoked over you?

8 You, though,^{f} do well when you fulfill the royal law found in Scripture:^{g} "Love your neighbor as yourself." 9 But when you show favoritism, you commit sin and are implicated by the law as lawbreakers. 10 Anyone who obeys the entirety of the law yet fails at one point becomes guilty of all of it. 11 The one who said, "Do not commit adultery" also said, "Do not commit murder." Accordingly, if you do not commit adultery but do commit murder, you have become a lawbreaker.

12 Speak, therefore, and act as people who are to be judged by the law of freedom. 13 After all, judgment will be merciless for anyone who has not shown mercy. Mercy triumphs over judgment.

a. James 2:1 bristles with translation and interpretive challenges. *Echete* (you possess) could be rendered as an imperative or an indicative. *Pistis tou Kyriou . . . Iēsou Christou* could be taken as an objective genitive, "faith in the Lord Jesus Christ"; or subjective genitive, "the faith/fulness of the Lord Jesus Christ." And it is not altogether clear what *tēs doxēs* (of glory) modifies (see the summary of proposals in Allison 2001, 541–43 n. 43; Allison 2013, 382–84). Even so, James's point is not in doubt: the utter incompatibility of following Jesus and showing favoritism toward the wealthy and well-positioned at the expense of the marginal, lowly, impoverished (cf. McKnight 2011, 180). I have translated *prosōpolēmpsiais* as "acts of favoritism" (as opposed to a disposition toward favoritism, for example) to reflect James's use of the plural noun.

b. James introduces this scenario with *gar*, signifying "continuity with supporting explanation" (Adam 2013, 35).

c. James's use of a conditional sentence should not be taken to mean that he is thinking in hypothetical terms only. The general prospective conditional clause refers to "something one can and must generally expect" (von Siebenthal 2019, 525).

d. James's term *anēr* commonly designates a man (and not a woman); a reference to a male in this cotext would be congruent with James's interest in portraying someone in terms of Roman canons of status honor.

e. I am taking both *tō kosmō* (according to worldly standards) and *en pistei* (in terms of faith) as datives of perspective or vantage point (cf. Boas, Rijksbaron, Huitink, and de Bakker 2019, §30.52).

f. Many translations take *mentoi* in its emphatic sense, so speak of those who "*really* fulfill the royal law" (CEB, NRSV; cf. NIV: "*really* keep"); I have taken it in its adversative sense: The wealthy do this, but you do well when you . . .

g. James's use of *nomos* in 2:8 likely refers to the whole of God's Instructions (or Torah) and his use of *hē graphē* (sg.) probably refers to the whole of Israel's Scriptures, with the subsequent citation of Lev 19:18, "Love your neighbor as yourself," an epitome of God's Instructions.

James begins this brief essay with a carefully constructed argument against acts of partiality that favor the wealthy and disparage the poor.[4] First, he lays out his thesis: the typical Roman practice of deferring to society's rich and elevated is incompatible with allegiance to Jesus Christ (v. 1). Second, he documents the impetus for his argument by referring to practices, whether actual or potential, within the assembly of these Jewish messianists (vv. 2–4). Third, James supports his thesis with additional claims in the form of questions for which the answers are embarrassingly obvious, and damning (vv. 5–7). Then, fourth, he grounds his thesis in the love command (vv. 8–11). Finally, he identifies the basis for end-time judgment in terms of mercy on behalf of the needy (vv. 12–13). Whatever else it might mean to work out one's hyphenated identity (messianist-Jewish-Roman), James urges that some conventional life patterns cannot be negotiated or creatively transformed; they are simply irreconcilable with following Christ. His readers and hearers must choose between acting toward the lowly and impoverished according to Roman standards or according to God's standards.[5]

[2:1] James sets the stage for his warning and instruction to those who exercise favoritism in two ways. The first is his initial appeal to his "brothers and sisters" (2:1). Since he repeatedly refers to his audience in this way,[6] we might overlook how this mention of *siblingship* anticipates, even grounds, his instruction.

Address forms generally communicate either hierarchical power (or control) on the one hand, or solidarity on the other hand. James opts for the latter, though this is not to say that his designation of his audience as brothers and sisters lacks rhetorical power. From the wider perspective of cultural anthropology, siblingship runs deeper than friendship, identifying people who are parts of each other, whose lives are cojoined and interdependent. From culture to culture, siblings "participate intrinsically in each other's existence"; they practice a "mutuality of being."[7] Siblingship cannot be reduced to blood relations since siblings are

---

4. Whether James is as accomplished a rhetorician as some analyses of this section imply, the progression of this section is easily recognized: see, e.g., Watson 1993a; Wachob 2000, 59–113; Hartin 1999, 124–28; Mongstad-Kvammen 2013, 103–204.

5. Cf., e.g., Mongstad-Kvammen 2013, 146–47; Green 2022, 300–301.

6. See Jas 1:2, 9, 16, 19; 2:1, 5, 14; 3:1, 10, 12; 4:11; 5:7, 9, 10, 12, 19.

7. So Sahlins 2013, ix (and throughout). He thus privileges "intersubjective being over the singular person as the composite of multiple others" and speaks of "partibility plus co-presence" (28). Sahlins defines a *kinship system* as "a manifold of intersubjective participations, . . . a network of mutualities of being" (20).

"made" in a variety of ways. In the present case, James has earlier observed that the siblingship he has in mind is the consequence not of shared biology but of divine agency in the birthing of God's people by means of God's true word (1:18).

In the Roman Mediterranean, sibling language generally negated notions of structured hierarchy in favor of mutuality. This is not the same thing as strict egalitarianism, however, since differences among siblings are obvious—age, for example, or economic disparities, or abilities like public speaking. Accordingly, we find references to "greater" and "lesser" siblings, even if the aim was for brotherly and sisterly love to displace such distinctions in the service of status symmetry and oneness. In his work *On Brotherly Love*, the Greek philosopher Plutarch (ca. 46–ca. 120 CE) recognizes inequities that inevitably arise among brothers; then he observes:

> One would therefore advise a brother, in the first place, to make his brothers partners in those respects in which he is considered to be superior . . . ; in the next place, to make manifest to them neither haughtiness nor disdain, by deferring to them and conforming his character to theirs, to make his superiority secure from envy and to equalize, as far as this is attainable, the disparity of his fortune by his moderation of spirit. (484D)[8]

He goes on to urge that superior brothers ought to share with the inferior, dampening divisions between them (484D–485C), and the inferior ought not degrade themselves in relation to the superior, nor place them too high on a pedestal (485C–486A). Siblings should aspire to avoid conflict by refusing to judge each other and overcome conflict through practices of leniency (mercy, compassion, forgiveness) toward each other.[9]

Recognizing that kinship language projects onto relationships a desired outcome but also serves powerfully to shape relationships in the direction of that ideal, we can see how James's appeal to his audience bolsters his theological interests. On the one hand, in the background we might hear the words of Jesus: "Whoever performs God's will is my brother, sister, and mother" (Mark 3:35 AT; cf. Matt 12:50; Luke 8:21). "Brothers and sisters," he says, but what James means is "those of you who pattern your lives after God's will." On the other hand, he has already drawn attention to God's having transformed James's audience into siblings, birthing them by means of God's true word (1:18), and thus making of them a people called and enabled to live in counterworldly ways.

---

8. Helmbold 1939, 283.
9. See the discussion in Aasgaard 1997; Aasgaard 2005; Sandnes 1997; Clarke 2004. Batten (2017) understands siblingship under the general heading of *friendship* yet might have done more to tease out the ramifications of James's use here of familial rather than friendship language. Mongstad-Kvammen (2013, 105–11) is helpful in this respect.

Naming his audience as "brothers and sisters," then, James lays the groundwork for his emphasis on life patterns congruent with Jesus's faith. You are brothers and sisters, we might hear him say, so act like it.

The second way James sets the stage for his instruction is by referring to "the faith of our glorious Lord Jesus Christ" (2:1). As in the opening to the letter as a whole (1:1: "the Lord Jesus Christ"), so here, James's phrasing identifies the interpretive lens through which to read what follows: Jesus's unveiling of God's agenda and the faithfulness for which it calls. As the second of only two explicit references to Jesus in the letter, this all the more underscores its importance here: it provides a christological plumb line by which to correct the patterns of thinking, believing, feeling, and behaving characteristic of the faithful scattered outside the Jewish homeland.

Notwithstanding the challenges swirling around how best to translate this verse, the interpretive importance of James's reference to Jesus here is clear enough. We get a sense of the issues by placing two standard translations alongside my own:

AT: My brothers and sisters, do not hold the faith of our glorious Lord Jesus Christ together with acts of favoritism.

CEB: My brothers and sisters, when you show favoritism you deny the faithfulness of our Lord Jesus Christ, who has been resurrected in glory.

NRSV: My brothers and sisters, do you with your acts of favoritism really believe in our glorious Lord Jesus Christ?

Rather than enter the debate regarding the best translation, we can simply admit that each of these, and others besides, are grammatically conceivable while recognizing that, despite their differences, they each point the finger at *the incompatibility of allegiance to the Lord Jesus and acts of favoritism*.[10] Additionally, I call attention to some of the consequences of the translation I have adopted.

First, although the translation offered by the NRSV might pass muster as a paraphrase, James's sentence is a command rather than a question.[11] This is important because the NRSV leaves open the possibility of a negative answer,

---

10. For the translation issues, see Adam 2013, 33–35. In different ways, my rendering is influenced by, e.g., Wachob 2000, 64–70; L. Johnson 1995, 220–21; Hartin 1999, 116–17; Lowe 2009.

11. *Echete* could be read as an indicative in 2:1 (as in the CEB: "When you show favoritism you deny . . ."), though the result would parallel the imperative (as in the NIV: "believers . . . must not show favoritism"). Punctuating the opening to ch. 2 as an interrogative is not impossible, but our writer typically provides a directive followed by an example (note the use of *gar* in 2:2: "For if . . .").

as if James's audience might respond, "No, really, we don't do that," when, plainly, they do. As James's next comments make all too clear, his audience is double-minded. They want to claim their allegiance to the Lord Jesus *while at the same time* exercising favoritism.

Second, James most probably refers to *Jesus's faith* and neither to *Jesus's faithfulness* nor to *faith in Jesus*. James otherwise never refers to faith *in Jesus*, but rather refers to faith in God (cf. 1:6–8; 2:19, 23). (This is an issue of syntax, not theology, since James's high Christology allows that faith in God entails faith in the Lord Jesus.) It is possible that James is referring to the whole of Jesus's life, and thus to his "faithfulness," since Jesus's ministry clearly embraced those who would not typically be included among their communities' esteemed members. Perhaps even more important, though, is the way Jesus, in word and deed, expressed his faith in God's purpose and power to overturn conventional judgments about what sort of people are up or down, what sort of people are inside or outside—and who, himself, as 1 Peter observes, "handed himself over to the one who judges justly" (1 Pet 2:23 AT), to the "Father who judges impartially" (1:17 AT). Indeed, James immediately goes on to declare God's choice of "the poor according to worldly standards": they are "rich in terms of faith" and "heirs of the kingdom he has promised to those who love him" (Jas 2:5). As Jesus proclaimed, "Happy are you who are poor, because God's kingdom is yours" (Luke 6:20 CEB). One cannot celebrate and emulate Jesus's faith in God's purpose and power to overturn judgments based on favoritism while continuing to practice favoritism.

Third, naming Jesus as Lord and Christ activates two overlapping schemas: the household over which Jesus is Lord and the dominion over which Jesus exercises royal rule as the Christ. This is significant for the way it identifies the household or dominion within which such and such patterns of life are deemed fitting. The household or dominion of Rome has its ways, but so does the household or dominion of the Lord Jesus Christ, and these two are not always compatible.

This last point is made all the more emphatically by James's allusion to Lev 19:15.[12] We read here: "Do not act unjustly in judgment. Show neither favoritism to the debased poor nor reverence to the influential rich. Judge your neighbor justly" (LXX, AT). Israel's Scriptures deny that God plays favorites when God judges and urge that humans must model themselves after God in this respect (e.g., Deut 1:17; 10:17; 16:19; 2 Chr 19:7; Ps 82:2; Prov 24:23; Mal 1:8; 2:9). The concept in question, *partiality*, derives from the idiomatic phrase (rooted in common practice), *to lift up the face as a sign of esteem*, and is always

---

12. When James cites Lev 19:18b LXX, he contrasts neighbor love with the exercise of favoritism (Jas 2:8–9), thus disclosing the influence of Lev 19:15. See L. Johnson 2004d; Lockett 2020, 460–62; Akiyama 2018, 156–58.

regarded negatively in Israel's Scriptures and in early Christian literature.[13] Of course, this is not to say that, for James (or for the Bible more generally), justice is blind, as "Lady Justice" is portrayed today in many parts of the world. As James is about to clarify, showing favoritism relates above all to how people treat those whom they regard as their social superiors, whereas God's eye is on the poor (Jas 2:5).[14] Note how Lev 19 punctuates its admonition against partiality with the declaration: "I am the LORD" (19:16)—an affirmation repeated like a chorus throughout the chapter, underpinning Yahweh's call to holiness (Lev 19:2, 3, 4, 10, 12, et al.). James mirrors the language of Lev 19, tying the rejection of favoritism to Jesus's lordship, even referring to Jesus as the "glorious Lord" and so highlighting the honor due him. This is ironic since this honorable Lord has aligned himself not with those who receive honor according to worldly standards but with the despised and degraded poor (Jas 2:5; cf. 1:9–11).[15]

[2–4] James identifies the motivation for his theological directive against showing favoritism (stated in 2:1) by introducing what is likely a recognizable practice in the gathering of these Christ-followers. Even if the scene that James paints is dramatized by the appearance of people from the social ladder's uppermost and bottommost rungs, his audience is likely to recognize themselves in it. Two people enter the assembly, and those gathered allocate their seating assignments on the basis of judgments concerning their relative importance. In Luke's Gospel, Jesus similarly critiques conventions around seating arrangements. Jesus relates a parable concerning seating assignments after observing how those invited to a meal were seeking places of honor at the table (Luke 14:7–14). And he criticizes the Pharisees and legal experts who sought prestigious seats in the synagogue and at dinner gatherings (11:43; 20:46; cf. Matt 23:6; Mark 12:39). It should not escape our notice, though, that the Christ-followers James portrays are doing nothing more than what would be expected in a Roman household. In this way, then, James unveils a case study in the conflict between life patterns (evaluations and practices) appropriate

---

13. Berger 1993, 3:179–80; Lohse 1968, 6:779–80. James uses the noun *prosōpolēmpsia* (favoritism) in 2:1 and its verbal form, *prosōpolēmpteō* (I show favoritism), in 2:9. In the NT, cf., e.g., *prosōpolēmptēs* (one who exercises favoritism) (Acts 10:34); *prosōpolēmpsia* (Rom 2:11; Eph 6:9; Col 3:25); *prosōpon + lambanō* (I show favoritism) (Gal 2:6); *aprosōpolēmptōs* (impartially), an adverb (1 Pet 1:17).

14. Similarly, note the story Jesus relates in Luke 18:1–8, in which a judge who apparently practices blind justice as "a judge who neither feared God nor respected people" (18:2; cf. 18:4) is nonetheless regarded as an "unjust judge" (18:6 CEB) on account of his ongoing refusal to grant justice to a widow (to one [along with orphans and immigrants] identified in Israel's Scriptures as the very personification of "the poor"). Interestingly, as in Jas 2:5, so also in Luke 18:7, we read of those whom God has *chosen*. In James, God has "chosen [*eklegomai*] the poor"; in Luke "the chosen ones" (*eklektos*) are "people [like this widow] who cry out to him day and night."

15. Cf. R. Martin 1988, 61.

to Christ-followers and life patterns deemed appropriate in Roman antiquity. What makes this all the more insidious is how easy it is for those who benefit from favoritism and those who participate in granting privilege to do so without noticing that they are doing so.[16]

Clothing was not merely a means of outward adornment in antiquity but broadcasted what or who one is in relation to others. It is hardly surprising, then, that James characterizes the two people who enter this gathering with reference to what they wear, using words that would immediately trigger status and role recognition on the part of James's audience. We can compare Jesus's story contrasting "a certain rich man who was clothed in purple and fine linen" with "a poor man named Lazarus, . . . who was covered with ulcers" (Luke 16:19–31 AT). In both instances, we seem to be dealing with the top and bottom of the scale determined by wealth, power, and privilege.[17]

This association with Luke 16 is helpful in another way, too. It serves to shine the light on how the terminology and wider concept of poverty are often used (both in antiquity and today).[18] What might appear to be an economic term, pure and simple, is often amplified by other criteria, such as disability and other health-related status, networks of relationships, social esteem, and more. Lazarus, the poor man in Jesus's story in Luke's Gospel, is placed at the gate of the wealthy man's compound,[19] indicating that Lazarus required help when coming to this location; as Jesus's story in Luke clearly states, he also is ulcerated (Luke 16:20). James's wealthy person is clearly a male, as would befit someone holding or ambitious for a position in the upper echelons of Roman society. But James does not tell us whether the poor person is male or female, nor does he fill in the blanks with other poverty-related measures. Male or female? Young or old? Disabled? Diseased? Questions like these rise in interest when we recall that women, the impaired, and children are disproportionately represented among those lacking in adequate economic resources. It is no stretch to imagine that, when James rails against discrimination in this section of the letter, he includes among the impoverished just such persons.[20]

We might wish James had said more. After all, it is not clear whether one or both of these two people are (or claim to be) Christ-followers. We have evidence elsewhere that such assemblies might include "outsiders or unbelievers" (1 Cor 14:23), but James's appeal to behavior among and toward siblings (2:1) and his choice of the phrase "among yourselves" (2:4) might tip the balance

---

16. Andria 2006, 1511–12.

17. Wealth and poverty are wedded to considerations of status, so much so, e.g., that senators and equites were distinguished from others by minimum standards of net worth. At stake was relative wealth, but even more so the power and privilege that accrue to the wealthy. See Whittaker 1993.

18. See Green 2020a.

19. Luke 16:20 uses a passive form of the verb *ballō* (I toss/place). NIV: "was laid."

20. Cf. Albl 2017, 430–45.

in favor of our identifying the impoverished person, at least, as a fellow messianist; thus we all the more strongly hear James's criticism of the behavior of those gathered (see further, below, on 2:5–7). James refers to the gathering with a word that might be translated *synagogue*, a reference to their *assembly* that would suggest that these Christ-followers are using language typical of Jewish assemblies for teaching, prayer, and community life to identify their own.[21]

The first person introduced appears in the garb of an elite Roman, one with equestrian status, a spectacularly wealthy person granted seating privileges and brandishing a gold ring, who may well have been a candidate for political appointment.[22] Since assemblies of Christ-followers would have been classified alongside the gatherings of other voluntary associations in urban settings (e.g., trade guilds, immigrant groups, and clubs oriented around deities), it makes good sense to picture such a man visiting in order to win support for his political ambitions. Even though no ballots would be cast by these Christ-followers, people with political ambitions depended on widespread backing from those over whom they would exercise office. This support took the form of their indebtedness to him, won by him through his tangible support, and chief among their obligations would have been the duty publicly to extend to him the honor appropriate to his station. Simply put, the philanthropy of the wealthy elite came with strings attached, sometimes heavy-handed and always servile, promulgating inequities of status, power, and privilege. James's critique of their offering the man an honorable seat, then, rebuts acts of favoritism in general and, more particularly, rejects the web of patron-client relations serving as the glue that held together the vast network of relationships in the Roman Mediterranean. Indeed, practices related to patron-client relationships would have been so common that they would be reflexive, unthinking, simply taken for granted, and this underscores the degree to which James's message is counterworldly.

---

21. *Synagōgē*: "gathering," "a building for an assembly," etc. The language of judgment peppers this section of the letter: *diakrinō* (I distinguish), 2:4; *kritēs* (judge), 2:4; *kritērion* (court), 2:6, *krinō* (I judge), 2:12; *krisis* (judgment), 2× in 2:13, perhaps leading us to think that James speaks of a judicial assembly. However, the first and last instances of this terminology (2:4, 12–13) refer to *playing favorites*, not practicing jurisprudence; the courtroom is in view only in 2:6, where we find no hint of a judicial role for the messianist-Jewish assembly. Cf., however, Ward 1969.

22. Persons of equestrian status included those with substantial landed wealth in the Roman Empire, second only to the senatorial order. On the identification of the man whom James describes, see the summary in Mongstad-Kvammen 2013, 127–28 (cf. 73–100): the gold ring signifies the equestrian order, senators and equites had seating privileges, and the expression *esthēs lampra* (fine clothes) can refer to the toga of a political candidate. See Kloppenborg Verbin 1999, 765–68. Even if one doubts the identity of this wealthy man as one with political ambitions, remaining is the critique of the patron-client relational system, in which goods and services are provided but ensnare recipients now obliged to reciprocate with myriad expressions of honor and support. Cf. Edgar 2001, 114–25; Batten 2017.

The second person who enters the assembly is the politician's negative image: "a poor person dressed in filthy rags." Our modern attempts to define the level of this person's impoverishment may hide the fact that structural poverty was the order of the day for most people in Roman antiquity. By some estimates, 90 percent or more of the empire's population lived at, near, or below subsistence level. Even more optimistic assessments of income distribution identify perhaps 80 percent of the empire's inhabitants in the category of those struggling to obtain basic necessities. Poor households would have comprised the vast majority of the population in urban centers.[23] This second person, then, could have been most anyone, though it is also true that those "filthy rags" portray this person as so down-and-out (say, the bottom 30 percent) that they intensify the contrast with the first man (a member of the Roman world's top 1 percent). To the shame of those Christ-followers gathered, this contrast forms the basis of their treatment of these two persons in the assembly. Whereas the one-percenter is ushered to "this excellent seat," the poor person has no place to sit at all, or is allowed to sit on the floor at someone's feet. This behavior—which, again, would pass without comment in a conventional Roman setting—warrants James's case against playing favorites. Clearly, it works against the mutuality and family-status symmetry expected among brothers and sisters, and it denies Jesus's faith in God's purpose and power to overturn such judgments and their attendant practices.

James provides one long sentence, first painting the scene, then interpreting it. Although people embedded in Roman culture would likely not give a second's thought to James's description of these expressions of favoritism (2:2–3), James unleashes a two-part, biting criticism (2:4). (1) They are making the very distinctions that Christ-followers must not and indeed cannot make; in doing so, (2) they make of themselves evil-minded judges. Together, these two aspects of James's analysis demonstrate the organic relationship between being and doing, between patterns of thinking and patterns of behavior. They are like the roots, stem, and leaves of a plant, so interconnected and interdependent that one cannot claim genuinely to believe one thing while doing another. Practices shape thoughts, beliefs, and feelings just as they are shaped by them. Accordingly, James's audience betrays the true character of their convictions through the way they behave toward these two people.

The term I have translated as *made distinctions* appeared earlier in the letter, where it signified *doubting* (1:6–7), and it could have this sense (or perhaps the sense of *wavering*) here as well.[24] In that case and in a more abstract way, James would be drawing attention to his audience as double-minded and unstable. In the present instance, though, the sense of *distinguishing* is activated by the

---

23. See above, on 1:9–11.
24. The term in question is *diakrinō*. The verb appears in James only in 1:6 and 2:4.

clear admonition against exercising favoritism (2:1) and by the clear practice of doing just that within the assembly (2:2–3). We might imagine that a stunningly wealthy man and a poverty-stricken beggar would distinguish between themselves by their self-presentations, so it is worth recalling that the issue at hand centers on the community's response to what differentiates the one from the other. Rather than prioritizing help for this impoverished person outfitted in filthy rags, they busy themselves with the supposed needs of a wealthy man of influence. (One can almost hear in the background the words of the enthroned king in the end-time scene Jesus paints: "Lord, when did we see you hungry or thirsty or a stranger or needing clothes . . . and did nothing to help you?" [Matt 25:44 AT; cf. Jas 2:15–16].) Their responses to the opportunity before them run counter to James's appeal to the familial character of his audience, with its ideal of mutuality and status symmetry. Even more so, it defies the faith of Jesus, grounded in God's aim and power to overturn common norms for determining who is up or down, in or out, and the practices that accompany those norms.

Making distinctions is an act of evil-minded judgment. The problem is twofold. First, as James will later clarify, such behavior by human beings comprises an attempt to unseat God from God's role as judge: "There is one lawgiver and judge, and this one is able to rescue and to destroy" (4:12); and Jesus's role as end-time judge: "The judge is standing at the door!" (5:7–9).[25] Second, this behavior is tied to cognitive patterns that are out of sync with Jesus's counterworldly faith. Making distinctions based on economic resources and political influence may have a cozy home in the broader world of James's brothers and sisters, but it does not represent the way of the messianic community. As James will go on to demonstrate, the wealthy are called to set aside any interest in evaluations of status or the cycles of gift and obligation that accompany them and, instead, to extend their resources on behalf of the needy without expectation of return. Read as a whole, James's letter places wealth under a dark cloud of suspicion, holds that wealth is short-lived, rejects the use of wealth in the service of coercive power or to curry favor and privilege, and sets aside any notion that wealth, even wealth tied to immense landholdings, is a consequence of divine approval (cf. 1:9–11).[26] Redistribution of goods and services on behalf of the hungry and dispossessed—this marks the way forward.[27] Luke similarly describes the community of those who believe in Jesus as having "one heart and mind," not holding tightly to their possessions but distributing to those in need,

---

25. Faber (1995) traces the juridical sense of the NT use of the term *prosōpolēmpsia*, "favoritism."

26. That this way of thinking runs counter to common perspectives is underscored by the disciples' response to Jesus's declaration, "Truly I tell you, a wealthy person will enter the kingdom of heaven only with difficulty": "When the disciples heard this, they were thunderstruck, saying, 'Then who can be saved?'" (Matt 19:23–25 AT; cf. Mark 10:23–26; Luke 18:24–26).

27. See the summarizing comments in Wheeler 1995, 91–106; Gordon 1989, 60–61.

with the result that "there were no needy people among them" (Acts 4:32–35 AT; cf. 2:44–45).

[5–7] For emphasis, James again refers to his "brothers and sisters" as he works to draw his readers and hearers in, beckoning their close attention. He wants them to *listen*, a directive that might recall for some the Shema: "Israel, listen! The LORD your God, the LORD is one" (AT), calling on Israel to love God "with all your heart, all your being, and all your strength" (Deut 6:4–5 CEB). Following this pattern, James pairs the command to *listen* with a reference to "those who love him"—that is, those who love God (Jas 2:4–5); and shortly, he will recall the Shema in his reference to the oneness of God (2:19). Others might also hear an echo of Jesus's words, "Those who have ears to hear should listen!" (Luke 8:8; 14:35; cf. 9:44; Mark 4:23; Matt 11:15; 13:9, 43). This is a call to pay attention, to be sure, but also to consider carefully, to ponder, and to respond accordingly.

James now furthers his thesis against favoritism (2:1) with a series of supporting claims that follow an A-B-A pattern:

> A God has chosen the poor. (2:5)
>   B You have dishonored the poor. (2:6a)
> A' The wealthy oppress you (the poor). (2:6b–7)

Ironically, "you"—that is, James's brothers and sisters—are mostly among the 80–90 percent of the empire's residents who live at, near, or below the subsistence level; yet, almost inconceivably, they side with the wealthy rather than with God in their convictions and practices concerning the poor. They participate in societal structures that inflict self-harm as well as maltreat their siblings; in doing so, they oppose God's agenda.

James's claims regarding God and the wealthy each make use of questions whose grammatical form anticipates an affirmative answer. (Has God not chosen the poor? Yes, of course! Do the wealthy not tyrannize you? Yes, of course! And so on.) The first question sets out two consequences of God's choosing the poor that parallel and help to interpret each other (2:5):

> Has God not chosen the poor according to worldly standards
>   to be rich in terms of faith, and
>   to be heirs of the kingdom he has promised to those who love him?

This claim concerning God's action on behalf of the poor triggers at least two concerns important to James's rhetoric. On the one hand, God's choosing the poor draws deeply on Israel's Scriptures, according to which God chose Israel and, in doing so, liberated and raised up the poor and oppressed; accordingly, God's regathering of Israel can be captured in the phrase "good news to the poor." This historically grounds James's affirmation in Israel's story (Deut

7:6–8; 26:5–9), in Israel's celebration of God's faithfulness on behalf of the poor (e.g., 1 Sam 2:8; Pss 12:5; 34:5–6; 140:12), in God's instructions to Israel regarding their own practices vis-à-vis the poor (e.g., Lev 19:10; 23:22; Deut 24:17, 19–21; Prov 14:31; 19:17; 22:9, 16; Amos 2:6–8; Zech 7:10), and in Israel's hope for God's deliverance (e.g., Isa 61:1–2).

On the other hand, James's declaration that God has chosen the poor ensures our understanding that the impartiality about which James has written (2:1: "Do not hold the faith of our glorious Lord Jesus Christ together with acts of favoritism") cannot be reduced to an abstract notion of impartiality nor to a call for fair or equal treatment of all. Impartiality, in the biblical witness, targets the privileged treatment of the high and mighty, of those whose wealth is tied to vast holdings of land and domestic animals, of the social and political elite. Accordingly, God does not put his finger on the scales of justice to favor such people, and neither should God's people.[28] That is, God challenges and indeed overturns pervasive social and political structures that favor the elite. "[God] has pulled the powerful down from their thrones and lifted up the lowly," Mary's Song has it, and "has filled the hungry with good things and sent the rich away empty-handed" (Luke 1:52–53 CEB). Much earlier, Hannah's Song announces: "The bows of mighty warriors are shattered, but those who were stumbling now dress themselves in power! . . . God raises the poor from the dust, lifts up the needy from the garbage pile. God sits them with officials, gives them the seat of honor!" (1 Sam 2:4–9 CEB). James's emphasis is furthered by his use of the phrase "according to worldly standards," since this phrase does not speak only of the actual, impoverished life situation of those whom God has chosen. It also speaks of the worldly systems that use indicators of rank and possessions to appraise people and, then, to slot impoverished people into social hierarchies of dominance that lead to their oppression.

If "according to worldly standards" refers to pervasive worldly systems hostile to God's ways, James's parallel phrase, "rich in terms of faith" (2:5), introduces an alternative viewpoint from which to evaluate humans. Throughout this letter, James is relentlessly negative in his understanding of the world (1:27; 2:5; 3:6; 4:4 [2×]), so it is important to keep in mind that he does not use the term *world* (*kosmos*) of God's creation or the human family or even the Earth. Instead, the term signifies something like *lifeworld* (from *Lebenswelt* in German philosophy), the world as a people understand and experience it, their shared values and practices shaped and transmitted from generation to generation, typically at a preconscious level. For James, "in faith" identifies a divinely sanctioned, counterworldly perspective that challenges and seeks to overturn

---

28. Cf. Kloppenborg Verbin 1999, 765: The "seemingly blatant expression of partiality on God's part" in Jas 2:5 "ceases to be so once 'impartiality' is understood as an explicit effort to challenge and negate prevailing arrangements of power and status"; cf. Tamez 1990, 36.

what would have passed for the empire's taken-for-granted lifeworld. In other words, James presents his audience with a topsy-turvy, right-side-up portrait of life that (1) characterizes the community of those who follow Christ. Those who are rich in faith, then, are those whose hope rests in God's promise of God's royal rule and who align their lives accordingly.[29] And sadly, (2) James's analysis puts his audience on the wrong side of history since, rather than "hold[ing] the faith of our glorious Lord Jesus Christ" (2:1), they are up to their necks in a lifeworld that favors the privileged and influential, a lifeworld against which God has set himself.

Perhaps the best commentary on James's phrase "rich in terms of faith" is its parallel (2:5): "heirs of the kingdom he has promised to those who love him." It is hard to miss James's allusion to Jesus's announcement "Happy are you who are poor, because God's kingdom is yours" (Luke 6:20 CEB; cf. Matt 5:3). Like the beatitude in Luke, so James's announcement speaks to the present and not only to an end-time reversal of things, relating not so much how things ought to be as how things actually are—when observed through the proper lens. Both define a lifeworld appropriate to God's royal rule as this is disclosed in Jesus's coming. Both encourage a counterworldly perspective according to which the poor can be regarded as "happy" rather than "hapless." Both encourage a counterworldly perspective according to which the poor are those who are thriving in the household over which Jesus is Lord, the domain of Jesus's royal rule (2:1), rather than assigned to the lower rungs or farther reaches of their communities by those enmeshed in now-pervasive, wrongheaded socioeconomic systems. Thus James highlights how this counterworldly *vision* of the world discloses God's royal rule in the present. He *invites* people to align themselves with the valuation of things characteristic of God's royal rule. Both vision and invitation communicate hope to people with subsistence-level lives while at the same time issuing an alert to those who live (or want to live) "the happy life" in the present—happy, that is, when measured according to a world system turned against God and God's ways. Those who measure the goodness and worth of their lives according to the now-outdated order of things will be caught unawares.[30]

Recall that, as James uses the term, *wealthy* should not be reduced to a judgment about income, property and livestock holdings, net worth, and so on. Rather, it must be understood relationally, with the wealthy characterized by their resources and rank, yes, but also and especially by the attitudes and behaviors that accompany them (see above, on 1:9–11). In fact, James is about to name the evils to which wealth drafts human beings—to humiliate, tyrannize, and abuse the poor (2:6)—a sketch to which he will later add further atrocities

---

29. Cf. Tamez 1990, 37.
30. In this paragraph, I have borrowed language from Green 2020d, 245–46.

(cf. 5:1–6). *Wealthy*, then, refers to landholdings and the like, *and* to the life patterns characteristic of those identified with this term.

In the same way, there is more to the *poor* whom God has chosen than their lacking the resources required for life's comforts. This becomes clear in James's reference to the promised inheritance of God's royal rule, where God's choice of the poor is interpreted with the phrase "those who love him" (2:5; cf. 1:12, "the garland of life God has promised to those who love him"). James thus glosses God's liberative choice of the poor with the call embedded in the Shema to love God with one's whole being (Deut 6:4–5). Recall how Jesus, drawing on Torah, fused together love of God and love of neighbor (Matt 22:35–39; Mark 12:28–31; cf. Luke 10:25–27; Lev 19:18), opening the door for James explicitly to bind the Shema together with neighborly love (2:8–18). Of course, having just identified his audience as "dear" or "beloved" (*agapētos*) brothers and sisters (2:5), James has already pointed the way toward coupling love for God and familial love.

In a perhaps unanticipated way, then, James's language is social, economic, and religious all at the same time. The Roman world was structured, however formally, around asymmetrical patron-client relations: a patron provides goods and services, and the client is obliged to respond with loyalty, support, and acclaim. This unequal relationship is ongoing since the debt thus accrued by the client is never fully satisfied. (What is more, this Roman system of relations was divinely sanctioned, with the gods serving as the emperor's patrons.) But James presents an economy that pulls the rug out from under this endless and debilitating cycle of so-called gifts and obligations. That is, James undermines an economy based on patronage, the relational web of the Roman world that served the wealthy at the expense of the needy. In its place, James presents an economy grounded in familial relations, an economy of shared resources.[31] James puts forward an economy based on God's liberative choice of the poor and the call embedded in the Shema to love God with one's whole being (Deut 6:4–5), a choice and a love that now governs (or ought to govern) life within the community of God's people.

James's pronouns, *you* (that is, *y'all*) and *they*, serve like a warning siren, alerting his audience to the seriousness of their situation (2:6–7). They, the wealthy, they are your abusers. They count you as worthless. They trample on

---

31. Sahlins (1972, 194) helpfully discusses the correlation of material exchange and social relation. In the case of what he calls *generalized reciprocity*, "the material side of the transaction is repressed by the social," in the manner of genuine altruism or hospitality. "It usually works out that the time and worth of reciprocation are not alone conditional on what was given by the donor, but also upon what he [*sic*] will need and when, and likewise what the recipient can afford and when." Generalized reciprocity (or, perhaps, "indefinite reciprocity" [1972, 193 n. 4]), is characteristic of close, familial relations.

you, taking advantage of you.[32] They use their energies to mandate your presence in the courts, likely using their wealth and influence to demand the repayment of debts—a particularly abhorrent practice given Scripture's emphasis on loans as means of helping the needy and thus outside the demands of reciprocity or obligation.[33] Of course, it almost goes without saying that jurists were themselves members of the wealthy elite, and court hearings regularly practiced the very favoritism toward the influential affluent against which James protests, with the result that recourse to the law was avoided by most people other than those of high rank, who could manipulate so-called justice to their own benefit.[34]

Furthermore, with such behaviors they insult (or malign) "the good name invoked over you." This could be a reference to God, whose name was sacred among God's people. "Do not use the LORD your God's name as if it were of no significance" is the second of God's Instructions (or Torah; Exod 20:7 CEB). Indeed, Jesus taught his disciples to pray, "Our Father who is in heaven, let the holiness of your name be upheld" (Matt 6:9 AT; cf. Luke 11:2). Given the reference to the glorious Lord Jesus Christ at the outset of this section (2:1), however, James more likely refers here to the name of the Lord Jesus Christ, the name above all names (Phil 2:6–11);[35] the name central to the earliest credo of his followers: Jesus is Lord (Rom 10:9; 1 Cor 12:3); the name invoked over the baptized (Acts 2:38; 10:48; 19:5); the name by which people are saved (Acts 2:21, 36; 3:16; 4:12).

Against this backdrop, James's indictment of his brothers and sisters is especially sharp: "You have dishonored the poor" (2:6a). The contrast is alarming: God did this, but you did that (2:5–6a). Equally startling, perhaps, is the company that James's audience seems to have chosen for themselves, for the attitudes and behaviors of the wealthy so easily map onto James's siblings. Consider the irony: God has chosen the poor, you are the poor whom God has chosen, you are the poor whom the wealthy harass, yet you humiliate the poor. Additionally, where James writes "insulting the good name invoked over you" (2:7), we might hear echoes from Ezekiel: "I will make my great name holy, which was degraded among the nations when you dishonored it among them. Then the nations will know that I am the LORD" (Ezek 36:23 CEB; cf.

---

32. The term James uses, *katadynasteuō*, "to oppress, govern tyrannically" (MGS 1051), appears in the NT only here and in Acts 10:38, where it speaks of those whom the devil oppresses. In Exod 1:13 LXX, the term is used of Egypt's oppression of Israel; similarly, in Neh 5:5 LXX, it signifies enslavement and abuse. Cf. Luke 22:25 NRSV: "The kings of the Gentiles lord it over [*kyrieuō*] them."

33. Cf. Exod 22:25: "If you lend money to my people who are poor among you, don't be a creditor and charge them interest" (CEB); Matt 5:42; Luke 6:34–35; Goldingay and Green 2011. Cf. R. Martin 1988, 66, who refers to "such matters as debts, rents, wages, and the prevalence of usury."

34. Veyne 1987, e.g., 166–68. Cf. Shiavone 1993.

35. Bede 1985, 23.

36:16–32). The Lord Jesus's name is upheld, we might say, when those who bear it embody his message. But through their acts of favoritism, these people have patterned their lives "according to worldly standards," not "in faith," and certainly not in ways congruent with "the faith of our glorious Lord Jesus Christ." And so they insult this excellent name.

[8–11] Having just made the case that James's siblings have positioned themselves with the wealthy against the poor and, therefore, against God, James takes the further step of grounding his argument against demonstrations of favoritism (introduced in 2:1) in Scripture. Though he refers explicitly to what is written in Scripture (2:8), by the end of this subsection James will identify what is written with what God has voiced: God spoke God's Instructions (or Torah; 2:11). These are God's words. They express God's will. We might say, then, that just as James's brothers and sisters disregard God's choice of the poor, so they neglect God's Instructions—spoken by God, written in Scripture.

The form of James's argument underscores the Jewish identity of his audience. They are Jewish messianists for whom following Torah is both a matter of course and a matter of consequence. Even if James has a more profound theology of sin than many of his peers in the world of Second Temple Judaism, he agrees with other Jewish theologians (1) that people are sinners not only because their hearts are bent toward the wrong (see above, on 1:13–15) but also because they actually sin as "lawbreakers" (2:9, 11) and (2) that Torah has ongoing significance for those who set out in faithfulness to thwart sin. Written in the late first or early second century CE, 2 Baruch, for example, speaks of those who neglect God's Instructions: "Those who do not love your Law are justly perishing"; the book emphasizes personal responsibility: "Adam is, therefore, not the cause, except only for himself, but each of us has become our own Adam" (2 Bar. 54.14–19).[36] James's perspective is similar, though James has already taught that the antidote to sin is the birthing of God's people by means of God's true word (1:18). For him, then, keeping the law remains key, as within Second Temple Judaism more generally, and is the way God's people faithfully respond to God's faithfulness. Again, we might wish James had more to say at this point, perhaps to clarify further the continuing status of the law among Christ-followers generally. He presumes that the law remains significant among his audience of Jewish messianists while saying nothing of the importance of Torah for gentile followers of Jesus. Nor does he hint that all is lost if they fail to keep the law perfectly. We might wish he had something to say here about forgiveness for breaking the law, for example, perhaps, in the manner of 1 John: "If we confess our sins, he is faithful and just to forgive us our sins and to cleanse us from all unrighteousness" (1:9 AT). However, James's concern here is neither with the applicability of Torah among gentile followers

---

36. ET: Klijn 1983. See further, Green 2017.

of the Lord Jesus nor with sin management. Instead, he is directing his audience's attention narrowly on one thing: the wickedness of playing favorites at the expense of the poor. He wants to persuade his readers and hearers that acts of favoritism transgress God's Instructions (or Torah); such acts constitute sin.

James begins this subsection with an acknowledgment of his readers and hearers' mixed record concerning God's Instructions (or Torah). On the one hand, they apparently do fulfill the royal law of Scripture (and so they do well). On the other hand, they show favoritism (against Scripture's royal law; and so they commit sin). James thus pulls back the curtain on their double-mindedness and instability (1:7–8; cf. 4:8). Their contradictory behaviors both enliven and reveal their lack of integrity.

The character of the royal law is clear enough: James cites the love command in Lev 19:18, following the wording of the LXX: "Love your neighbor as yourself." He also interprets the love command for his setting when he (1) explicitly juxtaposes it with its antithesis, showing favoritism (2:8–9); and (2) implicitly identifies "your neighbor" with the poor. (Recall Jesus's story of the Samaritan who, through his compassion, care, and financial provision, proved himself a neighbor to a man left half dead on the road from Jerusalem to Jericho—this as an elaboration of a legal expert's citation of Lev 19:18 alongside the Shema [Luke 10:25–37].) Less clear is the significance of the term "royal" that modifies "law."[37] Several possibilities come to mind, and we need not imagine that we must choose one over the others:

- The language James uses, *basilikos* (royal) evokes James's earlier mention of the *basileia* ("kingdom" or "royal rule," 2:5). Since Jesus's advent marks the definitive disclosure of God's royal rule, it makes good sense to read James's reference to the royal law as his way of qualifying the nature of faithful allegiance to the king and so the character of service in God's kingdom.

- James has twice referred to Jesus as "Christ" (1:1; 2:1), prompting his audience to identify Jesus as the king over the domain of God's royal rule—with *domain* understood less as a geographically bounded area and more as a field of influence and activity in which people experience, participate in, serve, and join the community formed in relation to the kingdom.[38] This is God's

---

37. See Allison 2013, 402–5; Akiyama 2018, 163–66.

38. In the Synoptic Gospels, statistically, what happens most frequently with respect to God's kingdom is that it is *entered* (Matt 5:20; 7:21; 8:11; 19:23, 24; 21:31; 25:34; Mark 9:47; 10:23, 24, 25; Luke 18:17, 24, 25; John 3:5; cf. Matt 11:12; Luke 16:16), with the result that people can be *in* (Matt 5:19; 11:11; 13:43; 18:1, 4; 20:21; 26:29; Mark 14:25; Luke 7:28; 13:28, 29; 14:15; 22:16, 30), *not far from* (Mark 12:34), or *out of* the kingdom (Matt 23:13). Cf. Acts 14:22; Col 1:13; 1 Thess 2:12; 2 Pet 1:11.

kingdom, yes, and it is the kingdom of King Jesus. Upholding the faith of the glorious Lord Jesus Christ entails loving one's neighbor.

- *Royal* might refer to the ultimate importance of the love command, in which case James's use of this law signifies the whole of God's Instructions (or Torah), and his use of *in Scripture* (sg.) includes the whole of Israel's Scriptures. Accordingly, Lev 19:18, "Love your neighbor as yourself," serves for James as an epitome of God's Instructions.

In the background one can almost hear Mark 10, Jesus's exchange with the rich man, who claims that he has kept God's Instructions (or Torah)—"Do not murder," "Do not commit adultery," "Do not steal," "Do not bear false testimony," "Do not defraud," and "Honor your father and mother"—from childhood. James's directive to his brothers and sisters tracks well with Jesus's response: "You are lacking one thing. Go, sell what you own, and give the proceeds to the poor" (10:18–22 AT). James's audience might respond to James similarly: But we *do* observe God's Instructions! In fact, it makes good sense of Jewish life in the Roman world that the question of what faithfulness to God's goodness entails would be reviewed and deliberated. Clearly, though, James regards his audience of messianists as having reached a decision on this question prematurely. He does not deny that they *do* follow God's Instructions sometimes or in a general sense, but he insists that they have failed to keep the law when they do not practice the love command. More particularly, they violate God's Instructions when they "take special notice of the one wearing fine clothes, saying, 'Sit in this excellent seat,' while saying to the poor person, 'Stand over there' or 'Sit at my feet'" (2:3). Just as selling one's possessions and giving to the poor signifies, for the rich man, relational identification (or friendship) with the poor in Mark's account, so in James neighbor love entails care for the poor. Even if one were to point to one's record—"I have not committed adultery!"—however admirable this might be, one has not been faithful to God's Instructions if one falters with regard to the royal law of love.

Why these two commandments concerning adultery and murder? Why does James develop his point with reference to these two? Perhaps the choice of adultery and murder represents nothing but chance. Perhaps, though, the different lists of God's Instructions read in Matthew's story of Jesus's encounter with the rich young man (19:18–19, including the love command!), Mark's account of the rich man (10:18–19), and Luke's narration of the rich ruler (18:20) should press our question further. Conceivably, James uses these commandments metaphorically to place the spotlight on (1) his audience's friendship with the world, leading him to brand them prophetically as adulterers (4:4); and on (2) their quarreling with and warring against each other (4:1–3). That is, James might be spiritualizing the one command, *adultery*, to speak of the troubled relationship between God and God's people (see Hosea!); and, in a way reminiscent of the Sermon on the Mount (Matt 5:21–22), radicalizing the other command, *murder*, with talk of anger and slander. This reading is conceivable but doubtful. At this juncture of his argument, James's language provides no indication that he refers to adultery as anything other than marital unfaithfulness. We find no hint of a metaphoric use of *adultery* either in the citation of God's Instructions, "Do not commit adultery," or in the follow-up clause, "If you do not commit adultery" (2:11). At this juncture, moreover, James seems willing to admit that his audience is not engaged in adultery. In short, we ought to take James's reference to God's Instruction regarding adultery at face value rather than figuratively.

But if we take James's reference to adultery at face value, would we not be inclined to read his reference to murder in the same way?[39] In fact, James later identifies murder as an issue among these Christ-followers: "You condemned and murdered the righteous one" (5:6). Apparently we cannot reduce James's choice of the prohibition of murder to its use as a metaphor for quarrels and skirmishes. Instead, we must regard murder, alongside quarrels and skirmishes, as an expression of his audience's dark cravings (4:1–3). At this point of his argument, we can justifiably imagine that those on whom such violence is enacted are the poor. And James will go on to sketch two scenarios, turning away the naked and starving (2:15–16) and withholding wages from the field-workers (5:4), that are hauntingly reminiscent of the ethical instruction of the Wisdom of Sirach: "The needy person's bread means life for that poor person; whoever withholds it is a murderer. Whoever takes away a neighbor's living commits murder, and whoever deprives a worker of wages sheds blood" (Sir 34:25–27 CEB).

James has thus furthered his argument against favoritism by grounding it in the royal law of neighbor love. At least, he puts favoritism in the company of adultery and murder, insisting that honoring the wealthy elite at the expense of the poor is as bad as these other forms of violence. Shockingly, too, it seems that James comprehends the horrific ends to which their convictions and behaviors lead and so insists that their acts of favoritism result in violence against the poor, even to the point of wrongful death.

[12–13] James concludes this subsection of his letter with a strong reminder of the actuality and the terms of end-time judgment. These words should be read within the flow of his argument and not as free-floating claims. James 2 begins with a striking contrast between Roman-style favoritism and faithful patterns of life inspired by Jesus's own faith—patterns that reflect his audience's

---

39. Cf. R. Martin 1988, 70; Cargal 1993, 116; McKnight 2011, 216–18.

siblingship, that lean into God's choice of the poor, and that embody Scripture's royal law (2:1–13): "Love your neighbor as yourself" (2:8, citing Lev 19:18). We can summarize his argument as follows:

- James states his thesis that the standard Roman practice of deferring to wealthy and prominent people is incompatible with holding to Jesus's faith (v. 1).
- James documents the need for his argument by referring to recognizable acts of favoritism within the assembly of these Jewish messianists (vv. 2–4).
- James supports his thesis by insisting that those who show favoritism have aligned themselves against God's will (vv. 5–7).
- James grounds his thesis in fidelity to the law and especially to the royal law, the love command (vv. 8–11).
- James concludes with his affirmation of the priority of mercy in relation to the lowly poor (vv. 12–13).

From beginning to end, then, this section of James's short essay (i.e., 2:1–13, within the whole of ch. 2) insists that his readers and hearers must choose acting toward the lowly and impoverished *either* according to Roman ways *or* according to God's ways.

End-time judgment casts its shadow over the whole of James's letter.[40] Here this shadow takes a more discernible form with reference to what will be judged and the basis on which judgment will be executed.

1. What will be judged? *Speaking* and *acting* refer to the full range of human behaviors. James's point, of course, is not that Christ-followers should exhibit such and such through their external behaviors. The contrast between the interior and exterior of humans is relatively modern (and Western) and had little purchase in the ancient Mediterranean world[41]—and, if anything, even less cachet with James. His concern for human wholeness, human integrity, translates into his insistence that patterns of thinking, feeling, and believing, *and* patterns of behavior, flow in and out of each other. They are inseparable. Accordingly, he begins this concluding comment by repeating the term *therefore*. We could translate, "Speak, therefore, and act, therefore, as people" (2:12).[42] Allegiance to the Lord Jesus Christ, embracing God's choice of the poor, orienting life around neighbor love—these cannot be reduced to good ideas or inner beliefs.

---

40. See, e.g., Jas 4:12; 5:9, 12. Cf. Eng 2020.
41. See Berger 2003, 60–81.
42. *Houtōs laleite kai houtōs poiete:* "*So* speak ye, and *so* do" (AV, emphasis added).

They generate and are themselves generated by corresponding practices in relation to the poor.

2. On what basis will judgment be executed? The measure by which judgment will be exercised is "the law of freedom." We encountered this phrase earlier, where it referred to the good news through which Christ-followers live conversionary lives, through which they thrive, even amid trials, as God's messianic people scattered throughout the world (1:25). To this, James now adds further significance, though we must not neglect the importance of that earlier claim. Whatever else it might signify, the *law of freedom* effects the liberation of people from the overpowering inclination toward the evil characteristic of the human family. As James now presses the point further, therefore, he does so while recognizing that he is calling his siblings not to the impossible or the unlikely, but actually to live in ways they have been set free to live. And the life to which they are called is encapsulated in the love command, the royal law, the law of freedom: "Love your neighbor as yourself" (2:8).

This is the portrait James paints of his audience of Christ-followers: Through the good news, they are set free *from* their sinful cravings *to* practice faithfully God's Instructions (or Torah), the epitome of which is neighbor love. They are ushered into the domain of God's royal rule, we might say, where they are enabled and expected to speak and to do neighbor love. His appeal, then, is set against the norms of Roman society relative to extending favorable treatment to the wealthy elite at the expense of the degraded poor and is aligned with the faith of "our glorious Lord Jesus Christ" (2:1). This is Jesus who directs God's household as Lord and oversees God's kingdom as Christ, who himself proclaimed good news to the poor through his speaking and acting, who put into practice his belief in God's purpose and power to overturn prevailing judgments about what sort of people are up versus down, what sort of people are welcomed, perhaps even coddled, versus being held at arm's length.

James does not develop an end-time schedule for *judgment*. He thinks of judgment in the future without here identifying the horizons of end-time judgment as either near or far. Likely his language is indicative of a belief that end-time judgment could occur at any moment. What is more, judgment is certain even if it is not mapped onto human-made calendars.

When the judgment comes, its basis will be neighbor love, which James goes on to gloss with reference to *mercy*. If James's language turns our thoughts to the Jesus tradition as this is represented in the Gospels (and James has certainly taught his audience to think with him about Jesus's teaching through his own reflections in this letter),[43] then numerous texts may come to mind. For example:

---

43. See the introduction, "Reading and Hearing the Letter of James."

- Speaking of those who thrive under God's royal rule, Jesus announces that people who show mercy receive mercy (Matt 5:7).
- Jesus relates a parable in which the master, showing mercy, forgives the colossal debt of his servant, but later hands him over to the prison guards after the servant refuses to show mercy (18:23–35).
- Jesus describes a scene in which, from his judgment throne, the king separates sheep from goats based on their treatment of the hungry, the thirsty, strangers, the naked, the sick, and the imprisoned (25:31–46).
- Of special interest are the concluding words of the legal expert who asks Jesus concerning whom the law of neighbor love refers. "Who is my neighbor?" he wants to know. This is followed by Jesus's parable of the Good Samaritan, in which a priest and a Levite bypass an injured man, but a traveling Samaritan, "moved with compassion," cares for the injured man's wounds, carries him on his donkey to an inn, and leaves him in the innkeeper's care after promising to cover further costs. Who was the neighbor? "The legal expert said, 'The one who practiced mercy toward him'" (Luke 10:25–37 AT).

We might also reflect on the closely related practice of *almsgiving*, a term that derives from the word *mercy* and signifies giving "to those in need as an act of mercy."[44] It follows that, in the community James envisions, showing mercy entails providing resources to the needy in ways that follow from and solidify the familial social structure James envisions.

James's final comments here take the form of proverbial affirmations grounding his claim that people will be judged by the law of freedom. Their proverbial form is clear from both the conciseness of those final words and the shift from second-person plural (2:12, "y'all") to the third person (2:13, "the one who"). These two verses are tightly intertwined, though, with the proverbial material supplying the basis for his directive concerning how his audience should speak and act. Judgment comes to the fore, with mercy identified as the basis and potential outcome of judgment. Christ-followers who show mercy will receive mercy. Those who are merciless will not receive mercy. To understand that practices of mercy win the case in the courtroom (and that failure to practice mercy leads to condemnation), we need look no further than those examples from Jesus's teaching sketched above.

---

44. L&N §57.111. "Mercy" translates *eleos*, while "almsgiving" translates *eleēmosynē*. Cf. Matt 6:2–4; Luke 11:41; 12:33; Acts 3:2–3; 3:10; 9:36; 10:2, 4, 31; 24:17.

2:14–26 Practicing Faith

2:14 What good is it, my brothers and sisters, if someone claims to have faith but has no deeds?[a] Such faith cannot save such a person, can it? **15** If a brother or sister[b] is naked and lacking daily food, and **16** one of you were to say to them, "Go in peace! Stay warm! Eat well!" yet you do not provide for their bodily needs, what good is it? **17** Just so, faith by itself, if it has no deeds, is dead.

18 But someone might claim, "You have faith and I have deeds." Show me your faith without deeds, and I will show you my faith by my deeds. **19** You believe that God is one. Good! Even the demons believe this, and they tremble in fear.

20 You thickheaded person, are you now ready to grasp[c] that faith without deeds is fit for nothing? **21** Abraham our father—was he not shown to be righteous by his actions when he offered his son Isaac on the altar? **22** See, his faith was acting in concert with his deeds, and his faith was made complete by deeds. **23** Thus the Scripture was fulfilled that says, "Abraham believed God, and God regarded him as righteous." And he was called God's friend. **24** See, a person is shown to be righteous by deeds and not by faith alone. **25** In the same way, was Rahab the prostitute not also shown to be righteous by deeds when she welcomed the messengers as her guests and sent them on by another road? **26** As the lifeless body[d] is dead, so faith without deeds is dead.

a. *Ergon/erga* (2:14, 17, 18 [3×], 20, 21, 22 [2×], 24, 25, 26) is traditionally translated as *work(s)* (e.g., AV, ASV, NRSV), but contemporary English usage prefers *action* or *deed*, as in the word-pair *word and deed* (cf. MGS 814).

b. Elsewhere in James, I take the author's reference to *adelphoi* (brothers) as inclusive of both brothers and sisters. Here, James actually refers to a "brother or sister" (*adelphos ē adelphē*); it is worth reflecting on how perilous the lot of the naked and hungry is compounded when those thus described are also identified as women.

c. *Theleis de gnōnai*: The *de* (now) builds on the former paragraph (2:18–19) not as a conclusion but as a further development of James's thought. *Thelō* is usually translated as "I want" but can have the sense "I am ready" (cf. BDAG 447–48; CGL 422–23). *Ginōskō* is typically associated with *knowing* or *understanding*, rather than *showing* (e.g., CEB, NRSV), but the English phrase "to show something" can describe the process of teaching and learning—and thus *coming to know*. The question is whether James's interlocutor is ready or willing to give the evidence its due (cf. Davids 126).

d. The parallelism works better in Gk:

    to sōma chōris pneumatos nekron estin, "The body without spirit is dead."

    hē pistis chōris ergōn nekra estin, "The faith without deeds is dead."

However familiar this translation might be (e.g., NIV, NRSV), it too easily allows or encourages the assumption that James operates with a dualist portrait of the human

person (with the body and spirit understood as separable [ontologically discrete] enti-
ties). However, *pneuma* is used only twice in the letter (here and in 4:5, a highly ambiguous text [see below]), so James provides insufficient evidence for such a judgment (contra, e.g., Adam 2013, 59). In Israel's Scriptures and in contemporary Greco-Roman usage, *pneuma* more typically carries the sense of *breath* or *air*, or *inner life* or *life force* (for background, see the summary in D. Martin 1995, 21–25, 117–20; also, e.g., von Staden 2000)—hence, my translation: "lifeless body."

In the short essay comprising Jas 2, James first contrasts acts of favoritism with faithful patterns of life congruent with and inspired by Jesus's own faith: patterns appropriate to the audience's status as a community of brothers and sisters, patterns following from God's choice of the poor, embodying Scripture's royal law: "Love your neighbor as yourself" (2:8, citing Lev 19:18), and putting mercy into play (2:1–13). James follows his critique of acts of favoritism toward the privileged powerful with four exhibits concerning faith and deeds more generally. The *first* is the appalling, cartoonish example of bogus Christ-followers who pronounce well-being, shalom, over a brother or sister whom they send away hungry and naked (2:14–17). This first case ends with the proverbial claim, "Faith by itself, if it has no deeds, is dead" (2:17). The *second* is a scathing contrast between demons, whose confession of the Shema, "God is one" (2:19; cf. Deut 6:4), leads to their trembling with fear, and these alleged Jesus-followers, whose confession of the Shema leads nowhere. In both instances, belief rings hollow (Jas 2:18–19). This second case leads to a proverbial claim, "Faith without deeds is fit for nothing," phrased as a question: "Are you now ready to grasp that faith without deeds is fit for nothing?" (2:20). Apparently James's audience requires further proof of this truism, and this is precisely what James sets out to provide with his *third* and *fourth* cases: Abraham and Rahab, both of whom, for James, are shown to be righteous by what they do.

James's argument pushes his audience to identify at a visceral level with Jesus, Abraham, and Rahab, and with Scripture's royal law. This is because of the way his examples recruit negative and positive associations (or feelings) that intuitively encourage (or subconsciously bias one toward) one form of response over another.[45] If the alternative to the faith of Jesus, the actions of Abraham and Rahab, and Scripture's royal law is the disturbing disconnect between word and deed on display among inhospitable Christ-followers, what choice is there, really? If faith isolated from deeds, and specifically from acts of mercy, is fit for nothing more than decaying remains destined for the grave, then faith working in concert with deeds is surely the better option, right? If we must pick between Jesus's faith, Rahab and Abraham, and Scripture's royal

---

45. Cf. Slingerland 2005; more broadly, Damasio 1994.

law, on the one hand; or keeping company with demons, on the other—really, what choice do we have?[46]

Excursus: James and Paul

With good reason, interpreters across the centuries have raised questions about whether and, if so, how James is in dialogue with Paul.[47] If we set a few well-known Pauline texts side-by-side with James's claims in this portion of the letter, we immediately see why such questions might arise. (In the following, I have provided my own translation of Pauline texts and adjusted my translation of material in James to show more clearly the parallels with Paul.)

Paul	James
"We hold that a person is justified by faith apart from the deeds of the law" (Rom 3:28). "We know that a person is not justified by deeds of the law but through the faithfulness of Jesus Christ [or: through faith in Jesus Christ]" (Gal 2:16).	"See, a person is justified by deeds and not by faith alone" (Jas 2:24).
"If you confess with your mouth that Jesus is Lord and believe in your heart that God raised him from the dead, you will be saved. For believing with your heart leads to justification and confessing with the mouth leads to salvation" (Rom 10:9–10). "By grace you are saved through faith. This is not by your own doing—but is God's gift—not by deeds, so that no one can boast" (Eph 2:8–9).[48]	"What good is it, my brothers and sisters, if someone claims to have faith but has no deeds? Faith cannot save such a person, can it?" (Jas 2:14)

More generally, the language of *justification* (that is, *being justified*) in the NT is very much associated with Paul but is also found three times in Jas 2 (2:21, 24, 25). Unlike Paul, James explicitly ties justification to deeds. Likewise, *deeds* are important to both theologians, but they have different interests. In Paul's reasoning against deeds, "works of the law," he targets obedience to the Mosaic law (God's Instructions) that mark a separation between Jew and gentile in the Jewish Diaspora—thus centering, especially, on food laws, circumcision, and the Sabbath (see above, on 1:1). Moreover, Paul recognizes that deeds resulting from keeping God's Instructions are unable to free people from their bondage to Sin (cf. Rom 5–6). For James, though, "a person is justified by deeds and not by faith alone" (Jas 2:24). We might use Paul's language, "works of

---

46. This paragraph is adapted from Green 2020b, 347.

47. See the surveys in Gowler 2014, 173–203; Allison 2013, 426–36.

48. Irrespective of their questions concerning the Pauline authorship of Ephesians, many take this text as summarizing Paul's perspective on these matters.

the law," to describe James's interests, since the deeds James has in mind are in fact the consequence of living out God's Instructions (or Torah), and especially the royal law, which epitomizes God's Instructions: neighbor love (2:8). If we were to do so, though, we would be using Paul's terms but not his lexicon. Again, these two theologians are focused on different concerns. In the NT, Paul uses the phrase "apart from deeds"—with the Greek term *chōris* (without, apart from)—to indicate that justification is not the consequence of deeds. James uses the same term, *chōris*, to insist that faith "apart from deeds" is "fit for nothing" (2:20), "dead" (2:26). To these examples of word usage, we might add the striking fact that Paul presents Abraham as the consummate exemplar of faith (Rom 4; Gal 3) who, clearly, was not justified by his deeds (Rom 4:1–8), whereas James draws on the story of Abraham to prove that "a person is justified by deeds and not by faith alone" (2:24).

From these data it seems incontrovertible that James is somehow in dialogue with Paul. Caution is in order, though, as we try to characterize that dialogue. If James has Paul's teaching in view, can we be assured that he has rightly understood Paul? Given the nature of these parallels, might it be that, rather than conversing with Paul or with Paul's letters, James has his sights on Pauline catchphrases interpreted and repeated by others? Must we not allow for the possibility that James is responding to Paul's message as this has been represented (or misrepresented) to him by others? If so, must we not also admit that we do not know whether those others from whom James might have heard are Paul's supporters or opponents? This means the following:

- We have no firm basis for urging that James's letter is his attempt to correct Paul on Paul's own terms. Maybe he is correcting those whom he regards as having misunderstood Paul, or maybe he himself has not fully grasped what Paul teaches.
- Attempts to trace historically any sort of give-and-take between Paul and James (and/or those who represent them in the first decades after Jesus's death and resurrection) may interest the curious but in the end entail layer upon layer of speculation.
- We have no real need to defend Paul against James or James against Paul (though we might learn something from both about how the other could be represented or misrepresented).
- Our first and primary focus should be on asking what these two figures teach about faith, justification, and deeds.

(Of course, this also means we should not allow later, especially Protestant-based, arguments about "faith alone" or "works righteousness" to shape or determine how we read these two theologians.)

In my translation and in the discussion below, I have tried to hear James as much as possible from within his own argument. At least two immediate consequences follow. First, I have translated the passive form of the verb *dikaioō* as "shown to be righteous." On the one hand, this verb signifies a range of actions (like "vindicate" or "to prove to be right") that allows for this rendering. The sense, then, would be James's effort to identify human practices that conform to and display God's character and will (including God's choice of the poor [2:5]). This sense is present earlier when our author introduces the negative of the related noun *dikaiosynē* (justice, righteousness): human anger does not conform to, or does not exhibit, God's righteousness (1:20; cf. 3:18). On the other hand, this translation makes room for the practice of linguistic *compression*, in which a momentary action signals an entire process. Consider the statement "We got married." For many, this simple declaration hides an astonishingly complex set of actions across a sometimes-lengthy timeline, maybe a pathway that often seems less linear and more twisted, or perhaps a journey reminiscent of a bumpy, jerky, unnerving roller-coaster ride. In the same way, James's use of the verb *dikaioō* might suggest what happened in a moment in time when a timeline is in view. As James's examples suggest, the translation "shown to be righteous" opens the door to faith-full processes that cultivate faith-full deeds.

This notion of compression/decompression is most apparent in James's claim concerning Abraham. According to the narrative timeline of Genesis, the almost-sacrifice of Isaac takes place much later (Gen 22) than the time when "Abram believed God, and God regarded him as righteous" (Gen 15:6 LXX, AT). James decompresses Abraham's "justification," which otherwise might erroneously be regarded as an act completed in a single moment. Instead, as James interprets the story, Abraham's "faith was made complete by his deeds" as his faith acted "in concert with his deeds" (2:22).

Second, this translation attempts to represent faithfully how James relates faith and deeds. Elsewhere, when James envisions the relationship between inner character and outward expression, he writes, "Can a fig tree produce olives or a grapevine figs?" (3:12). The metaphor on which he draws is organic, not mechanical, and this helps us understand the case he wants to make concerning faith and deeds. In a mechanical metaphor, we might picture "deeds" as an add-on to "faith." "Bolt those deeds on here. Screw them down there. Spot weld them here, here, and here." However, grapes are not accessories to grapevines, as though the work of friendly insects or viticulturists might be to affix grapes to vines. Grapevines simply produce grapes and fig trees figs. Even those who cannot tell the difference between grape and cantaloupe leaves or distinguish a gnarled olive tree from a twisted mesquite can nevertheless recognize these plants easily enough by their fruit. Organic metaphors conjure no images of hierarchical systems or assembly lines or divisible parts, but invoke images of integration, interrelation, and interdependence. It follows, then, that deeds do not occupy a space outside faith but are themselves integral to faith. For James, a reference to faith necessarily entails a reference to deeds, and a reference to deeds necessarily entails a reference to faith. Faithful deeds reveal faith, and faith is known through its faithful deeds, with the one shaping and animating the other. James inseparably binds together "is" and "does," calling the "is" into question only when it wants to exclude the "does." "As the lifeless body is dead, so faith without deeds is dead," James concludes (2:26).

The biblical-theological question is whether James and Paul can be understood together.[49] In my view, this question can and should be answered in the affirmative, even if their different audiences and situations pressed them to articulate matters in different ways. That is, their emphases, when contextualized in their own settings, are more complementary than competitive or contradictory. Key to recognizing the relative correspondence between Paul and James on these matters is allowing them their own

---

49. See McKnight 2023 for helpful orientation to and discussion of these matters.

dictionaries, so to speak, so that we hear their message within their own thought worlds. Crucial, too, is the significance of recent work on *faith* in the Roman world and in Paul, scholarship that moves away from more narrowly circumscribed notions of interior acceptance, inner conviction, or reasoned acquiescence, but understands faith more in fully embodied (or wholistic), relational terms concerned with entrustment and allegiance.[50] After all, was it not Paul who wrote that "what matters is faith expressing itself through love" (Gal 5:6)?

[2:14–17] James opens with three questions (2:14, 15–16), with each presuming a negative answer and receiving it, finally, in proverbial form (2:17). Some readers might discern an abrupt shift in James's argument, marked here by his address to "my brothers and sisters"[51] and the apparent turn toward faith and deeds. Rather than elaborating on 2:14–26 as a new section, however, it is better to see these verses as continuing the argument begun with the thesis stated in 2:1: "My brothers and sisters, do not hold the faith of our glorious Lord Jesus Christ together with acts of favoritism." At stake is what it means to have the sort of faith Jesus had. James now begins to insist that this kind of faith must be lived (faith *and* deeds) and not simply claimed. Accordingly, the opening phrase, "What good is it . . . ?," does not introduce an abstract truism but follows directly on the previous concern with end-time judgment. For people who will be judged according to the "law of freedom,"[52] what good is it if their claims to faith are devoid of deeds? The parallel James develops aligns the law of freedom (2:12), the royal law of neighbor love (2:8), with showing mercy (2:12–13) and with faithful deeds (2:14). The *faith* at which James takes aim, then, must be something like *declaration of belief*—not a bad thing, but clearly inadequate by itself. Such a faith is inconsequential at the end-time judgment. It "cannot save" (2:14)—that is, neither does it showcase in the present the transformation of believers by God's word (1:18–21), nor in the future will it preserve them for the afterlife.

Woven into the fabric of this short text is something of the metaphorical reach of *death* (*nekros*).[53] The most natural, biological sense of *death* would be the certain and tragic destiny of the desperate brother or sister who receives no help (2:15–16): DEATH AS THE END OF LIFE'S JOURNEY.[54]

---

50. E.g., Bates 2017; Gupta 2020; Morgan 2015.

51. See Jas 1:2, 16, 19; 2:1, 5, 14; 3:1, 10, 12; 5:12, 19; cf. "brothers and sisters" in 4:11; 5:7, 9, 10 (all as AT).

52. That is, those whom God's true, implanted word has freed from their sinful proclivities (1:18–21) and enabled them to practice neighbor love (2:12).

53. Here and in 2:26 (2×), James has *nekros* (lifeless/dead). In 1:15 and 5:20, he uses the semantic cousin, *thanatos* (death).

54. Given James's interest in the afterlife, it may be better to think in terms of DEATH AS PASSAGE (or DOOR). (The typical style in cognitive linguistics for designating metaphors is with all capital letters.)

To speak of a dead faith is to draw attention to its inefficacy, its pointlessness—and, in this context, its incapacity to put into play the quality of life God wills (2:17); like a corpse, this faith is inactive, inert, impotent: DEATH AS POWERLESSNESS. The shadow of death also covers those whose faith is by itself, devoid of deeds; possessing a faith that cannot save, they will be handed over to death at the end-time judgment (2:14; cf. 2:12–13): DEATH AS SEPARATION.

We can hardly exaggerate the significance of James's reference to "a brother or sister" (*adelphos ē adelphē*). In much of the NT writings (and ancient writings more generally), authors habitually use words like "brother" (*adelphos*) or "man" (*anthrōpos*) in ways that can refer also to their female counterparts, leading contemporary translators to use words like "brother and sister" or "siblings," or "human" or "humanity."[55] But here James unambiguously refers to both male and female members of the messianic community. This is worth contemplation for at least two reasons. The first is the significance of masculinity in Roman antiquity. Though various cultures today have differing perspectives, those in the West have traditionally thought in binary terms, male and female, each with distinguishing characteristics. In recent decades, though, this binary has been complicated through recognition of a range of biological and gendered complexities. Even so, today we might think of locating ourselves along a horizontal spectrum based on conventionally male and female traits. Contrast this with Roman antiquity, where men and woman were arranged vertically from more masculine to less, with the "man's man" at the pinnacle, the ideal. Some women could achieve a measure of manliness, and most males would fall short of the ideal on account of any number of status measures: wealth, education, physical attractiveness, disability, virtue, and so on. Given this way of thinking, the basic criterion of masculinity is mastery: mastery of the self and of others; manliness remains under construction as one proves oneself in relation to others; and manliness is endowed with moral significance, so that "being manly" is always positive (for a woman or a man), and "being effeminate or soft is morally reprehensible."[56] With no real fanfare, then, James challenges what might pass for male privilege in the Roman world—first, by placing a sister on the same level as a brother (rather than locating them vertically, one above the other, in terms of their

---

55. Cf. Strauss 2010. *Adelphē* (sister) appears a handful of times in letters attributed to Paul (Rom 16:1, 15; 1 Cor 7:15; 9:5; 1 Tim 5:2; Phlm 2); among these the closest parallel to Jas 2:15 is probably 1 Cor 7:15: "If the unbelieving spouse departs, let them depart. The brother or the sister is not bound in such instances" (AT). Also relevant are the references in the Synoptic Gospels to brothers and sisters (et al.) in references to the makeup of the community of Jesus's followers (Matt 12:50; Mark 10:30).

56. Ivarsson 2006, 165–66. See B. Wilson 2015, 39–75.

relative status); and second, by recognizing the importance of caring even for a man, "a brother," who in his dire need has fallen far short of any Roman measure of manliness. Within the messianic community, James thus assumes a systemic rejection of proclivities toward characterizing people in terms of Roman manliness. Second, the inclusion of "a sister" in this way accounts for the hard reality that women generally experience heightened trauma when their circumstances force them onto the street, hungry and naked. This might be for many reasons, including how, in a man-centered world, women in these circumstances typically have fewer options for self-support and self-care, plus the reality that women are often vulnerable to more dangerous and debilitating forms of abuse.

The urgent need of this brother or sister is developed in two interconnected ways. "Naked" could refer to "inadequate clothing," so the picture would recall the poor person of whom James spoke earlier: "dressed in filthy rags" (2:2). Either way, such a person is marked by poverty and humiliation (e.g., Gen 3:7; Rev 3:17–18), vulnerable, barely a human being at all,[57] certainly unable to receive the blessing "Stay warm!" offered by "one of you" (2:16). Providing them with clothing is a sign of genuine faith, an act of mercy (e.g., Isa 58:6–8; Tob 4:16). The immediacy of this person's dire circumstances is signaled by James's use of the term "daily" in the phrase "lacking daily food." This person's need is not for an occasional meal to carry them over, or for a little protein now and then to subsidize the diet. Rather, he or she lives in a perpetual state of crisis. Similarly, James later refers to the failure of people within the messianic community to assist even with the "bodily needs" of this brother or sister. We might rightly think they require far more than food and clothing, given their state of emergency, but they need this at the very least. In the hypothetical scenario James describes, we hear echoes of Jesus's words in Matt 25:42–43: "I was hungry and you gave me no food to eat. . . . I was naked and you gave me no clothes to wear" (AT).

James continues to paint this scene by turning to the hypothetical response of someone from within his audience of Jewish messianists, "one of you." His word choices suggest he is speaking of what might happen,[58] rather than of what is presently taking place, but the force of his lengthy question (2:15–16) rests on the prospect that this is exactly what can be expected of those who say they have faith but have nothing to show for it. Given the direction James is taking his readers and hearers, we can hardly expect anything other than hollow words that flow from an inert faith. "Go in peace" mirrors usage in Israel's

---

57. Cf. Hamel 1990, 73–75.

58. The form of the word *legō* (I say) James uses in 2:16 is subjunctive: *eipē*, "if one were saying" or "should one say."

Scriptures where both greetings and departures include a wish for *shalom*—
that is, for thriving, well-being, happiness, prosperity, good health.[59] The wish
for peace is scattered across the landscape of the NT, too, even finding its way
into the standard letter greeting.[60] "Go in peace"—these are celebrated words.
The same can be said of the other examples of well-wishing: "Stay warm! Eat
well!"—kind words that reveal their speaker as one who correctly recognizes
the needs of this brother or sister. But these goodly words are empty. They
are offensive for the way they use virtuous language to obscure a failure to
act on behalf of someone with the severest of needs. Here is an example of
"those who think they are devout," but "do not control what they say," nor do
they "come to the aid of orphans and widows in their trouble and suffering";
they have been "contaminated by the world" in that they allow themselves to
be guided by worldly life patterns rather than those at home within their faith
(1:26–27).[61]

[18–19] James's case takes a step forward with the introduction of an imag-
ined debate partner, an unnamed "someone." This person's opening statement,
"You have faith and I have deeds," may puzzle us since we might expect the
opposite claim from someone disputing James's point.[62] Because this style of
argumentation presumes a negation of James's claim, would we not anticipate
a response like this: "I have faith and you have deeds"? Should we suppose that
James's dialogue partner actually agrees with James? In fact, the counterargu-
ment is even more basic, urging, against James, the possibility that one person
can have faith, another deeds. In other words, this debate partner proposes the
very thing that James denies. Those who take their cue from Jesus's faith (2:1)
must realize that faith and deeds cannot be separated or partitioned. Faith as
allegiance expresses itself wholistically, integratively, in entwined patterns of
thinking, feeling, believing, and behaving. If someone were to attempt to show
faith without deeds, James has a ready response: "Faith by itself, if it has no
deeds, is dead" (2:17). He therefore counters that his faith is not a matter of
hollow claims but active allegiance. James thus rejects a portrait of the human
person, such as one so pervasive in the modern West, that identifies the "real"

59. In Gk. usage more generally, James's term, *eirēnē*, signifies "peace" or tranquility. However,
under the influence of the LXX, in which *eirēnē* translates most appearances of the Heb. term *šālôm*
(shalom), *eirēnē* refers more broadly to well-being, flourishing, etc. Cf. *TLNT* 1:424–38.

60. E.g., Exod 4:18; Judg 18:6; 1 Sam 1:17; 20:42; 2 Sam 15:9; Matt 10:12–13; Mark 5:34;
Luke 7:50; 8:48; Rom 1:7; Eph 6:23; 1 Pet 1:2; 2 John 3; 3 John 15; Jude 2; Rev 1:4.

61. L. Johnson 1995, 239.

62. Dibelius (1976, 154) famously identified this as "one of the most difficult New Testament
passages in general," though James's own position is scarcely in doubt. Allison (2013, 468–71)
briefly documents the various options for making sense of 2:18a. See the thorough discussion in
McKnight 1990; my reading tracks with his.

person with his or her interior.[63] Deeds bring to light one's deepest allegiances. As the shoot and root systems of a plant are indivisible and interdependent, so one's tightly held convictions and deeds are indivisible and interdependent. James will now demonstrate this truth pointedly with an appeal to Israel's confession of the oneness of God, the Shema.

James raises the stakes of his argument by referring to the inadequacy of reciting the Shema when doing so entails nothing by way of honoring God's Instructions (or Torah), epitomized in the command to love one's neighbor. According to the Shema, God is one: "The LORD your God, the LORD is one" [AT]; and Israel shall love the one God singularly: "with all your heart, all your being, and all your strength" (Deut 6:4–5 CEB). By the first century CE, the Shema was integral to Jewish liturgical practice, with the phrase "Recite [these words] when you lie down and when you rise" (6:7 NRSV) giving rise to the practice of reciting the Shema twice daily.[64] Israel's daily profession of faith and covenantal allegiance is set firmly within the framework of learning, teaching, and obeying God's Instructions (or Torah) (6:1–9). Read together, the Shema's various forms in Israel's Scriptures (Num 15:37–41; Deut 6:4–9; 11:13–21) identify the Shema as the basis of Israel's vocation to keep God's Instructions.[65] Accordingly, a declaration of belief in the one God, the God of Israel, clearly entails allegiance to this God in the form of love and obedience. To put it more pointedly, "Israel's belief in one God was expressed in obedience to Torah."[66] Although this was broadly the case with those practices that distinguished Jews from others in the Greek and Roman periods—circumcision, food laws, and Sabbath-keeping (see above, on Jas 1:1)—for James, belief in the one God, the God of Israel, was expressed above all in the royal law, the law of freedom: "Love your neighbor as yourself" (2:8, citing Lev 19:18).

James does not quote the Shema and the love command in the same breath,[67] but in his letter we find solid testimony that he has been influenced by Jesus's union of the calls to love God wholly and to love one's neighbor (Matt 22:35–39; Mark 12:28–31; cf. Luke 10:25–27):[68]

---

63. In his magisterial 1989 study of the making of personal identity in the West, C. Taylor notes the pervasive view that persons have an inner self, which is the authentic self.

64. Cf., e.g., Let. Aris. 158–60; Josephus, *Ant.* 3.91

65. See Schiffman 2009.

66. MacDonald 81 2013.

67. Cf. T. Iss. 5.2: "Love the Lord and your neighbor; be compassionate toward poverty and sickness" (ET: Kee 1983, 803).

68. This chart is adapted from McKnight 2011, 241. Akiyama (2018, 155–69, esp. 158) overstates when he claims that James has not combined neighbor love (Lev 19:18) and love of God (Deut 6:5); the data make clear that love of God is more than "implicit" (Akiyama's word) in James's discussion of neighbor love.

God is one	Deut 6:4–5: "The LORD your God, the LORD is one" (AT).	Jas 2:19: "You believe that God is one."
Love God	Deut 6:4–5: "Love the LORD your God with all your heart, all your being, and all your strength" (CEB).	Jas 1:12: "They will receive the garland of life [God] has promised to those who love him"; 2:5: "Has God not chosen the poor . . . to be heirs of the kingdom he has promised to those who love him?"
Love your neighbor	Lev 19:18: "Love your neighbor as yourself" (NRSV).	Jas 2:8: "Love your neighbor as yourself."

As James has just claimed, "I will show you my faith by my deeds" (2:18)—or, to paraphrase, "I will show you my belief in the oneness of God by the way I act on behalf of my neighbor, and especially the poor."

The absurdity James identifies is benchmarked with reference to the faith of demons. Notice, first, the partial parallel James articulates:

You   believe that God is one.
Even the demons   believe [that God is one], and they tremble in fear.

Belief that God is one—this is not a bad thing. What makes it absurd is when such belief is nothing more than words spoken, when this belief omits the vocation of love and allegiance within which such belief has meaning in Israel's Scriptures and in contemporary liturgical practice, when this belief is devoid of the vocation of neighbor love that Jesus binds together when asked to name the greatest of God's Instructions (or Torah). In the parallel above, such belief falls short of even demonic faith, since the faith of demons leads to some sort of action, trembling, whereas the belief James censures apparently leads to no action at all. And second, of course, demons in the NT are known both for their right belief and for their opposition to God's agenda (e.g., Mark 1:24; 5:7). Even their faith cannot save, therefore (cf. Jas 2:14). This kind of faith, then, is doubly blameworthy. In no way does such faith emulate Jesus's faith (2:1) in God's purpose and power to overturn judgments and deeds rooted in favoritism, a faith expressed in word and deed in Jesus's life.

[20–26] The short essay comprising Jas 2 now reaches its climax. Thus far, James has contrasted acts of favoritism with faithful patterns of life congruent with and inspired by Jesus's own faith (2:1–13). Following this, James turned more generally to discuss faith and deeds, not because he is changing subjects but because he wants to drive home the character of Jesus's faith, and therefore the reality that faith and deeds are indivisible, with the one animating and shaping the other. To make his case, James provides four exhibits: (1) the incredible-yet-conceivable, scandalous example of so-called Christ-followers who speak words of shalom over a brother or sister whom they send away hungry and naked (2:14–17); (2) a scathing comparison of demons and alleged Christ-followers whose credo, the Shema, "God is one" (2:19; cf. Deut 6:4), rings hollow because it assumes a wedge between faith and deeds where no wedge is possible, since faith and deeds are organically united (Jas 2:18–19). Pressing further, as if this were not proof enough, James asks, "Are you now ready to grasp that faith without deeds is fit for nothing?" (2:20). Apparently, James's debate partner is so thickheaded (or *empty*-minded,[69] perhaps as reflected in the interlocutor's *empty* words [2:19; cf. 2:16]) that further testimony is required. This brings us to his final exhibits: (3) Abraham and (4) Rahab, both of whom, in James's interpretation, are shown to be righteous by what they do.[70]

James pairs Abraham and Rahab through his introduction of the adverbial phrase "in the same way" (2:25): Rahab and Abraham demonstrate, both in the same way, that "a person is shown to be righteous by deeds and not by faith alone" (2:24).[71] Of these two exemplars, the relevance of James's reference to Rahab may be the easier to understand. Within her world, Rahab's social rank would have been at best ambivalent,[72] this in spite of the likelihood that she was forced into a life of trading sexual pleasures for money as one of the few options available to her as a single woman challenged with economic calamity. Her life situation would have been strongly correlated with poverty and abuse.[73] According to Joshua, Rahab's house occupied space on the outer wall of the city (Josh 2:15); her physical location, then, was a metaphor of her place on the fringe of her world. In terms of status, then, Rahab would be located toward that end of the spectrum also occupied by the poor of whom James writes.

Significantly, then, Rahab demonstrates precisely the behavior to which James has just called his audience: receiving God's people as if they were one's own family, even provisioning them when they depart. Is this not the very extension of openhanded hospitality James has just counseled? Though socioreligiously an outsider—a woman in a man's world, a prostitute, harassed, impoverished—she exemplifies "the royal law" that epitomizes God's Instructions (or Torah): "Love your neighbor as yourself" (Jas 2:8; citing Lev 19:18).

---

69. *Kenos*, "empty"; see LSJ 938.

70. This last point, "in James's interpretation," is important since the material in Genesis (Abraham) and in Joshua (Rahab) does not develop the significance of these two figures in just this way.

71. *Homoiōs* (in the same way). This examination of James's comments on Abraham and Rahab is adapted from Green 2020b, 347–49.

72. See Josh 2:1; 6:17, 25; Matt 21:31; Luke 15:30; Heb 11:31. For orientation to the literary representation of Abraham and Rahab in Israel's Scriptures and Second Temple Jewish literature, see Foster 2014, 59–80, 104–13.

73. See Schottroff 1993, 150–55; Cohick 2009, 268–74.

She speaks and acts as someone who shows mercy (Jas 2:12–13). James thus reflects wider emphases available in early Jewish and Christian interpretations of Rahab, namely, that she "represents the least, last, and lost among us all, whose newly found devotion bears witness to the hospitable God who seeks and finds the outsider to save."[74]

We have reflected on Rahab first in part because her example illuminates James's comments on Abraham. James has written that Rahab's faithfulness is like Abraham's, but the opposite can be said, too. Abraham is like Rahab. At one level, this is nonsense. Is Abraham not Rahab's polar opposite? The life situation of someone like Abraham—a male, wealthy, a person of the highest acclaim—would seem a universe removed from hers. Even so, their stories intersect tellingly on two points. Both were shown to be righteous by their actions (according to James); second, both were celebrated on account of their hospitality (according to Jewish tradition).[75] Although James does not overtly refer to Abraham's hospitable practices, he does invite reflection on them. (1) He refers to Abraham as God's friend,[76] this in a sociocultural context in which friendship would be correlated with economic sharing and hospitality—that is, the very behavior James has just outlined. Especially interesting, then, are roughly contemporaneous references to Abraham as "friend of God" and to his celebrated hospitality, such as these: "[Abraham] is your friend and a righteous man, who welcomes strangers" (T. Ab. [B] 4.10; cf. 13.5);[77] and "Blessed is your father Abraham, for he has become the friend of God . . . because of his generosity and love of strangers" (T. Jac. 2.12).[78] If friendship with God is constituted through faithfulness to God, faithfulness to God entails acts of mercy on behalf of those in need.[79] (2) This emphasis is furthered by James's odd reference to Abraham's "deeds" (pl., Jas 2:21–22), which seems out of place since James explicitly mentions only one such deed, the binding of Isaac. Apparently, for James, the binding of Isaac may be the summation of Abraham's faithfulness, but it is not the whole of it. In Jewish tradition (as we have begun to see) and in the NT, Abraham's reputation is enlarged with reference to his hospitality.[80] Note how, in a perhaps surprising turn of phrase,

74. Wall 2001, 230.
75. See Ward 1968, 285–87; L. Johnson 1995, 245, 249.
76. That is, "he was called God's friend" (Jas 2:23)—cf. 2 Chr 20:7; Isa 41:8; Jub. 19.9; 3 En. 44.10; Philo, *Abraham* 273; Philo, *Sobriety* 55; Apoc. Ab. 10.5; et al., including numerous references in Testament of Abraham.
77. ET: Sanders 1983, 897.
78. ET: Stinespring 1983, 914.
79. See L. Johnson 2004a; Batten 2004; Batten 2017, 138–43.
80. In the NT, note the clear allusion to the story of Abraham's hospitality (Gen 18) in Heb 13:2: "Do not forget to show hospitality, because by doing so some have opened their homes to angels without knowing it" (AT). In Luke's Gospel, John the Baptist exegetes what *Abrahamic life* looks like in terms of sharing with those in need and resisting wrongful economic practices

the text James cites from Israel's Scriptures, "Abram believed God, and God regarded him as righteous" (Gen 15:6 LXX, AT), is "fulfilled" as "his faith was made complete by his deeds" and as "his faith was acting in concert with his deeds" (Jas 2:22–23). (3) James couples his reflections on Abraham with Rahab's exemplary hospitality. Just as *hospitable practice* is implicit in the case of Abraham, so *faith* is implicit in the case of Rahab. James speaks plainly only of her behaviors, but her faith is a necessary implicature of his argument. Her hospitable practices signify embodied faith. In the same way, James speaks plainly of Abraham's faith, but reflection on the nature of his faithful deeds is a necessary implicature of his argument.

It is easy enough to imagine James's coupling of Abraham and Rahab as an example of his interest in pairing male and female. Only a moment ago, he referred to "a brother or sister" (2:15), thus displaying a systemic rejection of any attempt to characterize God's family in terms of Roman masculinity. Similarly, from a typically Roman vantage point, Abraham and Rahab exemplify the top and bottom rungs of the ladder of prestige. Accordingly, their corresponding roles as exemplars of faithfulness undercut discriminatory attitudes and practices that accord privilege to those with gold rings and posh apparel at the expense of the needy who show up in filthy rags (2:2). James may well have been interested in other connections, too. Is not James concerned with how these brothers and sisters respond to the tests of exilic life (1:2–4)? It would be difficult to imagine a more demanding test than the one Abraham faced: "Take your son, your only son whom you love, Isaac, and go to the land of Moriah. Offer him up as an entirely burned offering there on one of the mountains that I will show you" (Gen 22:2 CEB). In his exposition of James's letter, the Venerable Bede emphasized the severity of Abraham's test: "For what greater temptation, except for those which concern injuries to one's own body, can happen than that someone, an old man, should be compelled to slay his only and most beloved son?"[81] Accordingly, Abraham may well provide Exhibit One of the nature of faithful response to tests of which James writes in the opening of his letter: "My brothers and sisters, consider the various trials you encounter as occasions for the greatest happiness, knowing that the testing of your faithfulness produces endurance. Let endurance complete its work so that you may be mature, whole, lacking nothing" (1:2–4). Moreover, Genesis identifies Abraham as the consummate exile. Addressing the Hittites, he observes, "I am an immigrant and a temporary resident with you" (Gen 23:4 CEB; see Gen 15:13; Acts 7:6). In other words, although Abraham's elite status

---

(Luke 3:7–14). And Zacchaeus's economic practices, giving half of his possessions to the poor and providing restitution for those defrauded in his business, lead to Jesus's identifying him as Abraham's child (19:1–10).

81. Bede 1985, 31.

and reputation might seem to put him out of reach as a model of faithfulness for James's audience, it turns out that Abraham is a stranger, a refugee, like them; and he is tested, like them. As such, his faith-in-action, his allegiance, can serve as a surprisingly down-to-earth exemplar of diasporic faithfulness to James's readers and hearers.

James opens and closes this subsection with two proverbial phrases, both of which trigger strong biases (or visceral reactions) aimed at forming James's audience in the image of his portrait of faith and deeds acting in concert for those in need. The first declares, "Faith without deeds is fit for nothing" (2:20). The second concludes this section and, indeed, the entirety of Jas 2: "As the lifeless body is dead, so faith without deeds is dead" (2:26). Both trade on hard-and-fast, uncompromising contrasts. In the first, James uses a play on words to state the obvious: Faith without deeds (Gk. *ergon*, "deed," "work") is deedless (Gk. *argon*, "not working," "idle"). It follows that a deedless faith contributes nothing and is fit for nothing. In the second, from Israel's Scriptures, James assumes that living creatures (human and nonhuman) are alive because God has given them the breath of life.[82] The point is that creaturely life does not consist of a body *plus* the breath of life; instead, creaturely life simply *is* the animated body. A living being cannot remain a living being sans the breath of life; one is left, instead, with decaying remains that belong in a grave. In the same way, faith cannot remain faith devoid of deeds; by way of analogy, one is left with a decaying carcass, not the sort of faith Jesus embodied and Abraham and Rahab practiced.

---

82. E.g., in the creation account, "the LORD God formed man from the dust of the ground, and breathed into his nostrils *the breath of life*; and the man became a living being" (Gen 2:7 NRSV, emphasis added). In the account of the flood, analogously, God undertakes "to destroy from under heaven all flesh in which is *the breath of life*." Noah brings onto the ark "two and two of all flesh in which there was *the breath of life*." The narrator tells us, "Every creature took its last breath: the things crawling on the ground, birds, livestock, wild animals, everything swarming on the ground, and every human being. Everything on dry land with *life's breath* in its nostrils died" (Gen 6:17 and 7:15 NRSV; Gen 7:21–22 AT; emphasis added).

James 3:1–4:12
Teaching Wisdom and Its Practices

This section of James's letter is set apart in two ways. First, James continues his practice of beginning a new segment with the formula "my brothers and sisters" along with a statement of topic.[1] Here, *teachers* are ostensibly the focus, though how James's opening salvo concerning teachers relates to the rest of this part of the letter requires clarification. Second, this entire section of the letter is framed by dual emphases on speech and judgment (3:1–12; 4:11–12).

Although speech practices and end-time judgment bracket this section, the two middle sections center less on patterns of behavior and divine approval (or disapproval) and more on theological and moral formation (3:13–18; 4:1–10). The purpose of James's *inclusio*, then, is not merely structural. It also highlights the integrative, tightly woven relationship shared by faith and deeds, by patterns of allegiance and patterns of behavior—or, perhaps better for this section of the letter, by wisdom and the way of life it engenders (cf. 3:13–18).

I am tempted to make "habits of the heart" the heading of this material. Alexis de Tocqueville (1805–59) famously used this phrase in 1835 when referring to the subconscious and often-unacknowledged mores that shape human perceptions, choices, and behavior.[2] In the present context, "habits of the heart" can draw valuable attention to James's transparent concern with communally shaped and mutually shared dispositions and practices. The community's perceptions and experiences are regulated by and, in turn, regulate its members' allegiances and dispositions, which are formed by and in turn give form to their behaviors. We might say that James is on the offensive in this section, contrasting habits of the heart more at home in wider Roman society with those appropriate to the messianic community. James is concerned, then, to inculcate in his hearers and readers transformed patterns of thinking and believing that (1) reposition the self in the world; (2) are fashioned among and shared with his siblings; (3) generate and maintain coherence within the messianic community

---

1. See above, on Jas 1:2–27.

2. See de Tocqueville 2000, 275. Bellah, Madsen, Sullivan, Swidler, and Tipton used de Tocqueville's 1835 phrase 150 years later as the title of their much-discussed and still-important analysis of middling America in 1985: *Habits of the Heart*. I reframed some material from this introduction for publication in Green 2023.

while identifying and animating responses that cohere with God's wisdom (as opposed to those hostile to God's wisdom); and then (4) are expressed in one's practices—realizing, of course, that practices are not only downstream from those patterns of thinking and believing but also serve to solidify and encourage them. (Angry speech is a manifestation of anger, we might say; yet angry speech can also bank the smoldering coals of anger, add coals to the fire, and like bellows make those coals burn hotter.) In addition, as James makes especially clear in this section, transformed habits of the heart (5) are not the result of human mastery but have their origin with God, in "the wisdom that comes down from above" (3:17). Recall James's earlier counsel: "Anyone among you who lacks wisdom should ask God, who gives to everyone without a second thought, without reservation, and it will be given to you" (1:5).

Of course, shared "habits of the heart" and characteristic behaviors are not theoretical interests for James. He names them. "The tongue . . . contaminates the body," for example (3:6). "Let them demonstrate their deeds through an honorable way of life distinguished by the gentleness that comes from wisdom" (3:13). "You crave something you do not have, you commit murder, and you hunger for something you cannot attain" (4:2). "You double-minded, purify your hearts!" (4:8). "Do not vilify each other, brothers and sisters" (4:11). James thus puts before his siblings an inventory of problematic dispositions and practices. On the positive side of the register, James unveils his commitment to a particular kind of theological and moral formation, centered on the virtues of practical wisdom and humility.

How does all of this relate to the banner that James provides for this large section of the letter: "Brothers and sisters, not many of you should become teachers, for you know that we teachers will be judged more stringently" (3:1)? We should note that (1) James refers to teachers in this letter only here, (2) James includes himself as a teacher when he writes "we teachers," and (3) he addresses his instruction not to teachers narrowly but more broadly to his "brothers and sisters" (3:1, 10; 4:11). Accordingly, we can say that his message operates on multiple levels:

- He warns teachers and those who aspire to be teachers about their enhanced culpability at the end-time judgment.
- He instructs teachers on (what should be) the nature of their instruction. (James thus performs as a teacher of teachers.)
- He himself engages in the work of teaching among any who hear or read his letter.

In short, we would be mistaken to think that James's concern with teachers is dropped after its initial mention, but we would also be shortsighted to think that what follows concerns teachers only.

We cannot help but notice that James here both teaches and emphasizes what must be taught. In this way he guides those teachers and would-be teachers who read or hear these words. What must be taught centers less on *content* and more on *telos*. That is, James does not concern himself chiefly at this juncture with formal (or factual or scientific) knowledge on a given subject, or even with first principles and what can be inferred from them—what someone might call *intellectual wisdom* (as if knowledge and subject-matter expertise might substitute for wisdom). Rather, he focuses on *practical wisdom*, with its dual interest in understanding (or discerning and savvying) well and doing well. This second kind of wisdom undergirds and is realized in human flourishing. For James, this wisdom is "pure, then peaceable, gentle, leadable, full of mercy and good fruits, lacking partiality, not double-faced" (3:17). Accordingly, the humility James commends (4:6, 10; cf. 3:13–14) is not only an antonym of arrogance or haughtiness, nor simply the converse of grasping for recognition and respect. This humility also entails one's teachableness, one's openness to (trans)formation, and indeed, one's capacity to welcome wisdom from above.

3:1–12 Speech Practices

3:1 Brothers and sisters, not many of you should become teachers, for you know that we teachers will be judged more stringently. 2 We all err in many ways. If someone does not err with respect to speech, this person is fully mature, able to harness the whole body.

3 If we bridle horses by putting bits into their mouths to make them obey us, we can guide their whole bodies as well. 4 Consider how ships—so large and driven by strong winds—are guided by a tiny[a] rudder wherever the will of the pilot desires. 5 So also the tongue is a small part of the body, and it boasts of great things.

See how small a flame sets such a large forest ablaze. 6 The tongue is a fire. The tongue is the world of wickedness set among the parts of our body.[b] It contaminates the entire body. It ignites the circle of life and will itself be ignited[c] by hell.[d] 7 Humankind takes charge—indeed, has already taken charge—of every kind of wild animal, bird, reptile, and aquatic life, 8 but no human is able to take charge of the tongue—a restless evil, full of deadly poison.[e] 9 With it we bless the Lord and Father, and we curse human beings made in God's likeness. 10 Blessing and cursing come from the same mouth—my brothers and sisters, things should not be this way!

11 Both fresh water and salt water do not flow from the same spring, do they? 12 My brothers and sisters, can a fig tree produce olives or a grapevine figs? Of course not, and neither does a saltwater spring yield fresh water.

a. *Elachistos*, the superlative of *elachys* (small), has an elative force (cf. Boas, Rijksbaron, Huitink, and de Bakker 2019, §32.2); compared to the size of the boat, the rudder is minuscule.

b. Although 3:6a is clear enough, the syntax of the rest of the verse (*hē glōssa . . . phlogizomenē hypo tēs geennēs*, "The tongue is . . . itself ignited by hell")—with one definite verb (*kathistēmi*, "to set," "to establish") and five nominative phrases (three of which are participial)—has long troubled interpreters. Dibelius (1976) referred to it "in its current form [as] among the most controversial in the New Testament" (193), for example, and claimed that "there are few verses in the New Testament which suggest the hypothesis of a textual corruption as much as this one does" (194). Among recent interpreters, Allison similarly voices his suspicion that "the text is corrupt" (2013, 535; cf. Bauckham 1998, 119 n. 1). However, we find no material support for textual emendation in the Gk. manuscript tradition, and therefore no good reason to rewrite the text so as to recover what later interpreters might imagine must have been original (cf., e.g., R. Martin 1988, 113–14; Moo 2000, 156). Contemporary translators and interpreters tend in the direction of the reading I adopt here (e.g., CEB, NIV, NRSV).

c. *Phlogizomenē* (from *phlogizō*, "I set on fire"), a present participle, is typically rendered in the present in English translations: "is set on fire" (CEB; cf., e.g., AV, NIV, NRSV). However, the present participle can have a future sense (see von Siebenthal 2019, 384–85; BDF §339), and I have adopted a future reading here for reasons I will note in the comments, below.

d. Or Gehenna (*geenna*).

e. These two final phrases clearly characterize the tongue, even though neither follows the expected form (*glōssan* is in the accusative, but *kakon* and *mestē* are nominative). Adam summarizes the situation well when he refers to the first as "a nominative absolute with an implied copulative" and to the second as a "nominative absolute" or, maybe, a "predicate nominative" (2013, 67–68).

This section of James's letter is carefully crafted as a short essay on speech practices especially, but not solely, as these are related to the role of teachers. The heading that James offers concerning teachers (3:1) urges a reading of what follows that does not reduce his instruction to personal speech ethics, as important as this might be, but a reading open to its communal ramifications. Repeated references to "the whole body," which can signify both the individual as well as humans in their social or communal contexts, speak to the broader significance of James's message, too.[3] After concluding this essay, James contrasts two kinds of practical wisdom (3:13–18), an emphasis for which he prepares with his final metaphors on what kind of water flows from different

---

3. For *holon to sōma* (the whole body), see Jas 3:2, 3, 6. *Sōma* (body) generally refers to the living body or the corpse of a human or nonhuman animal, but can also be used figuratively of a group of people united in some way (see *CGL* 2:1352–53; Schweizer 1993, 3:322, 324). Baker (1995, esp. 105–38) provides solid background for and a helpful analysis of 3:1–12, but, as his title announces, he does not much explore the communal or social significance of James's instruction.

kinds of springs and what kind of fruit grows from different kinds of plant life (3:11–12).

The relationship between this portion of the letter and the immediately preceding material (ch. 2) is less than straightforward. We look in vain for strong linguistic connections, for example, though we do find conceptual similarities. Consider, for example, James's wholistic or integrated understanding of the human person, his theological anthropology. In chapter 2, faith and deeds are inseparable just as, now, character and speech are conjoined. More noticeable are the ways James's introduction (1:2–27) identifies issues he now addresses in this short essay on speech habits. Among these connections are the obvious repetition of James's concern with the speech and the tongue (1:19, 26;[4] cf. 2:12) and James's ongoing interest in (moral) purity (1:21, 27; 3:6). Also at the conceptual level, we are reminded of James's general pessimism concerning the human capacity to counter the relentless pressure toward evil. Earlier, this was graphically portrayed in terms of the lure and seduction of human cravings (1:12–15). Here, after admitting that "we all err in many ways" (3:2), James asserts emphatically: "No human is able to take charge of the tongue—a restless evil, full of deadly poison" (3:8). Additionally, his earlier indictment of double-mindedness (1:7–8) comes to expression in his incredulous recognition that "blessing and cursing come from the same mouth" (3:10). Human integrity is again on the line.

Across his letter, James is surprisingly consistent in the way he develops his interest in the speech habits of his audience. He critiques his brothers and sisters over and over for their failed attempts at speaking.[5]

- 1:13: Do not say, "God is tempting me!"
- 1:19: Be slow to speak.
- 1:26: Control what you say.
- 2:3: Do not let words put into play your partiality toward the elite and against the needy.
- 2:8, 12: Speak in accordance with neighbor love.
- 2:14: Do not say you have faith but have no deeds.
- 2:16: Do not speak words of blessing while failing to help the needy.
- 4:11: Do not vilify or condemn each other.
- 4:13, 15: Speak humbly, not arrogantly.
- 5:9: Do not make complaints against each other.

---

4. Including the use of *chalinagōgeō* (to bridle/harness/control) with *glōssa* (tongue) in 1:26, and in 3:2 with reference back to *logos* (word). The related noun *chalinos* (bridle/bit) appears in 3:3.

5. I focus primarily on James's use of the following terms: *aucheō* (I boast), *glōssa* (tongue/speech), *laleō* (I speak), *legō* (I say), and *stenazō* (I complain).

In this section, James also adopts a wide-angle lens with which to critique the human family more generally:

- 3:2: Those who do not err with their words [if there were such people] are fully mature.
- 3:5: The tongue is modest in size, but "it boasts of great things."
- 3:6–7: "The tongue is a fire . . . the world of wickedness set among the parts of our body. It contaminates the entire body. It ignites the circle of life and will itself be ignited by hell."
- 3:8: "No human is able to take charge of the tongue—a restless evil, full of deadly poison."

This inventory contributes negatively to the issue that arises with James's every reference to "brothers and sisters" (e.g., 3:1, 10), namely, the poor quality of their communal life, their lack of relational integrity. James does not call out his siblings in comparison with the rest of humanity as though they were especially heinous in this regard. To the contrary, he seems to imply that they are too much like those human beings who have not been transformed by God's "true word," "the implanted word" (1:18, 21). (Note the irony around the contrast between God's liberating word versus these discordant, human words.)

With the gift of God's true word comes the vocation to practice, to hear and do, God's word. It is on this latter point that James finds his readers and hearers lacking (cf. 1:22–26). Given the way James attends to these matters, it almost goes without saying that his siblings need to cultivate fresh speech habits, even though it is also plain that he has no hope that, on their own, they will be able to do so.

Rather than providing the way forward in this section, James hammers away at the necessity of harnessing the tongue and, we should add, identifies the problem less with the tongue, taken in isolation, and more with one's integrated self, one's patterns of thinking, feeling, believing, and behaving. As in his earlier counsel about the human condition (1:12–18), resolution here requires intervention from outside the human person and from outside the human community. In the material that follows (3:13–18), James goes on to develop the nature of that intervention in terms of God's wisdom.

James's essay on speech habits is structured around his claim in 3:2: "We all err," especially "with respect to speech." This, together with the prospect of a more stringent judgment, is the reason Christ-followers should be slow to seek or exercise the role of teacher, so entangled is that role with words spoken (and sometimes written) (3:1). After this we find testimonies to the tongue's disproportional influence (3:3–5a) and destructive power (3:5b–10). Finally,

James provides two rhetorical questions, both of which anticipate a negative response; these drive home the duplicitous nature of the speech habits he has discussed (3:11–12).[6]

[3:1–2] Although James begins this short essay on speech ethics with reference to teachers, what he has to say is clearly not directed to them alone. This is plain from his opening appeal to his "brothers and sisters" (3:1)—which elsewhere in the letter refers to the entirety of James's hearers and readers—followed by the phrase "we all" (3:2).[7] With respect to speech, he writes, *everyone* errs, and not only teachers. This comports well with proverbial declarations like Prov 10:19: "With lots of words comes wrongdoing" (CEB; see Prov 10:18–21) and, especially, Sir 19:16: "Who hasn't sinned with the tongue?" (CEB). James may well have been influenced by these earlier texts, but also by reminiscences of Jesus's teaching, such as we read in Matt 12:36–37: "I tell you that people will have to answer on Judgment Day for every useless word they speak. By your words you will be either judged innocent or condemned as guilty" (CEB).[8] On the one hand, this means that the threat of judgment is tied to everyone's speech (and not only that of teachers), a note that James sounds earlier in the letter, in 1:19–20: "Let everyone be quick to listen, slow to speak, slow to anger. This is because a person's anger does not produce God's righteousness"; and in 1:26: "If those who think they are devout do not control what they say, then they deceive their own hearts; their devotion is a sham." Even so, on the other hand, James draws particular attention to the enhanced judgment facing teachers so that he can drive home his more general concern with speech. "Teachers," then, would be a subset within the community of Jewish messianists, and James's reference to them allows for a firm warning regarding end-time judgment. This is because teaching involves speaking (and writing, as in the case of James himself), a role that opens teachers to expanded opportunities for erring in their speech.

It is tempting to regard teachers as a special class with a presumed elevated status within the community. If we take this route, then we might take the further step of claiming that James has thus elevated his own status among these Christ-followers by making of himself a teacher, yes, but even more: a teacher of teachers. This reading is problematic for two reasons, however.

---

6. For analyses of James's rhetoric, see Hartin 1999, 181–88; Watson 1993b. Watson's level of detail helps to illuminate the specifics of this text, though Hartin grasps better how the overall argument develops.

7. James uses the term *hapantes*, an intensive form of *pas* (all/whole). For references to "brothers and sisters," see 1:2, 16, 19; 2:1, 5, 14; 3:1, 10, 12; 4:11; 5:7, 9, 10, 12, 19.

8. DeSilva (2012, 82–83, 256) observes the close association of Ben Sira and James on the topic of controlling one's speech. The case for dependence on the Jesus tradition is heightened by the further parallels between Jas 3:10–12 and Matt 7:16–20; 12:33; Luke 6:43.

First, James has previously shown little interest in status markers, identifying himself simply as a "servant of God and of the Lord Jesus Christ" (1:1) in an apparent bid to call his audience to a single-minded allegiance to the Lord like his own. Along the same lines, James here and repeatedly throughout the letter refers to his audience as "brothers and sisters," language that emphasizes mutuality rather than hierarchy.[9] Second, among early communities of Christ-followers, "teacher" was less an office and more a role or function. James does not write, as Paul or Peter might,[10] of the exercise of spiritual gifts, but he can still refer to the formative role of teachers who nurture communities in appropriating their scriptural traditions and their identification as Jesus-followers. In this context, *teachers* refers less to what we might think of as professionally trained, designated instructors and more to those with practical wisdom for bringing the Scriptures and traditions about Jesus to bear on faithful living.

Importantly, James provides no hint here that he is troubled especially by the character of those among his readers and hearers who teach, nor the character of what they teach. (He is troubled, clearly, but his interest lies with the way words are used among everyone in his audience and not only by teachers.) Instead, he draws attention to those who teach in order to emphasize his primary concern, namely, the problem of speech. As those who help to shape the lives of these communities of Christ-followers, they will receive a greater judgment—not a harsher judgment, but a more rigorous one. That is, in the end-time judgment (note James's use of the future: "will be judged"), they will be thoroughly examined on account of their heightened opportunities to stumble, and thus to encourage stumbling among others, with respect to speech.

James's comment about universal human failure (3:2a) would be recognized as a truism in all times and places,[11] so much so that the immediately following conditional sentence, "If someone does not err . . . ," seems to introduce an impossibility. Yes, we might say, whoever does not stumble with regard to speech would be able to show themselves to be fully mature, but we have to admit there is no real chance of this happening in anyone's life. Indeed, James himself will declare, "No human is able to take charge of the tongue" (3:8a). Such pessimism on James's part is mitigated, however, by two aspects of his message in the letter's introduction.

---

9. See above, on Jas 2:1.

10. Cf. Rom 12:4–8; 1 Cor 12; 1 Pet 4:10–11.

11. E.g., L. Johnson (1995, 256) notes that James's phrase, "We all err in many ways," is "a Hellenistic commonplace," but this sentiment was also well-known in the Jewish world. See further, Watson 1993b, 55–56 n. 41; Allison 2013, 523.

First, our author does hold to the possibility of full maturity, which, we may recall, refers to ongoing, uncompromising devotion to God and God's ways (1:4). Maturity, then, is not for James the superhuman capacity for self-control, but the sort of consistency and integrity of heart and life in devotion to God hammered out amid life's adversities.[12] James does not portray *perfection* as the sort of flawlessness judged by a fixed blueprint of the sinless life. Nor does he relegate human wholeness and integrity to the next life, even if he is concerned with God's eschatological approval of his readers and listeners. The Venerable Bede thus points in the right direction when he concludes that we must understand James as allowing that God's people "are able to offend even in many things and yet remain perfect."[13] This is because perfection—or better, integrity and wholeness—refers to the direction and progression of one's life, the journey on which one is embarked, and not (simply) to one's having arrived at such and such a destination.

Second, we may recall James's overall sense of the human situation. True, our theologian espouses a pessimistic anthropology. Humans lack the resources to master cravings that lead to sin and death. Their natural capacities are inadequate for attending to God's will (1:12–16). However, God "has chosen to give us birth by means of his true word so that we might be a kind of foretaste of what would become of everything he created" (1:18). That is, the people who comprise James's audience are not left to their own devices. They have God's own wherewithal for the journey of integrity and wholeness; if they are found lacking, they are urged to request the same from a gracious God (1:5, 18).

Though James's instruction here at the beginning of his short essay on the tongue is aimed at everyone in his audience, it is not hard to imagine the fierceness of his gaze on those who share the role of teaching among these far-flung Christ-followers. Given the centrality of words to their vocation, are they not all the more responsible to embody and to cultivate in others this full maturity? And if so, should they not harness their whole selves as well as safeguard and guide the whole community of God's people?

[3–5a] James takes the next step in his essay on speech ethics by introducing two similes, the purpose of which is to underscore the outsized influence of the tongue. In parallel ways, working horses and steering ships can be compared to human speech practices.[14] The parallels are not precise, but they are suggestive.

---

12. See above, on Jas 1:2–4.
13. Bede 1985, 36.
14. James begins 3:5 with the term *houtōs* (in this way).

Horses (3:3)	Ships (3:4)	Humans (3:5a)
The person who drives horses, the charioteer	The person at the ship's helm, its pilot	
	Amid strong winds	
A bit in the horse's mouth	A tiny rudder	The tongue, a small body part
Guide the whole horse	Guide the large ship	
	Wherever the pilot desires	
		Boasts of great things

Here, James draws on stock images in his world to emphasize the tongue's disproportional leverage.[15] James's readers today with an agrarian background will recognize what almost everyone in Roman antiquity would know, namely, that the bit is a horizontal rod placed in a horse's mouth and held there by rope or leather straps over and around the head. In its early history, the bit might be made of organic material, like bones or antlers, but in time these were supplanted by metal bars, allowing the rider or the driver of a wagon or chariot to turn the horse with a slight tug in one direction or the other.[16] James's concern seems tightly focused on the ability of a small bit to guide (and even control) a large animal weighing on average more than 1,000 pounds. In antiquity, marine navigation used steering oars attached to the rear of a craft, at its stern; or toward the rear of the boat on its side as "a quarter rudder," providing a simple technological solution to the problem of steering even those vessels that would have been regarded in the Roman era as extraordinarily large.[17] Depending on the length and capacity of the craft, these could be quite large and heavy. Accordingly, James uses the superlative of *small* in order to make a point similar to what he has said about horses and bits. Comparatively speaking, the rudder is dwarfed by the boat's enormous mass, "so large." Guiding horses and ships— both analogies serve to contrast the comparatively modest size of the tongue with its mammoth power over the whole person (and then, over the community within which one is nested).

James's maritime analogy takes us further still. First, the phrase "driven by strong winds" (3:4) identifies the necessity and aim of words. What is

---

15. For the traditional status of these analogies in the Greco-Roman world, see, e.g., Dibelius 1976, 186–90; Watson 1993b, 58 nn. 55–58.

16. See Timothy, T. Taylor, Tuvschinjargal, and Bayarsaikhan 2016.

17. See Casson 1971, 224–28; Mott 1997.

needed is not complete silence but rather words well chosen. This is because winds carry sailing vessels downwind, irrespective of the crew's anticipated destination. Rudders mitigate the wind's force, guiding the ship in the desired direction. James allows that people, too, can be "driven and tossed by the wind" (1:6), so they require guidance, which takes the form of words well spoken: "quick to listen, slow to speak, slow to anger" (1:19; cf. 1:26). Second, James plainly observes that rudders allow ships to be steered "wherever the will of the pilot desires" (3:4). Writing in a way that is not easy to capture in English translation, James highlights both the pilot's inclination or disposition (*hormē*) and the pilot's purpose or intention (*boulomai*). By way of analogy, James thus emphasizes that speech habits show the importance of one's allegiances and dispositions. Extending the analogy along the lines he develops in his short essay on speech ethics, we should add that he targets especially the incongruity between fidelities and inclinations, on the one hand, and actual behaviors, on the other hand. His audience's practices with words expose their wrongly directed dispositions, so he points to the scarcity of fully mature persons among his readers and hearers. They are not whole. They lack integrity. They continue to be tempted, lured away, seduced by their cravings (cf. 1:14).

The comparison with speech is made explicit when James admits that the tongue is a small body part, yet it "boasts of great things" (3:5a). With this observation, James supports two interrelated judgments. First, although James can use the language of *boasting* in an ironic sense, as he does in 1:9–10 (which I translated as "express confidence"), here it has the sense of self-important pomposity.[18] Shortly, our author will further lambast the kind of pride that expresses itself in hubris (4:1–16). This pride entails inclinations and efforts toward belittling others and minimizing their needs as unimportant to someone of our station or to demonstrate our mastery over them. It is also the abject

18. Cf. Ps 12:3–4: "May the Lord destroy all deceitful lips and a boastful tongue, those who say, 'Our tongue we will magnify; our lips are our own—who is our lord?'" (NETS).

In 1:9–10, James uses the term *kauchaomai* (I boast/brag), but in 3:5 he uses *aucheō* (I boast); LSJ (285) offers the picturesque "plume oneself," and MGS (350) has "vaunt." *Kauchaomai* also appears in 4:16, where it is paired with the noun *kauchēsis* (boasting) and has a clearly negative sense: "all such boasting is evil."

Watson sketches when boasting was and was not acceptable in the Greco-Roman world (2016, 90–93): "Self-praise was generally considered repugnant. . . . Boasting was appropriately used in only a few well-defined circumstances" requiring "great delicacy" (90–91). In Israel's Scriptures and Second Temple Judaism, boasting should never be anthropocentric: "The Lord proclaims: the learned should not boast of their knowledge, nor warriors boast of their might, nor the rich boast of their wealth. No, those who boast should boast in this: that they understand and know me" (Jer 9:23–24 CEB). Cf., e.g., 1 Kgs 20:11, Pss 52:1; 94:1–4; Prov 27:1–2; Isa 10:12–14.

refusal to recognize and embrace our need for and dependence on God. "Boasting of great things" plainly participates in this kind of pride.[19]

Second, in addition to the more obvious idea that a small organ can have disproportional influence on the whole, we hear James's charge that horses and ships can be controlled but the tongue seems out of control. Notice again James's wording: "*It* boasts of great things" (and not, say, "*With it we* boast of great things")—as if the tongue had a mind of its own. And the mind it exercises is a self-congratulatory, condescending one, putting into play patterns of life that James goes on to identify as earthly, unspiritual, even devilish, life patterns marked by jealousy, status-grabbing, and swagger (3:14–15). According to James's assessment, his audience is removed from full "maturity" by a country mile, an evaluation supported by their inability to "harness the whole body" (3:2).

[5b–10] James continues his analysis of the tongue. Its disproportional influence remains in focus,[20] but James supplements his assessment by emphasizing the tongue's destructive power (3:5b–8) and duplicity (3:9–10). This small body part is powerful, and dangerously so. It is a fire. It is a world of wickedness. It is uncontrollable. And it is deceitful.

James's first comparison, the fire-like tongue, is proverbial, enhancing his message through alliteration (*hēlikon . . . hēlikēn hylēn*)[21] and emotional impact (3:5b–6a). We can work through the significance of his metaphor in two steps. First, although *fire* is capable of a range of associations (including such positive, bodily associations as *warmth* or *food preparation*, or more abstract ones like *zeal* or *passion*), James emphasizes only two: small flame/large forest and smoldering destruction. In this way, he invites his readers to visualize the destructive power of a single spark, which can cause a firestorm that decimates an entire forest.[22] This is the image he wants his audience to share when he asserts, "The tongue is a fire" (3:6a). The tongue, we might say, is an arsonist, a firebug that ignites an inferno.

Second, metaphors like this one often function as *somatic markers*—that is, they trigger bodily responses that tag emotionally significant events and provide

---

19. Readers of James today need to take seriously James's own discourse situation when reflecting on his concern with prideful boasting. R. Niebuhr famously identified *pride* as the basic or primary sin (*The Nature and Destiny of Man*). This is not James's position. Clearly, our author does not call the degraded poor to self-abasement but rather affirms them as having been chosen by God and calls on Christ-followers to relate to those in need accordingly. At the same time, James's rhetoric regarding boasting, pride, and humility takes aim at the wealthy and well-positioned, and at those who curry their favor (see above, on Jas 2). See further, Feldmeier 2014, 88–93.

20. Verse 5b: large/small; v. 6: part/parts, part/entire.

21. James 3:5 uses the term *hēlikos* with two different senses: "how small [a fire] . . . how great [a forest]."

22. On these two associations in Greco-Roman and Jewish sources, see Allison 2013, 532–34. Allison also notes that Israel's Scriptures associate forest fires with catastrophe and judgment (e.g., Ps 83:13–18; Isa 9:18–19; Ezek 15:6–8).

continuing, autonomic guidance. We might think of our own reflexive, instinctive responses of disgust or joy, which we experience as gut feelings of attraction or repulsion.[23] Accordingly, at a subconscious level, James's identification of the tongue as an incendiary device might recruit feelings of dismay, dread, and despair. Associating the tongue with these negative feelings, his audience is urged to form a mental image of the fire-tongue as an uncontrolled, intense, destructive force, and to respond (quite apart from reasoned analysis or debate) just as they would to imminent danger: run away, not toward. Hopefully, then, this first metaphor both opens the eyes of these Christ-followers to the harmful role the tongue plays in human communities and also triggers in them that sinking feeling that can lead one to seek help.

James first compares the tongue to a fire, destructive and out of control. Second, he calls the tongue "the world of wickedness set among the parts of our body" (3:6b). This phrase may continue the emphasis on the disproportional influence of the tongue—now portrayed as a "world" in relation to the body's various parts. More to the point, though, is the way James construes the "world" (*kosmos*) here and elsewhere in the letter.[24] *World*, in his usage, does not refer to the earth or its inhabitants. Rather, the term consistently has the sense of *lifeworld*—that is, a culture's complex web of taken-for-granted values, rituals, and practices; the universe as a given people understand, experience, and practice it; a society's common ideals and habits shaped and transmitted from one generation to the next, typically unselfconsciously. And his portrait of these life patterns is unfailingly negative, so much so that he identifies friendship with the world in opposition to friendship with God (4:4). He extends that negative portrayal here, giving the tongue-world the quality of *wickedness* (3:6).[25]

Although this is James's only use of the term *wickedness* in this letter, he develops the idea earlier in his short essay on favoritism, where he expounds on the unjust treatment of the degraded and impoverished (Jas 2). Sharply put, the lifeworld that he targets is characterized by judgments and practices that fail to see that allegiance to Jesus is incompatible with acts of favoritism (2:1), that fail to account for God's choice of the poor (2:5), that fail to follow Scripture's royal law of neighbor love (2:8–13), and so on. This connection to James's earlier concern with favoritism toward society's upper echelons (Jas 2) is encouraged by James's references to speaking in that earlier essay: Do not let words put into play your partiality toward the elite and against the needy (2:3). Speak in accordance with neighbor love (2:12). Do not say you have faith but have no deeds (2:14). Do not speak words of blessing while failing to help the needy (2:16). Plainly, for James, the destructive power of the tongue is realized as

---

23. Somatic markers are ably discussed in Slingerland 2005; more generally, Damasio 1994.
24. Jas 1:27; 2:5; 3:6; 4:4 (2×). See above, on 1:26–27.
25. *Adikia*, "wickedness," "injustice."

it infects human beings—and, indeed, human communities—with patterns of thinking, believing, feeling, and behaving set in opposition to God.

James documents his concern with the tongue-world by adding three more clauses: (1) "it contaminates the entire body"; (2) "it ignites the circle of life"; and (3) it "will itself be ignited by hell" (3:6c). The first two underscore the tongue's damaging influence, the third its condemnation.

1. The tongue introduces a *pollutant* into and among human beings, infusing people and their communities like an infectious disease. The image of the tongue as a contagious contaminate meshes well with the view, widespread in antiquity, that those who voice evil thoughts of falsehood and deceit are morally defiled and defiling.[26] Their moral impurity is realized in their duplicity. With their words, they represent themselves as righteous when in fact they are acting apart from God's Instructions (or Torah).

In the extended introduction to his letter, James's message drew on the metaphor MORALITY IS PURITY, with the abstract notion of morality grasped in terms of the bodily experience of cleanliness.[27] He triggers the same metaphor here, though now focused even more dramatically on speech.[28] As with the image of the devastatingly destructive fire (3:5–6), so now, James's metaphor drives his readers and hearers away from their present speech habits. Humans are not attracted by pollution and contamination. They instinctively back away from it. Accordingly, James's language biases his readers and hearers toward moral purity in their speech practices.

For James, the ingredients of this pollutant are Roman values and practices that work against God's agenda and contaminate Christ-followers and their communities. (James will delve into these problematic dispositions and behaviors further in 3:13–18.) This "world of wickedness," the tongue, opposes "devotion that is pure and unsullied in God the Father's eyes." That kind of

---

26. See Blidstein 2022. For the psalmist, e.g., "You are not a God who delights in wickedness; evil will not sojourn with you. The boastful will not stand before your eyes; you hate all evildoers. You destroy those who speak lies; the LORD abhors the bloodthirsty and deceitful. . . . For there is no truth in their mouths; their hearts are destruction; their throats are open graves; they flatter with their tongues" (Ps 5:4–9 NRSV). The letter to the Ephesians similarly conflates images of wrongdoing, including evil speaking, and purity: "But sexual immorality and impurity of any kind or greed must not even be mentioned among you, as is proper among saints. Entirely out of place is obscene, silly, and vulgar talk; but instead, let there be thanksgiving. Be sure of this, that no sexually immoral or impure person or one who is greedy (that is, an idolater) has any inheritance in the kingdom of Christ and of God. Let no one deceive you with empty words, for because of these things the wrath of God comes on those who are disobedient" (Eph 5:3–6 NRSVue). That this association was known outside the Jewish world is clear from the instructions to those who want to enter a Gk. temple in Rhodes: "With pure hands and mind, and with a truthful tongue, come in, not through washing, but pure in mind" (Blidstein §2).

27. See above, on Jas 1:19–27.

28. Blidstein 2022, §3.2.

devotion is marked not by duplicity but by care for the vulnerable and needy, and keeping "ourselves from being contaminated by the world" (1:27).

2. James uses a common image, "the circle of life,"[29] to identify the comprehensive, destructive power of the tongue. Like a *fire* that chases fuel wherever it can find it, so every chapter of life's story is subject to its reach.

3. The tongue is set for end-time *punishment*. Here, "ignited by hell" is an image of divine judgment that captures, again, James's earlier reference to the prospect of God's eschatological approval and disapproval (3:1). More often than not, English translations of this third clause (rendered here as "ignited by hell") leave the impression that hell is the *source* of the tongue's fire. For example: "it is set on fire of hell" (AV), "is itself set on fire by hell" (NRSV, NIV), or "the tongue itself is set on fire by the flames of hell" (CEB). This is a possible reading. It wants to underscore the wickedness of the tongue by tracing it back to diabolic influence (see 3:15–16). However, an emphasis on the wicked tongue's *fate*, rather than its *origin*, is far more probable.[30]

Hell is *Gehenna*,[31] a term not used in contemporary literature to refer to the home of the devil and his minions. In the OT, Gehenna is the Valley of Hinnom, site of the sacrifice of children, proclaimed unclean under Josiah, made into a trash heap, and then associated with fiery, end-time judgment.[32] This last sense continues beyond the OT. For example, a Jewish text from the late first century CE portrays *Gehenna* as "the pit of torment," where one finds "fire and torments": "The pit of torment shall appear, and opposite it shall be the place of rest; and the furnace of Gehenna shall be disclosed, and opposite it the paradise of delight. Then the Most High will say to the nations that have been raised from the dead, 'Look now, and understand whom you have denied, whom you have not served, whose commandments you have despised. Look on this side and on that; here are delight and rest, and there are fire and torments.' Thus he will speak to them on the day of judgment" (2 Esd 7:36–38 NRSV). For James, the tongue that blazes will itself be set ablaze in the scorching, end-time judgment, following the notion that punishment is proportional to and modeled on the offense. With respect to the tongue, other texts similarly promise

---

29. The roots of this image in Orphic philosophy, with its interest in the repeated migration of souls, is much discussed, but scholars also recognize the migration of this image from its origins to the wider, more popular sense of "the whole course of life." See summaries in, e.g., Davids 1982, 143; L. Johnson 1995, 260.

30. This is demonstrated in Bauckham 1998.

31. The English term *hell* sometimes translates the Gk. word *hadēs* (Hades), which refers to the "place of the dead" or the "netherworld," which may or may not signal judgment in the afterlife. See Bauckham 1992, 3:14–15.

32. On the Valley of Hinnom, see Josh 15:8; 18:16. On the sacrifice of children, see 2 Kgs 16:3; 21:6. For that valley under Josiah, see 2 Kgs 23:10. For Gehenna's association with judgment, see Isa 31:9; 66:24; Jer 7:31–32; 19:6; Rev 14:7–13. Cf. Watson 1992, 2:926–27.

fiery judgment, including the Sermon on the Mount in the First Gospel: "And if they say, 'You fool,' they will be in danger of fiery hell [Gehenna]" (Matt 5:22 CEB).[33]

James's analysis of the tongue identifies it is a "fire," first, and then as "world of wickedness." Third, he declares that the tongue is uncontrollable (3:7–8). Previous emphases remain: the disproportionality of a person's tongue when compared with the entire animal world and the tongue's noxious power. To these James now adds that the tongue is indomitable.

The notion of *taming* the tongue (e.g., CEB, NIV, NRSV) may be too weak. The only other use of James's verb in the NT refers to the impossibility of overpowering or subduing a demonized man (Mark 5:4).[34] Essentially, James's image locates human beings at the apex of the animal world rather than depicting humans as having domesticated every creature.

The entirety of the animal kingdom is in view, with James using a fourfold classification—beasts, birds, reptiles, and aquatic life—reminiscent of the creation account in Gen 1:26: "Let us make humanity in our image to resemble us so that they may take charge of the fish of the sea, the birds in the sky, the livestock, . . . and all the crawling things on earth" (CEB; cf. Gen 9:2; Deut 4:17–18). Moreover, for James, humanity's charge over the animal world seems timeless, occurring in the past and continuing still. The aim of this portrait of human charge-taking is not so much to countenance how humans have behaved toward other animals as it is to provide a harsh contrast with the human incapacity to subdue the tongue. And James underscores this contrast with his language choices: people have exercised control over *every* kind of animal, but *no one* can exercise control over the tongue. In short, humans may want to take pride in their place at the pinnacle of the animal world,[35] but they are reduced to utter helplessness when it comes to mitigating the feral destructiveness of this little organ, the tongue.

We might wish that James would provide an antidote to the dire situation he has set before his audience, a medicant that would reverse what at this point seems the inescapable prospect of fiery judgment. He will begin to do so shortly (beginning with 3:13), but he has not yet finished painting humanity, Christ-followers included, into a horrific corner with his analysis of the tongue. Why is the tongue uncontrollable? It is, he now adds, "a restless evil, full of deadly

---

33. See also, e.g., Pss. Sol. 12.1–4: "Lord, save my soul from . . . the criminal and slandering tongue that speaks lies and deceit. The words of the wicked man's tongue (are) twisted so many ways; (they are) as a fire among a people which scorches its beauty. May God . . . destroy the slanderous tongue in flaming fire far away from the devout" (ET in Wright 1985, 662). See further, Allison 2013, 541–42.

34. *Damazō* (I overpower/subdue/tame) is used 3× in 3:7–8. See MGS 453.

35. Watson documents the ancient world's pride in taming the animal world (1993b, 60, 60–61 n. 76).

poison" (3:8). James's pessimistic anthropology again comes to the fore. Previously, he associated restlessness, or instability, with double-minded people (1:7–8). Soon he will, again, connect instability or disorder with evil; both are grounded in jealousy and devious self-promotion (3:14, 16).[36] The problem with the tongue, then, is that it makes public one's inner dispositions; for James's audience, the dispositions made visible are mixed, unstable, not at all single-minded in their devotion to the Lord. Double-minded, these messianists are also double-tongued,[37] and this brings harm to the messianic community. The tongue is "full of deadly poison"; this image likewise implicates human beings as purveyors of social disorder, wreaking havoc among others like a venomous snake (cf. Ps 140:1–3). Apparently, the modifier "deadly" is not used in hyperbole, given James's earlier interest in God's Instruction (or Torah) concerning murder (Jas 2:11) and his later reference to murdering the righteous (5:6). The life cycle of *craving*, after all, culminates in death (1:15). Not for nothing does James find himself needing to refer to his audience repeatedly as *brothers and sisters*, reminding them again and again of the kinship they share on account of the saving word they have received and urging that they live accordingly.

The pinnacle of James's message regarding speech habits (3:9–10) pinpoints what we might call the problem of the double tongue, itself deeply rooted in double-mindedness. The brutal irony rests in the tongue's duplicity, recognized in its use in both blessing and cursing. "My brothers and sisters" (3:10) recalls the opening address of this short essay (3:1). With these words, James slows the processing of his message so that he can accentuate an appalling oxymoron in which kinship and community are set alongside damning words spoken over each other. "Things should not be this way!" (3:10)—indeed! James goes further, though, pressing his finger into the speech-caused wounds of these communities. They bless the Lord and Father,[38] but damn their siblings, human beings made in God's likeness. In his extended introduction, James signaled his interest in Gen 1–3—recalling God's work in the creation of light and of heavenly bodies that illumine the earth (Jas 1:17; Gen 1:3–5, 14–18), evoking God's affirmation of creation's goodness (Jas 1:17; Gen 1:4, 10, 12, 18, 21, 25, 31), writing of "everything God created" (Jas 1:18), and reflecting on Adam

---

36. The noun *akatastasia* (disorder) appears in 3:16, the adjective *akatastatos* (unstable) in 1:8; 3:8.

37. Although James does not use the term *double-tongued*, we find it in the Didache (late first century) and the Epistle of Barnabas (late first or early 2nd century): "Do not be double-minded or double-tongued [*diglōssos*, double-tongued, deceitful], for the double-tongue is a deadly trap" (Did. 2.4; Barn. 19.7 AT). See also in LXX: Prov 11:13; Sir 5:13–6:1; 28:13; cf. 20:16.

38. Given the allusion to Gen 1 that follows, "Lord and Father" is almost certainly an example of hendiadys, two words referring to God, rather than a reference to the "Lord" (Jesus) and also to the "Father" (God). Cf., e.g., Gen 9:26; 24:27; Isa 63:16.

and Eve as he works through the problem of testing.[39] Now he uses the rare word *homoiōsis* (likeness),[40] alluding to Gen 1:26–27: God made humanity "according to our image and . . . likeness [*homoiōsis*]" (NETS). James thus draws on the opening chapters of Genesis to characterize God, to reflect on the human condition, and now especially to ground his call for ethical comportment. In doing so, James reaches beyond the circle of kinship shared among these brothers and sisters, speaking instead of their common humanity before God. How can it be that God's people denounce other human beings who, from God's perspective, are godlike? Is this not the same thing as denouncing the God who made them?

[11–12] James turns, finally, to the worlds of hydrology and food production to drive home the nature of the problem with the tongue. He moves from explicit metaphors, like a fire or deadly snake, to implied simile; meanwhile he continues to bank on common experience to energize his prosecution of human speech habits. In doing so, he adopts an ABA pattern:

> A Both fresh water and salt water do not flow from the same spring, do they?
> B My brothers and sisters, can a fig tree produce olives or a grapevine figs?
> A' Of course not, and neither does a saltwater spring yield fresh water.

This ABA pattern opens and closes with the kind of water issuing from its source in the ground, drawing the closest analogy to the mouth (and thus the heart) from which flows, unimaginably, two kinds of speech, blessing and cursing. Although salt water mixes with fresh water in an estuary, where a river empties into the sea, it is unthinkable that both salt water and fresh water might claim the same source. Couched between these references to water and its source (3:11, 12b) is an agrarian metaphor (3:12a) well-known in the Jesus tradition. Jesus is speaking of false prophets in this part of the Sermon on the Mount, but his maxim applies more generally: "You will know them by their fruits" (Matt 7:16 NRSV). He goes on to tie good fruit to good trees and bad fruit to bad trees, and to deny that grapes are gathered from thorny weeds or figs from thistles, then claims, again: "Thus you will know them by their fruits" (7:20 NRSV). The link to James's message is even more obvious later in Matthew's Gospel: "A tree is known by its fruit. Children of snakes! How can you speak good things while you are evil? What fills the heart comes out of the mouth" (12:33–34 CEB; cf. Luke 6:43–45). We can think through James's images in two ways. On the one hand, our author traces speech habits

---

39. See above, on 1:12–18. The fourfold division of the animal world in 3:7 recalls Gen 1, too (see above), so this helps to ready us for the more direct allusion in 3:9.
40. The term appears in the NT only here.

back to their source, promoting an integrated portrait of life and its patterns. Good speech habits flow from a good heart. Bad speech habits flow from a bad heart. Speech habits reveal their source in one's inner life, one's deeply held commitments, allegiances, and dispositions. On the other hand, he portrays speech habits as the effortless yield of one's inner life. Fig trees do not decide to produce figs rather than olives. Indeed, fig trees do not decide to produce anything at all. Fig trees simply produce figs. This is their nature. In the same way, a person's interior life simply is on display in her or his behavior; here this is so in speech practices. James, therefore, is not issuing an imperative, as if his message were something like this: "Don't speak that way! Speak this way!" Instead, his message centers here on the indicative: "How you speak reveals who you really are."[41]

Excursus: The Tongue and Moral Identity (Reprise)

Although the ancient world identified a small range of functions for the tongue, James concerns himself with only one: the tongue as the organ of speech.[42] Even so, James is not interested in the flexing and twisting of the tongue in support of different speech sounds. Rather, *tongue* is synecdoche, first, for the many body parts implicated in speech (the larynx, the diaphragm, the lungs, the mind,[43] and so on); and second, for the human being understood wholistically. Luke's Gospel reports Jesus's words concerning the role of the eye as the body's lamp: "If your eye is healthy, your whole body is full of light, but if it is unhealthy, your body is full of darkness" (Luke 11:34 NRSVue). James writes similarly, though referring to the tongue rather than the eye and therefore shining the brightest light on habits of speech. Accordingly, the tongue is key to James's portrait of the human person, and particularly of human moral identity. Who a person is—one's character, one's dispositions, one's allegiances, one's patterns of thinking, feeling, and believing—are not hidden away in a person's interior but are continuously on display in one's behavior.[44] One can only do what one is. This does not mean that the traffic is one way, as though one could trace movement only from internal to external, however, since one's practices are themselves formative of one's identity. One's speech habits flow out of one's inner life but also help to shape that inner life further. In a sense, James's focus on the tongue presses further than Jesus's emphasis on the eye, since speech habits shape the person doing the speaking as well as provoke immediate and ongoing consequences among one's community.

---

41. See Berger 2003, 76–77.

42. A survey of ancient Gk. and Lat. literature shows that, apart from medical texts (e.g., the earlier Hippocrates and the later Galen), *tongue* typically refers to one's voice (or words or speech) or to the language one speaks.

43. I refer to the *mind* since those parts of the brain implicated in speech would not have been known to an ancient audience.

44. See Berger 2003, 74–78.

The metaphors that shape James's portrait of the tongue are crucial, then, because they provide a window into the interiority of individual and community life. These are not similes, as though the tongue could be compared to this or that. They are not ornamental or flowery language James uses to embellish his message. Rather, they are *metaphors* that show how James wants to conceptualize (and how he wants his audience to conceptualize) the tongue. The tongue *is not like* a fire, for example. It *is* a fire.

Of course, James blends his metaphors so that some but not all qualities associated with the tongue are in view, just as some but not all aspects of fire are in view. James is not concerned with the tongue's role in digestion, for example, or in taste. In the same way, James does not develop an interest in every element associated with fire. His instruction is unconcerned with heat or light or smoke, for example. Instead, bringing tongue and fire together, James conceptualizes what otherwise might seem like ordinary speech but actually triggers a clear and present danger, so much so that immediate action is urgent. And this is not his only (blended) metaphor:[45]

- The tongue is a fire.
- The tongue is a world of wickedness.
- The tongue is a pollutant.
- The tongue is a venomous snake.

What is at stake here? First, James's audience is not indicted because their speech habits are consistently abusive. They pronounce words of blessing as well as cursing (3:10). Second, though, it is precisely this unpredictability that is the problem for Christ-followers. Restless, disordered speech habits pull back the curtain to expose people whose inner lives are disordered, unstable (see 1:7–8). Double-tongued speech habits demonstrate and perpetuate double-mindedness. Speech habits perpetuate and demonstrate duplicity. What James wants to find among Christ-followers is integrity between one's interior and exterior (see 3:11–12). Whatever their claims about faith and faithfulness, James shows that their vocal displays demonstrate an interior turned more toward friendship with the world than friendship with God.

3:13–18 Authentic Wisdom on Display

3:13 Who among you is wise and learned? Let them demonstrate their deeds through an honorable[a] way of life distinguished by[b] the gentleness that comes from wisdom. 14 But if you have bitter rivalry and devious self-promotion in your hearts, then stop gloating and falsifying the truth. 15 This is not the wisdom that comes down from above, but is earthly, worldly,[c] diabolic. 16 Wherever there is rivalry and devious self-promotion, there is disorder and every contemptible deed. 17 But the wisdom that comes down from above is first pure, then peaceable, gentle,

---

45. For conceptual blending, see Evans and Green 2006.

leadable, full of mercy and good fruits, lacking partiality, not double-faced. 18 Those who make peace sow the fruit of justice peaceably.[d]

a. *Kalos* is usually rendered "good" but occupies a more expansive domain, including *beautiful, fitting, noble*, etc.
b. I am reading the phrase *en prautēti sophias* as a dative of manner, and *sophias* as a genitive of source.
c. *Psychikos* is used here in the sense of *pertaining to life in this world*, as opposed to *what is divine*; cf. L&N 79.2.
d. I am reading *en eirēnē* as a dative of manner (see, e.g., Baker 1995, 175).

The larger section of James's letter, 3:1–4:12, is bracketed by shared emphases on speech and judgment (3:1–12; 4:11–12), with the two middle sections (3:13–18; 4:1–10) concerned with theological and moral formation. The letter's prominent motifs crisscross in the present subsection, demonstrating both how interwoven are James's interests throughout the letter and, more importantly, the nature of his integrated understanding of human beings. Heart and life cannot be separated.

The central theme of this subsection is clearly *wisdom*, mentioned four times (3:13 [2×], 15, 17) and described twice (3:13, 17–18), as well as identified through its negation (3:14–16). James thus emphasizes wisdom and the way of life it engenders. This is not the first time James has placed the spotlight on wisdom, however, and it is important that we allow earlier material to shed light on this discussion (see 1:2–8). "The wisdom that comes down from above" (3:15, 17) is none other than God's wisdom, God's gift to those who ask in confidence. It is *practical wisdom*: the capacity both to understand and to act, to embody patterns of perception and performance that reflect God's ways. Wisdom from above includes the wherewithal to evaluate rightly and to act faithfully amid trials related to allegiance to the Lord Jesus within a world system that runs counter to God's ways. More particularly, it includes both recognizing the actual status of the degraded poor and the esteemed wealthy from God's vantage point and acting accordingly (1:9–12). Christ-followers are called to an integrity of heart and life, so that their patterns of thinking, feeling, and believing are fully synchronized with their patterns of behaving.

[3:13] Here and in the next subsection (4:1), James introduces his topic with a question. "Who among you is wise and learned?" reaches backward to 3:1, with its warning to anyone who might want to take on the role of teacher. However, *anyone* "among you" (and not only a teacher or would-be teacher) is caught in the net James casts. This is especially noticeable given the general interest in epistemology (what we know and how we know it) that pervades the letter.

The Language of "Knowing" in James	
"I show," "I reveal" (*deiknymi*)	2:18 (2×); 3:13
"I know" (*epistamai*)	4:14
"learned" (*epistēmōn*)	3:13
"I know" (*ginōskō*)	1:3; 2:20; 5:20
"Pay attention!" "Look!" (*idou*)	3:4, 5; 5:4, 7, 9, 11
"I know," "I understand" (*oida/eidō*)	1:19; 3:1; 4:4, 17
"wisdom" (*sophia*)	1:5; 3:13, 15, 17
"wise" (*sophos*)	3:13

Taken together, these references urge the view that James stakes his claim on the kind of insight he wants his hearers and readers to exercise.[46] His need to shape his audience's perception of the way things really are leads him to ground his message in a call for transformed patterns of thinking and believing that (1) reorient the self in the world, (2) are shaped within and shared by one's community, (3) generate and maintain coherence within the community and at the same time identify and enliven responses of resistance toward life patterns that oppose God's wisdom, (4) are demonstrated in one's practices, and (5) derive not from human ingenuity but from God's gracious gift. James wants his audience to envisage the world as God does and act accordingly, and to do so together.[47] In short, James's opening query is less a request for an answer and more an invitation to self-reflection: Are we, am I, wise and learned *according to these metrics*?

In fact, James provides his readers and hearers with no opportunity to respond to his query. We might call this a pseudoquestion—perhaps meant to undermine a position by framing it in doubt or to press the reader for a decision.[48] (It would help if we could hear the reader's intonation when performing this letter among the communities to which James addresses himself!) In any case, clearly, a verbal response will not do. One cannot say, "Yes, I am wise and learned." To the contrary, James seems to say that we already know who is wise and learned on account of the life they live. Wisdom and learning are not for James

46. See above, on 1:2–8.
47. In her examination of Frederick Douglass's reading of James, Aymer (2007, 72–73, e.g.) calls this "darkness reading": a call for James's audience not to identify with the darkness characterizing this world system but to cultivate a self-identity over and against the darkness, based on the wisdom from above.
48. Dupriez 1991, 371.

matters of specialized knowledge. This is practical wisdom (ways of perceiving and performing) and tacit learning (embodied, experienced knowledge that is hard to quantify).

On the one hand, we should remind ourselves how James earlier framed his message christologically, identifying allegiance to the Lord Jesus as the interpretive lens for all that follows in this letter (1:1) and identifying Jesus's faith in God's purpose and power, the sort of faith on display in Jesus's words and deeds, as the benchmark of faithful life patterns among God's people (2:1). The understanding he is after is crafted through hands-on engagement with Israel's Scriptures, as people are shaped by the Jesus tradition and single-minded allegiance to the Lord Jesus. So, this scriptural and christological orientation tells us something about who is wise and learned.

On the other hand, James summarizes the lifestyle of the wise and learned. First, to reiterate, people are known not through the claims they make about themselves but by their deeds. James thus reprises his prior instruction: "I will show you my faith by my deeds" (2:18; see 2:14–26). Put sharply, whether one has received "the wisdom that comes down from above" is not a matter of self-perception; it can be determined only through one's deeds.[49]

Second, these deeds are not assessed in an atomistic way or individually, but in the context of one's day-to-day life, the habitual patterns characteristic of one's life. So the wise and learned are not recognized through their self-claims nor through one or two heroic acts, but, as it were, through the stories told of them over time.

Third, note that what constitutes an *honorable* life depends on one's community of reference, the attitudes and behaviors that "we" count as respectable or admirable. Accordingly, just as James has insisted that God's valuation and choice of a people govern how God's people appraise and act toward people (see 1:9–12; 2:5–7), so this reference to an "honorable lifestyle" beckons for a transformation of the community's biases. Indeed, because James's world typically correlates elevated honor with elevated power and privilege, what he prioritizes by way of shared community dispositions and behaviors must have seemed bizarre. This strangeness rests in the way people are summoned to esteem those whom God esteems rather than those whom the Roman world esteems—and to act accordingly. To draw on two prominent aspects of James's message thus far, an honorable lifestyle will be displayed in engagement with those who inhabit society's fringes (1:26–27; 2:1–26) and in speech habits (1:19–21; 3:1–12).

Fourth, undergirding this honorable lifestyle, ultimately, is God's gift freely given to those who ask in faith—that is, God's wisdom, which gives birth to and nurtures gentleness. James's term for *gentleness* overlaps with the *humility*

49. See K.-W. Niebuhr 2016, 11–13; K.-W. Niebuhr 2013.

he will counsel shortly (4:6–10). In Matthew's Gospel, it characterizes the nature of Jesus's royal rule (11:29; 21:5) as well as those who "will inherit the earth," as Jesus declares in his third beatitude (5:5 CEB).[50] The virtue of gentleness stands in sharp contrast to the out-of-control, biting, venomous tongue James has just critiqued (3:1–12). Again, the gentleness of which James the ethicist writes cannot be reduced to the best human beings can muster in their relationships with each other. Rather, it is the fruit of God's gracious gift of wisdom. The proof of wisdom is an honorable lifestyle distinguished by gentleness.

[14–16] Before describing further what "the wisdom that comes down from above" is (3:17–18), James outlines what it is not. Apparently he is dismayed that some have such a misshapen view of the way things are that they fool themselves into thinking that they should be counted among the wise and learned.

Like wisdom, not-wisdom is recognized by its fruit: bitter rivalry, devious self-promotion, gloating, falsifying the truth, disorder, and every contemptible deed. Two of these—bitter rivalry and devious self-promotion—reside in the heart (3:14) *and* present themselves as behaviors (3:16). Their origins are earthly, worldly, and diabolic. Diagramming the relationships among behaviors, inclinations, and sources James seems to envision would be complicated, but this is precisely the point. Whatever is internal is externalized, and whatever is external is bonded to what is internal. James's theological anthropology is thoroughly integrated.

In James's world, the *heart* signifies the center of cognition (both intellectual and affective life), the site of commitment-making and moral formation. We therefore can think of movement from the center to its behavioral expression in community life. James presses even further. He traces misshapen dispositions to a phony wisdom that is earth-centered and earthbound (leaving no room for heavenly influence, no room for the wisdom from above), worldly (reflecting a lifeworld apart from allegiance to the Lord[51]), and diabolic (or devilish, hostile toward God and God's ways). This bogus wisdom takes root in the heart, and we recognize its influence through one's deeds.

Just as wisdom is demonstrated through the behavior it engenders (3:13), so not-wisdom is demonstrated through the behavior *it* engenders. Similarly, one's life patterns serve as a window into one's heart and, then, into the nature of the wisdom animating it, whether authentic wisdom from above or antiwisdom from below. James's penetrating gaze falls on examples of conduct promoting community disharmony. In part, these examples follow from the

---

50. Cf. the noun *prautēs* in Jas 3:13 and the adjective *praus* in Matt 5:5.

51. Recall that *lifeworld* refers to the world as a people understand and experience it, their shared values and practices shaped and transmitted through successive generations, typically at a preconscious level; see above, on 1:26–27.

nature of the world that he and his audience inhabit, known as it was for its agonistic character, with people engaged in an ongoing struggle to maintain or advance their social positions and social power. James's interest in these behaviors was announced earlier, in his remarks about status-seeking and politicking for position (2:2–4), as well as boasting (a sign of an uncontrollable tongue, 3:5).[52] He has spoken of disorder, too, when characterizing those who, lacking faith, cannot receive God's wisdom (1:5–8), and when describing the perilous tongue (3:8). The new addition here would be "falsifying the truth" (3:14). This contrasts with the honorable way of life that distinguishes the wise and learned (3:13). And this, together with James's phrasing,[53] suggests that he is interested not only in those who tell lies but also, indeed, in those whose whole way of life falsifies what is true. That is, he draws negative attention to those who claim they are wise and learned when, in fact, their lives are enmeshed in a bogus wisdom set against the true wisdom from above. James's final reference to "every contemptible deed" speaks to the open-ended nature of his list of telltale behaviors. Many other patterns of conduct, too, contradict the honorable way of life born of God's gracious gift of wisdom.

[17–18] The contrast between the way of bogus wisdom (3:14–16) and the way of wisdom is unmistakable. James plainly observes that his interest centers not only on such and such behaviors, however, but especially on the source of that behavior. Is it an antiwisdom grounded in what is "earthy, worldly, diabolic," or is it "the wisdom that comes down from above"? The virtue tradition might emphasize human practices that facilitate the formation of the virtues, but this is not the approach James takes. In an ultimate sense for James, the way of wisdom does not depend on human ingenuity or vision or effort. Wisdom is not the result of self-mastery. Instead, James insists that, whatever else it is, a virtuous life is first the consequence of a divine gift. For him, recipients of God's wisdom are marked by an ongoing way of life expressed in characteristic sensibilities and behaviors. The "wise and learned" (3:13) act not out of a sense of duty or commitment to social norms, but because they are becoming and have become wise people.[54] Put sharply, the virtues James enumerates would not be the cause of a community's moral excellence, but the effect of God's gracious gift, welcomed and put into play in day-to-day life.

James's lists of vices and virtues (3:14–17) are reminiscent of similar lists in the literature of the ancient Mediterranean, including the NT.[55] They might

---

52. James 3:5 uses the term *aucheō* (I boast), whereas 3:14 reads the more complex form, *katakauchaomi* (I boast against / gloat over [someone]). Either way, claims of superiority are in view.

53. James writes of "falsifying the truth" (*pseudesthe kata tēs alētheias*) in 3:14 rather than simply "lying" (*pseudesthe*).

54. See J. Wilson 2011, 812.

55. In the NT, e.g., 2 Cor 12:20–21; Gal 5:19–23; Eph 4:31–5:5; 1 Pet 3:8; 4:3. For a helpful discussion of this tradition, see Downs 2011.

perform a range of functions, though for James they target community formation and harmony. His letter sets vices and virtues side-by-side as a means of
identifying who is genuinely wise versus those whose lives exhibit antiwisdom.
Recalling his earlier words—"My brothers and sisters, can a fig tree produce
olives or a grapevine figs?" (3:12)—we have good reason to say that James
tells us less what wisdom and antiwisdom *are* and more what wisdom and
antiwisdom *generate*.

If pseudowisdom cultivates conduct detrimental to community life, the
opposite must be said of God's wisdom. Note how James's description of
genuine wisdom is tied to concerns expressed across the first three chapters
of his letter. For example, his lengthy introduction reaches its climax in references to "pure and unsullied" devotion and to keeping ourselves "from being
contaminated by the world" (1:27), and now he declares that the wisdom from
above is "first pure" (3:17). James lifts up mercy (2:13) and now identifies wisdom as "full of mercy" (3:17). He is on the offensive against words and deeds
of favoritism (2:1–13), and now he speaks of wisdom as "lacking partiality"
(3:17). And he writes explicitly of the double-minded (1:7–8) and implicitly of
those who are double-tongued (3:5b–10), insisting that wisdom is not "double-
faced" (3:17).[56] We see, then, that his choice of words to describe wisdom's
effects is very much tied to the community-centered circumstances motivat-
ing this letter. Evidently James is building a case against the life patterns on
display among at least some of his readers and hearers while, at the same time,
sketching a mural of what their communal patterns could and ought to be.
And in this context we should recall the interpretive lens James has provided
for understanding those patterns: allegiance to the Lord Jesus, with our faith
modeled on his (1:1; 2:1). Pushing further, we note how James the theologian-
ethicist highlights patterns of thinking, feeling, believing, and behaving that
work themselves out relationally. He names *social* virtues. True, his audience
of Jewish messianists must carve out the nature of allegiance to the Lord Jesus
in a world largely defined by Rome. Also true, James's audience must do so in
ways that bring to life *these* dispositions, *these* virtues. The outcome would be
a community of people—not only an individual here, another there—reflecting in that world "the wisdom that comes down from above." Accordingly,
we can say that what James describes is a gift from God, modeled after Jesus,
perfected (or habituated) in communal life.

We find a close parallel in Paul, who contrasts deeds of "the flesh" and the
"fruit of the Spirit" (Gal 5:19–23 NRSV). Comparison with Paul at this point
is telling, first, because both Paul and James trigger an organic (rather than a
mechanized) frame. Paul emphasizes love and James stresses purity without

---

56. *Anypokritos*, meaning "sincere/lacking deceit or fraud."

reference to inner self versus outer conduct, without a hint of linking disparate pieces together to assemble a "product." Instead, like fresh water from a freshwater spring, like olives from an olive tree, the virtuous life flows from God's intervention in our lives. Second, we see parallels between Paul's emphasis on the work of the Holy Spirit and James's on the work of divine wisdom. This, together with the personification of wisdom in Jewish literature (e.g., Prov 8), supports the view that James portrays wisdom—that is, God's presence to promote human thriving within and among God's people (cf. Jas 1:2–27)—in a way analogous to Paul's portrayal of the Spirit.[57] Third, Paul refers to the fruit (not fruits) of the Spirit and places *love* in the initial position, identifying it as a heading for the rest and implying that the others (joy, peace, patience, and so on) are extensions of love. Similarly, James names *purity* first, as though it were the key to the rest.[58] Yet this does not mean that James, in comparison with Paul, has decentered love. How could it, given James's prior, emphatic appeal to the royal law, the double command, of love (ch. 2)? Instead, in a way consistent with James's message more generally, he characterizes "wisdom that comes down from above" as uncontaminated by the ways of a world system out of step with God's agenda, wholeheartedly living in allegiance to the Lord Jesus, marked by a thoroughgoing integrity. This purity correlates with life-giving sensibilities and behavior that promote human flourishing and community (see above, on 1:19–27; cf. Prov 3:13–35).

Words in lists are often known best by the company they keep, and resist. *Purity*, then, would be the antithesis of "bitter rivalry and devious self-promotion," which trace their origins to what is "earthly, worldly, diabolic" (3:13–15). And *purity* would be further described by the series of virtues that follow, all of which promote community well-being:[59]

- "Pure, then peaceable." James used the closely associated term, *peace*, in 2:16, with a view toward thriving, well-being, happiness, prosperity, and good health. Here it contrasts with such community-corrupting behaviors as rivalry and disorder (3:14–16).
- "Pure, then . . . gentle"—or *considerate* or *gracious*, a term that finds a place in other NT virtue lists (1 Tim 3:3; Titus 2:2; cf. Phil 4:5; 1 Pet 2:18). For James, *gentleness* overlaps with the *humility*

57. On this correlation of Wisdom and the Holy Spirit, see Kirk 1969. More broadly, see Levison 1997.

58. Adamson 1976, 154.

59. James's impressive skill as a writer is on display in 3:17. The first three qualities are associated through alliteration: *epeita*, "then," followed by *eirēnikē*, *epeikēs*, *eupeithēs*, "peaceable, gentle, leadable." The second set shares the coordinating conjunction *kai*: "full of mercy *and* good fruits." The final two virtues share both a prefix (*a-*, alpha privative, negation) and suffix (*-kritos*, "judging/choosing"): *adiakritos*, *anypokritos*, "lacking partiality, not double-faced."

he will counsel shortly (Jas 4:6–10) and contrasts sharply with the out-of-control, biting, venomous tongue he has just critiqued (3:1–12).

- "Pure, then . . . leadable." Capturing the best sense of this word is difficult, given its rarity in the Greek Bible. The term qualifies a person as willing to listen, persuadable, ready to follow,[60] and so the opposite of being obstinate, arrogant, and unruly.
- "Pure, then . . . full of mercy and good fruits." James recalls his earlier counsel, where he extolled the virtue of mercy over judgment (2:1–13) and the necessity of faithful deeds (and not faith alone; 2:14–26). By evoking that earlier instruction, he lumps inhospitality and ungraciousness toward the needy together with the disorder and contemptible deeds that damage communities of God's people (3:16) and calls for their opposite.
- "Pure, then . . . lacking partiality." James captures the spirit of his earlier instruction regarding favoritism in a single word and so undermines the Roman practice of deferring to society's rich and elevated at the expense of the degraded poor. Such practices counter the faith of the Lord Jesus (2:1–13). Favoritism—and with it, "bitter rivalry and devious self-promotion" (3:14)—may be thoroughly conventional, expected, and assumed in the Roman world, but they have no place within and among Christ-followers, whose way of life flows out of God's gracious gift of wisdom.
- "Pure, then . . . not double-faced." The opposite of deceit, *not double-faced* labels what is genuine, sincere, authentic. Basically, *double-faced* signifies behaviors that camouflage God's character and ways.[61] For James, the wisdom that is pure accomplishes what human beings cannot accomplish on their own, namely, taming the tongue, so that blessing and cursing do not come from the same treacherous mouth (3:7–12). It is not double-minded and unstable (1:7–8) and it does not falsify the truth (3:14).

These last two adjectives describe what wisdom is not, speaking directly to the way the wisdom from above negates the pseudowisdom that merits the adjectives *earthly*, *worldly*, and *diabolic* (3:15). What is needed is the wisdom that God gives without reservation, the wisdom that results in maturity and wholeness (1:2–8), the wisdom that promotes "pure and unsullied devotion,"

---

60. See MGS 859; L&N §33.305; *CGL* 1:625. The adjective *eupeithēs* appears in the Greek Bible only here, but the noun *eupeitheia* (ready obedience) is found in 4 Macc 5:16; 9:2; 12:6; 15:9.
61. In the NT, see Rom 12:9; 2 Cor 6:6; 1 Tim 1:5; 2 Tim 1:5; 1 Pet 1:22. See Green 2011.

aid to "orphans and widows in their trouble and suffering," and keeping "our-selves from being contaminated by the world" (1:27).

James's closing statement is transitional: "Those who make peace sow the fruit of justice peaceably" (3:18). Our author has mapped the way of wisdom in terms of social virtues that cultivate and sustain community health (3:13–18). Next, he will pivot so quickly that his audience might suffer whiplash. He turns instantly to an assessment of the reality among those who receive this letter—not peaceful integrity and thriving community but conflict, craving, disputes, and fighting (4:1–3). Mapping the way of wisdom as he has, over against the way of antiwisdom, he also prepares for this most basic dichotomy: friendship with God versus friendship with the world (4:4).[62]

James's précis is marked by a proverbial brevity that requires unpacking. First, he riffs on Jesus's words: "Happy are people who make peace" (Matt 5:9 CEB).[63] The reference to "happy" fits well within James's message, provided we recall that happiness is not a fleeting response to one's good fortune but a pronouncement of communal well-being over lives lived before God (see Ps 1).[64] Adapting Jesus's words to his concerns, James insists that the messianic communities to whom he writes not only ought to do the things that support community well-being, but they should also do so in peaceful ways. Could he make his case against rage, duplicity, favoritism, neglect, intrigue, conceit, rivalry, and other such evils any plainer (see Jas 1:19–20; 2:1–17; 3:1–16)? Second, having earlier claimed that "anger does not produce God's righteousness" (1:20), he now declares that peacemaking does. Of course, one sows seeds, not the harvest of fruit, so James's reference to sowing the fruit of justice may sound strange to us. This is a case of compression, where an entire process (think: "We went to town" or "I got a job") is linguistically reduced to a single moment. Compression supports efficient communication, but only if we decompress. What does this process entail? What is involved in peace-ably sowing the seeds of justice? Decompressing: this is exactly what James has been doing in his letter thus far, and will continue to do, as he beckons God's people to conform their commitments and deeds with Jesus's faith and therefore with respect to God's choice of the poor, doing so with practices, including speech habits, congruent with love of God and love of neighbor. *This* is peaceably sowing the seeds of justice.

---

62. James's thought world is thus reminiscent of the prayer for understanding and wisdom that leads to friendship with God, which is more desirable than authority or status or wealth (Wis 7:7–14).

63. Matthew 5:9 uses *oi eirēnopoioi* (the peacemakers); Jas 3:18 has *tois poiousin eirēnēn* (those who make peace). Cf. Acts 7:26: *synēllassen autous eis eirēnē* (he "tried to make peace between them," NETS); Col 1:20: *eirēnopoiēsas* ("making peace").

64. See above, on 1:2–4.

4:1–10 Countering Contentious Cravings with Humility

4:1 What is the source of conflicts and skirmishes among you? Do they not arise from your cravings that war within you? 2 You crave something you do not have, you commit murder,[a] and you hunger for something you cannot attain. You struggle and fight. You do not have because you do not ask. 3 You ask and do not receive because you ask with bad intentions, namely, to indulge your cravings.

4 Adulterers![b] Do you not know that friendship with the world means enmity with God? Those who want to be a friend of the world set themselves up[c] as an enemy of God.

5 Or do you suppose Scripture is pointless when it says that the life[d] God establishes in us craves jealously,[e] 6 but God gives us more grace—that is,[f] when it says, "God resists the proud but gives grace to the humble."

7 Therefore, submit to God. Resist the devil and he will run from you. 8 Come near to God, and he will come near to you. Sinners, cleanse your hands! You double-minded, purify your hearts! 9 Lament, grieve, and weep. Let your laughter be turned into grief and your joy into gloom. 10 Humble yourselves before the Lord, and he will lift you up.

a. I have translated *phoneuete* (to murder) as one among a series (with each verb in the present active indicative), though it is also possible to read *murder* more explicitly as the consequence of craving (e.g., CEB, NIV, and NRSV).

b. *Moichalis* could be translated as *You unfaithful people!* (e.g., CEB) since it is used figuratively here. I have kept the more prosaic reference to *adulterers* in order to make more obvious the connection to prophetic references like Hos 3.

c. *Kathistatai*—My translation attempts to account for the parallel with 3:6: "The tongue is the world of wickedness *set* [*kathistatai*] among the parts of our body."

d. Or *life force*. *Pneuma* could also be translated as *spirit*, though in popular Western thought today this might lead one to imagine that James is working with a dualistic (body/soul) or trichotomic (body, soul, spirit) understanding of the human person. For the traditional, Heb. understanding of the person as an undifferentiated unity, see, e.g., Wolff 1974. See above, on 2:26.

e. The sense of 4:5–6 is much discussed, with a range of translation options dependent on a series of ambiguities. These are efficiently reviewed in Bauckham 2004, 271–77. (Bauckham's own proposal—"The Spirit of God in us loathes envy," which, on his hypothesis, derives from the lost apocryphal book of Eldad and Modad [2004, 277–81; cf. Allison 2013, 617–22]—is inviting but problematic since it depends on a mistranslation of an assumed Heb. source rather than on the Gk. text we have before us.) Having been influenced by McKnight (2011, 335–44) and Carpenter (2000), my translation takes its cue from the duplication of *legei* (what "the Scripture . . . says . . . says") and takes seriously both the role this material plays in James's rhetoric and the parallel between Jas 4:5–6a (an interpretive gloss on Prov 3:34) and 4:6b (a citation of Prov 3:34).

f. *Dio* is inferential, a marker of result. My translation attempts to draw out the importance of what precedes as an interpretation of the scriptural text James now cites.

The present passage is the third of a four-part section in 3:1–4:12 and concerns itself generally with the need for theological and moral reformation. Speech practices and end-time judgment bracket the section as a whole (3:1–12; 4:11–12). These opening and closing subsections underscore the necessity of deep change, though without detailing what transformation might mean or how it would be possible. The two middle segments (3:13–18; 4:1–10) take up the challenge of sketching that needed reformation. Overall, the shape of James's presentation in this larger section portrays the tightly woven relationship shared by patterns of allegiance and habits of behavior.

James has just outlined two paths, each marked by a kind of wisdom (or antiwisdom) and the way of life it engenders (3:13–18). Now he contrasts two ways of life, the one marked by pride, the other by humility; the one expressed in the language of hostility toward others and toward God, the other in the language of submission toward God (4:1–10). His argument comes with the implication that submission to God, rather than to one's cravings, will lead to communal well-being and flourishing among his audience of Christ-followers.

Excursus: Humility as the Central Virtue

As we interact with James's message concerning *pride* and *humility*, we ought to attend to James's dictionary, so to speak, rather than assume that James participates in the usage of certain key terms common in our contemporary communities. This means that we need to follow his argument rather than imagine that words like pride and humility are containers of meaning applying in every circumstance. Accordingly, for James, *pridefulness* simply must not be confused with modern notions of confidence or positive self-esteem, for example, nor with a healthy appreciation of one's self-worth or the feeling one has while watching one's child perform well in a ballet. Nor should we confuse James's imperative concerning *humility before God* and *submission to God* with historical demands that people (typically "others," like women or indigenous people, for example) submit to other human beings and their institutions.

Pride, for James, is associated with allowing one's cravings to rule. According to 4:1–10, pride manifests itself in all manner of interpersonal and social fighting, in idolatry, in solidarity with world systems set against God, and indeed in harmony with the devil, who opposes God.[65] *Humility* is pride's opposite, so it calls for submitting to God rather than to one's cravings. This submission is marked by purity in one's undivided allegiance to the Lord and concern for divine approval rather than acclaim according to a world system that privileges the powerful and wealthy.

---

65. Note the parallel in 4:6–7: God resists (*antitassō*) the proud, and James calls his readers and hearers to resist (*anthistēmi*) the devil. See L&N §39.1.

Outside biblical usage, the terminology for *one who is humble (tapeinos)* or *humility (tapeinōsis)* is generally negative.[66] Closely related words like *ignoble, contemptible, ignominious*, and *base* come to mind, as do *servile, sycophantic*, or *slavish*. Influenced by Israel's Scriptures and later Jewish texts, however, some NT writings and later Christian theologians counted *humility* among the virtues. In Mary's Song, for example, Mary declares that God "has looked with favor on the lowly state *[tapeinōsis]* of his servant," and that God "lifts up the lowly *[tapeinos]*" (Luke 1:48, 52 NRSVue). Reflecting on Mary's words, Origen later proclaimed that, "in the Scriptures, humility is declared to be one of the virtues."[67] Origen's interpretive move rejected the possibility that the negative connotations of *humble* or *lowly state*, like lewdness or depravity, might apply to Mary. Instead, she is a model of virtue. In a celebrated passage, Paul interprets *humility* christologically: "Found in appearance as a human, [Christ] humbled *[tapeinoō]* himself. . . . Therefore God exalted him even more highly" (Phil 2:7–9 NRSVue). Following this train of thought and using his topsy-turvy notion of the way things really are, James takes a term more probably at home in a smear campaign and uses it positively to distinguish genuine Christ-followers.[68] James's thought at this point is familiar from his earlier claims, such as we read in Jas 1:9: "Brothers and sisters who are of low status should express confidence concerning their high status"; and in 2:5: "Has God not chosen the poor according to worldly standards to be rich in terms of faith, and to be heirs of the kingdom he has promised to those who love him?"

Despite its importance in theological and ethical formation, the language of *humility* has been and remains vulnerable to abuse.[69] I have already alluded to one reason for this: the ease with which those in power are able to exercise control over others by calling them to be "Christlike" in their selflessness. "*We* will demonstrate to the world the victorious Christ," we can almost hear them say, "while *you* model Christ the humble servant." Second, humility can take the form of self-humiliation or self-degradation, or a pathological self-denial that minimizes or altogether negates what James has already made crystal clear: the dignity that accompanies the godlikeness all human beings share (3:9–10). Third, given the way James extols the virtue of humility, some might approach his instruction in transactional terms, duping themselves into imagining that humility is the ticket to prosperity and power. (After all, does James not say that the Lord will lift up those who humble themselves [4:10]?) This is antihumility, however, and it flows from the same craving for power and privilege that genuine humility counters. Perhaps more to the point, though, is the reality that humbling oneself before the Lord entails

---

66. See Grundmann 1974, 8:1–5; *TLNT* 3:369–71; Feldmeier 2014, 61–62; Becker 2020, 23–29.

67. Origen 20 (*Hom. Luc.* 8.4). Origen thus situates Mary's humility in relation to the four cardinal virtues of classical antiquity: justice, temperance (self-control), fortitude (courage), and wisdom. On scriptural antecedents to Mary's declaration, see, e.g., 1 Sam 2:7–8; Ps 113:7–8. On the language of humility in the LXX and NT, see Grundmann 1974, 8:6–26.

68. James can do this because of a long record of extolling the virtue of humility in Israel's Scriptures (e.g., Pss 18:27; 25:9; 149:4), including the tradition concerning the humble as the object of divine favor (e.g., Prov 3:34; see also, e.g., Luke 14:11; 18:14; 1 Pet 3:8–9; 5:5–6); and the example of Jesus (Phil 2:1–11; cf. 1 Pet 2:21–25).

69. Similarly, see Feldmeier 2014, 64–65. On the theological tradition more broadly, see Becker 2020, 29–50.

embracing God's valuation of others and of oneself. This means that, when God lifts up the humble, their raised-up status need not (and generally does not) map onto society's conventional roles at all. Pointedly, the humility James (and, with him, the rest of the NT) counsels has nothing to do with these kinds of misconceptions and abuses.

James's attention centers on conformity to God's character and mission rather than on canons of approval that mimic the norms of a wayward lifeworld or world system. James is concerned with people who, left to their own devices, war with each other in order to grasp at higher social standing and wealth. They step on and over each other in order to be counted among the high and mighty. The remedy James offers for such errant dispositions and behaviors is humility, together with God's gracious empowerment, with the result that one is raised up, yes, but in God's eyes rather than in the eyes of an idolatrous world.

[4:1–3] Those who approach James as a thematically integrated letter rather than a more-or-less haphazard collection of proverbs may experience a strong jolt here. Remembering that James is not himself responsible for dividing his writing into chapters and verses, we can see how abruptly, but adroitly, he pivots between peaceable peacemaking and combative warmongering (3:18 → 4:1). As in 3:13, he now begins a new section with a question that introduces his theme: "What is the source of conflicts and skirmishes among you?" In this first paragraph (4:1–3), he diagnoses the situation of his hearers and readers.

In the Greco-Roman world, *war* is the opposite of *peace*, and the intensity of this contrast is not lost when we account for the more textured notion of *peace* as *community thriving and well-being* characteristic of Israel's Scriptures and early Christian writings.[70] In fact, as James opens this portion of his letter, he uses militaristic terminology at home in the classical Greek and Roman worlds of prodigious battles and legendary wars:

War, combat, conflict	*polemos*	4:1
Clash, combat, skirmish	*machē*	4:1, 2
I serve as a soldier, I wage war	*strateuō*	4:1
I commit murder, I kill	*phoneuō*	4:2
I wage war, I battle	*polemeō*	4:2

James's language is obviously metaphoric, but this does not soften the harsh reality he describes. True, he does not concern himself with javelins and spears,

70. See above, on 2:16.

shields and helmets, or siege engines and catapults. But he remains concerned with violent intentions, aggressive acts, and by implication the ensuing devastation and chaos. Metaphors are not merely linguistic ornamentation. Rather, we use metaphors every day to conceptualize abstract concepts in light of our embodied experience. In this case, COLLECTIVE LIFE IS WARFARE, with human beings joining the rest of the animal world as they fight for what they want. Note, however, that James does not require readers to grasp community life in terms of the warfare metaphor. That is, social or community life need not be conceptualized in warmongering terms. He describes what is, not what should or must be. (Indeed, we can almost hear him say: "My brothers and sisters, things should not be this way!" [3:10b].) Nor does the community life he imagines and condemns resemble warfare in every way. For example, he does not identify battle lines carefully, nor does he inventory the armaments deployed in this combat. Instead, his militaristic metaphors characterize the ugliness of the situation he envisions and press his audience to acknowledge their urgent need for transformed patterns of life. With these metaphors and in no uncertain terms, he traces the profound distance between the way of wisdom he has just outlined (3:13: "an honorable way of life distinguished by the gentleness that comes from wisdom"; 3:17: "first pure, then peaceable, gentle, leadable, full of mercy and good fruits, lacking partiality, not double-faced") and the way of pseudowisdom (3:14: "bitter rivalry and devious self-promotion") now on display in messianic communities that, everyone must surely admit, are contaminated by worldly ways (cf. 1:27).

Among the list of militaristic words James uses (charted above), one is not like the others: murder. Including *murder* alongside *conflicts* and *war* may hint that it too carries a metaphorical sense in this context, but this need not be the case. Recall that, elsewhere in the letter, *murder* is tied to God's Instructions (or Torah; Jas 2:11).[71] Also recall that James accuses his readers and hearers of withholding wages from field-workers (5:4), condemning and murdering the righteous one (5:6), and speaking words of blessing over the hungry and naked without lifting a finger to care for their bodily needs (2:15–16). According to the second-century-BCE Jewish book of Sirach, one of James's influences, such actions are tantamount to murder: "The needy person's bread means life for that poor person; whoever withholds it is a murderer. Whoever takes away a neighbor's living commits murder, and whoever deprives a worker of wages sheds blood" (Sir 34:25–27 CEB). The way James links craving or envy with murder is likewise foreshadowed in the second-century-BCE work Testament of the Twelve Patriarchs: "Envy dominates a person's whole mind and lets him neither eat nor drink nor do anything that is good. It is continually suggesting to

71. See Exod 20:13; Deut 5:17 NRSV, "You shall not murder [*phoneuō*, 5:18 LXX]"; see above on Jas 2:8–11.

him that he should kill the person that is envied."[72] Although we might like to think that, among God's people, acts of murder would be unthinkable, James's language leaves the door open to even this form of violence as an expression of his audience's darkest cravings.

James first inquires into the source of "conflicts and skirmishes among you" (4:1a), then provides his own answer in the form of a question that presumes a positive response (4:1b): "Do they not . . . ?" In other words, James the prophet forecloses actual consideration of his opening question, as though daring his readers and hearers to challenge his assessment.[73] His diagnosis is a given, the baseline from which discussion can now proceed. James puts his finger on the cause of these battles with an array of related terms:

Craving, desire	*hēdonē*	4:1, 3
I crave, I strongly desire, I long for	*epithymeō*	4:2
I hunger, I strive after, I covet, I "experience strong envy and resentment"[74]	*zēloō*	4:2

In moral discourse generally, and certainly in James's moral dictionary, these terms all carry the negative sense of evil desire.[75] Earlier, he developed a chain of effects that shows how the human condition unravels from its penchant for evil (1:14–15):

$$\text{cravings} \rightarrow \text{temptation} \rightarrow \text{sin} \rightarrow \text{death}$$

Behind combative dispositions and practices, behind an atmosphere heavy with violence, stands the human bent toward evil. In support of this claim, James enters into evidence Exhibit A: the communal lives of his audience. Have their cravings not given birth to temptation, has not temptation grown into sin, has not sin matured into death?

James's message turns on what one does not have, what one cannot attain, and what one cannot receive—phrases woven together with the language of conflict and, perhaps surprisingly, with the language of prayer (4:2–3). He indicts his audience for the struggles that arise from their sense that the only way to get what one must have is to seize what others already have. This is wrong thinking, James insists. It assumes both earthbound ways of measuring what it means to flourish in this world and the utility of human beings in providing for their own overall personal and communal health. James's alternative is

---

72. T. Sim. 3.2–3 (ET: DeSilva 2012, 231). See DeSilva 68–70, 230–32. Cf. Gen 4:3–8.
73. Dupriez (1991, 370) explains a rhetorical question in these terms.
74. L&N §88.163.
75. See above, on 1:12–18.

as simple as it is profound. One needs instead, and only, to ask, with God as the implied object of one's request. "You do not have because you do not ask" (4:2). We might think immediately of the Jesus tradition: "Ask, and it will be given to you" (Matt 7:7; Luke 11:9 NRSV; cf. Mark 11:24). Clearly, though, this is not a carte blanche promise, as the Jesus tradition already implies. For example, Jesus seems to put some parameters around what God gives in response to prayer in the way he concludes an extended discussion of prayer: "If you, then, who are evil, know how to give good gifts to your children, how much more will the heavenly Father give the Holy Spirit to those who ask him!" (Luke 11:13 NRSV)—or, in Matthew's version: "How much more will your Father in heaven give good things to those who ask him!" (7:11 NRSV). James's approach is different though the idea is complementary: "You ask," yes, but your prayer comes from a place of "bad intentions." And those bad intentions are named: "to indulge your cravings" (4:3). Evidently, James has in mind that some are imploring God to provide them with prosperity, power, and privilege—ignoring the fact that these are not divine gifts, "from above," but instead reflect their association with what is earthly, worldly, and diabolic (3:13–18). To borrow imagery from 3:11–12, such prayers are like someone standing before a fig tree and demanding olives.

Closer to home than the Jesus tradition are the opening words of this letter. First, James identifies a process of maturity that begins with trials and ends in the greatest happiness (1:2–4). The lives of Christ-followers scattered throughout the world may encounter struggles, but these are formative, cultivating human maturity, integrity, flourishing. Second, he admits that the wherewithal for this kind of happiness might be lacking (1:5–8). This one possible deficit is wisdom: the capacity to understand and to act faithfully. Praying for wisdom, though, is so tied to God's character that those whose lives are in harmony with God receive what they ask for, whereas those whose lives are out of step with God receive nothing. God "gives to everyone without a second thought, without reservation" (1:5), yet the request must arise from single-minded allegiance to the Lord. Entrusting oneself to God's magnanimity entails a commitment to act in line with and on the basis of God's wisdom. Alternatives like wavering loyalty, double-mindedness, and instability—these are out of bounds. Skillfully, then, James ties his present analysis of his battle-minded audience to his introductory invitation to the process of human maturation and thriving, while at the same time demonstrating for the actual situation of combative messianic communities the immediate significance of that earlier invitation.

[4] James expands his portrait of interpersonal conflicts and battles among Christ-followers so that it includes conflict even with God. This is not surprising, given the direction his preceding comments on prayer took (4:2–3). If requests are being made, they are wicked insofar as they flow from human

cravings and not from allegiance to the Lord. James's opening charge is explosive: "Adulterers!" The term recalls Hos 3, where the Lord directs the prophet to take an adulteress as his wife as a sign of Israel's idolatry.[76] James sees how alleged Christ-followers chase after a substitute god, "the world." So they earn from him the scarlet letter of idolatry. Moreover, far from being God's friends, they have set themselves apart by their hostility to God as God's adversaries.

The force of James's analysis derives in large part from Greco-Roman notions of *friendship*. As Cicero (first century BCE) put it, "Friendship is nothing other than agreement in all matters, divine and human, joined with goodwill and affection."[77] In Roman moral philosophy, friendship referred to a level of agreement, solidarity, and allegiance that would disallow the idea that one could maintain union with these opposites, the world and God. Jesus's proverbial words in Luke 16 may come to mind: "No slave can serve two masters; for a slave will either hate the one and love the other, or be devoted to the one and despise the other" (Luke 16:13 NRSV). A parallel aphorism appears in 1 John: "If anyone loves the world, the love of the Father is not in them" (1 John 2:15 CEB). Our understanding of James's negative assessment of the world is predicated on our reminding ourselves that *world* (*kosmos*) does not for him refer to the world God created or to the creatures that inhabit it.[78] As we read James, we might think more accurately of the philosophical term "lifeworld": the complex web of taken-for-granted ideals, traditions, and habits shared by a people; the world as they understand and experience it, generally at a prereflective level. James's *world* therefore refers to shared, taken-for-granted perceptions of the way the world is and the way the world works. For him, then, friends of the world have calibrated their moral and relational compasses not on the true north of God's character and mission; through worldly interference, the compass needle points the wrong way. Friends of the world are not aligned with the revered Abraham, "God's friend" (Jas 2:23), for they are known more for their discriminatory attitudes, their pandering to the privileged, and their hunger to be counted among the community's elite than for their Abraham-like hospitality—yet in doing so injuring their own communities. The picture James paints is like Luke's mural depicting Jesus's warning to his followers: "Watch out for the legal experts. They like to walk around in long robes. They love being greeted with honor in the markets. They long for the places of honor in the synagogues and at banquets. They are the ones who cheat widows out of their homes, and to show off they say long prayers. They will be judged most

---

76. Cf. Ezek 23:45; Mal 3:5. According to Matthew's Gospel, Jesus used similar language when describing his interlocutors: "An evil and adulterous generation" (Matt 12:39; 16:4; cf. Mark 8:38).

77. Cicero, *Amic.* 20; ET in Williams 2012, 4. In addition to Williams, see, e.g., Konstan 1997.

78. In addition to 4:4, James uses the term *kosmos* in 1:27; 2:5; 3:6. Concerning James's negative evaluation of the world, cf. 2 Tim 4:10; 1 John 2:15.

harshly" (Luke 20:46–47 CEB). Friends of the world have chosen against the God who has chosen the degraded and impoverished (Jas 2:5).

[5–6] Although what James writes is difficult to unravel linguistically,[79] his aim is clear: He appeals to Israel's Scriptures to bolster his message. In doing so, he calls on his readers for a judgment about the theological soundness of Scripture. Imagine a question about the meaningfulness of Scripture in light of Isaiah's witness:

> My plans aren't your plans,
> > nor are your ways my ways, says the LORD.
> Just as the heavens are higher than the earth,
> > so are my ways higher than your ways,
> > and my plans than your plans.
> Just as the rain and the snow come down from the sky
> > and don't return there without watering the earth,
> > making it conceive and yield plants
> > and providing seed to the sower and food to the eater,
> so is my word that comes from my mouth;
> > it does not return to me empty.
> > Instead, it does what I want,
> > and accomplishes what I intend. (Isa 55:8–11 CEB)

This scriptural text underscores, on the one hand, the distance between the ways of "the world" (using James's language) and the ways of the Lord; and, on the other hand, the vitality, potency, and efficacy of God's word. Given the nature of his presumed audience of scattered Jewish messianists, James thus strongly reinforces his message even before he actually cites Scripture.

What does Scripture say? James gives two versions, the first comprising his contextualization of the scriptural text for his instruction, the second the text itself.

> (4:5–6a) James's contextual appropriation of Prov 3:34:
> "It says that the life God establishes in us craves jealously,
> > but God gives us more grace."
> (4:6b) Quotation of Prov 3:34:[80]
> "that is, when it says, 'God resists the proud
> > but gives grace to the humble.'"

James's letter echoes Prov 3 in many ways—for example, in its references to genuine happiness and well-being (Jas 1:2, 12; Prov 3:2, 13, 33), its pairing

---

79. See the translation above and esp. translation note e.
80. James's citation follows the LXX, though the LXX has "Lord" (*kyrios*) where James reads "God" (*theos*).

of wisdom and understanding (Jas 3:13; Prov 3:13, 19), its interest in speech and wealth (Jas 1:22–27; 2:1–17; 3:1–12; et al.; Prov 3:9–10, 14–16, 27–31), the way it privileges peace (Jas 3:17–18; Prov 3:17), and the way it eschews craving and violence (Jas 4:1–4; Prov 3:29, 31–33). Importantly, Prov 3 posits the Lord, and not human resourcefulness, as the basis of honor and well-being for the faithful. Moreover, James is working more broadly with an interest in the Two Ways for which this section of the book of Proverbs is known, with both Proverbs and James evidencing the strongest possible bias in favor of the Way of Wisdom.

James's own priorities recall the way the concluding section of Prov 3 draws a sharp line between divine approval of the wise and virtuous, and divine disapproval of people variously described as devious, wicked, violent, foolish, and, of course, prideful (3:33–35). James's gloss associates *the proud* with those who *crave jealously*—that is, those caught up in rivalry and devious self-promotion (Jas 3:14–16), those who are mastered by their cravings (4:1–3). That God "resists the proud" extends James's prior assertion that those who befriend the world set themselves up in opposition to God (4:4). James the sage has prepared for our proverb's interest in divine approval of the humble by means of his earlier reference to "an honorable way of life distinguished by the gentleness that comes from wisdom" (3:13; cf. 3:17). Now, James extols the virtue of humility as an antidote to arrogance and violence, indeed, as a solution to the situation of those who are called to allegiance to the Lord but are presently God's adversaries.[81]

James's reference to God's gift of "more grace," which parallels the promise of grace in Prov 3, is vital to the remedy for which he advocates. Note, first, how the letter's introductory chapter brings into focus the distance between God's gracious behavior and that of James's audience. God gives "without a second thought, without reservation" (1:5); but even when presented with the dire need of their siblings, some can only muster empty words: "Go in peace! Stay warm! Eat well!" (2:16). Second, James hints further at the magnitude of the chasm separating human and divine when he declares that God has given "us birth by means of his true word" (1:18). From God, they already have both the vocation and the wherewithal to act as God acts, but they have chosen a different way. Third, this means that God's *grace* is not simply the extension of divine favor but is itself (potentially) efficacious: it makes possible.[82] Accordingly, we see that humility remains possible because God has made it so. God's gracious gift of wisdom carries within itself what is needed to move from enmity to friendship with God, from aggression to peace, from pride to humility. James does not use conversionary or repentance-oriented language here, but he is nonetheless

---

81. See above, "Excursus: Humility as the Central Virtue."
82. See Barclay 2015, e.g., 73–74.

pressing for transformation—not a shift from one religion to another, of course, but a shift toward greater conformity and deeper allegiance to the Lord, who has called them. What this transformation looks like is already signaled by identifying *humility* over against *pride*, but James has more to say with his ensuing series of directives.

[7–10] James's negative assessment of life patterns animated by craving has been relentless, culminating in his claim that those who befriend the world set themselves up as God's adversaries (4:4). This is matched by his recognition, borrowing from Prov 3:34, that God opposes the arrogant (that is, those whose commitments and habits reflect the wider world rather than God's wisdom). Not least in light of the militaristic language permeating James's analysis thus far (Jas 4:1–3), it is not hard to see how James has extended his mural of communities of God's people warring among themselves to include their warring, too, with God. James's citation of Prov 3:34 introduces a much-needed hinge in his argument, a way out of or beyond this unseemly state of affairs: God gives grace to the humble (Jas 4:6). James now makes explicit what his audience may implicitly hear in the preceding paragraph. The way forward involves setting aside the way of self-gratification and self-promotion, turning from the violence it endorses and nourishes, and embracing the way of humility. With his introduction of *therefore* (4:7), James pivots sharply from what is to what must be. The vocabulary of repentance is absent, but the notion of a life redirection (reaching into a person's core) permeates this new subsection. In a series of ten imperatives, James explains what is needed.

Imperative 1: Submit to God (4:7a). The first and last imperatives, submit to God and humble yourselves before the Lord (4:10), frame James's instruction. This is not because these two directives are identical, though they surely overlap in meaning, but because they together drive home James's point that the fundamental crisis he names is *theological.* Yes, he depicts a social and relational and personal calamity, but it is first about God. Either it grows out of a basic misunderstanding of God's character and purpose, or it fails to see how allegiance to God entails aligning oneself with God's character and purpose. This is why the remedy is God's grace, God's wisdom. Undoubtedly, this underlying theological problem lies behind James's unyieldingly negative assessment of errant patterns of thinking, feeling, believing, and behaving that spans his teaching across this entire section (3:1–4:12). He wants to confront his audience with a mirror reflecting how they are mired in life habits that counter what they know and believe.

James's opening verb is usually rendered into English with reference to ongoing *submission* (e.g., AV, CEB, NIV), and this translation works well here. The term appears in NT household duty codes, too, though those texts are noteworthy for the ways they mitigate the ultimacy of one's submission to other humans or to human institutions. In those texts, human claims for submission must not supplant the ultimate claims of the Lord. James requires no such caveats, however, since he is uninterested in submission to other humans. In fact, he counters any suggestion that one might subordinate oneself to one's own cravings, to those of others, or to the world more generally. Accordingly, James's verb generally has to do with situating oneself properly in the recognized order of things, such as one's place in a detachment of soldiers or in a household, and acting accordingly.[83] This is important because of the way James has earlier recognized two overlapping schemas (or, we might say, two orders of things) within which he encourages faithful life in the world. These are the *household over which Jesus is Lord* and *the dominion over which Jesus exercises royal rule as the Christ* (see above, on 1:1; 2:1; cf. 2:5). To name these is also to shine the spotlight on patterns of life at home in this order of things, and those not at home. The household or dominion of Rome has its ways, but so does the Lord's household or dominion; as James has clarified in no uncertain terms, these two are not always compatible.

Imperatives 2–3: Resist the devil, and he will run from you. Come near to God, and he will come near to you (4:7b–8a). Earlier, James insisted that temptations originate in human cravings and do not derive from God or from the devil (1:12–18).[84] Now he has just restated this point: Conflicts and skirmishes among you—"Do they not arise from your cravings that war within you?" (4:1). Accordingly, this directive to resist the devil is less his attempt to lay responsibility for the ills of his audience at the feet of the devil and more his recognition that, as his readers and hearers allow their cravings to rule their lives, they have joined sides with the devil.[85] With the devil, they have become God's adversaries.

"Resist" (*anthistēmi*) has a militaristic sense, recognized in other NT texts that urge Christ-followers to adopt a defensive posture vis-à-vis the devil. "Therefore, pick up the full armor of God so that you can stand your ground [*anthistēmi*] on the evil day and after you have done everything possible to still stand" (Eph 6:13 CEB; cf. 4:27). "Like a roaring lion your adversary the devil prowls around, looking for someone to devour. Resist him [*anthistēmi*], steadfast in your faith" (1 Pet 5:8–9 NRSV).[86] This suggests that, even if the devil is not the ultimate source of temptation, he is responsible for fanning the flames of human craving. The basic sense of the Greek term *diabolos* is

---

83. *Hypotassō*. For its use in household codes, see Eph 5:21, 24; Col 3:18, 20, 22; Titus 2:9; 1 Pet 2:13, 18; 3:1, 5. Cf. Achtemeier 1996, 182. I take this and the following instances of the aorist imperative as references to an action as a single complete whole (Boas, Rijksbaron, Huitink, and de Bakker 2019, §38.30).

84. See above, on 1:2–18.

85. With different emphases, see Ellis 2019, 280; Green 2022, 302–3.

86. The extensive parallels between this material in James and 1 Pet 5:5–9 suggest that James and 1 Peter share a common tradition.

"slanderer," and this is noteworthy given James's focus on speech habits in Jas 3:1–12 (cf. 1:19–20; 4:11–12). In the NT more broadly, though, *the devil* refers to the personification or embodiment of evil characterized essentially by his opposition to God and God's ways, then also to God's people.[87] For James, this transcendent figure appears to operate indirectly, through a world system (including the commitments and behaviors characteristic of that system) set against God's agenda. Even so, James's reference removes the blinders that might support a reading of the troubles he addresses as merely human or earthly. His audience, he urges, are participants in a cosmic struggle.

The Venerable Bede, whose commentaries sometimes bring together the work of his predecessors, quotes at length "the words of the blessed Cyprian" (3rd century CE) concerning the devil's ways:

> He goes around us individually, and like an enemy besieging those shut up, he examines the walls and explores whether there might be some part of our members less firm and less trustworthy, by entrance through which a way inside may be effected. He offers to the eyes unlawful appearances and seductive pleasures, that he may destroy purity through sight; he tempts the ears by harmonious music, that he may get rid of and weaken christian [*sic*] strength by the hearing of a pleasant sound; he arouses the tongue to reviling, he urges the hand to capricious murder when it is excited by injuries; he provides unjust gains, that he may make a cheat; he piles up dangerous profits, that he may ensnare the soul by money; he promises earthly honors, that he [may] take away heavenly ones; he manifests false values, that he may steal away the true. And when he is not able to deceive secretly, he threatens clearly and openly, bringing forward the fear of violent persecution in order to overcome the servants of God; always restless and always hostile; [he is] cunning in peace, violent in persecution.[88]

Given James's interests, we might emphasize the possibility of "persecution" less than Cyprian does and highlight more how the devil "goes around us" relationally, socially, communally. Challenges to faithful living as God's faithful people scattered in the Roman world (i.e., "trials") ought to cultivate human maturity and wholeness; but craving is like a spark that, fanned by diabolic influence in the form of widely sanctioned beliefs and behaviors that oppose God's wisdom, erupts into a firestorm of sin and death (1:2–4, 12–15; cf. 5:20).

As weapons of resistance against the devil, James offers submission to God and drawing near to God. This coheres well with the larger portrait James has painted. The devil is an external influence, reinforcing and celebrating craving, with the result that God's people find themselves in solidarity with the devil. But God's influence is internal: God "chose to give us birth by means of his

---

87. E.g., Acts 10:38; Eph 6:11; 1 Tim 3:6–7; 2 Tim 2:26; 1 Pet 5:8.
88. Bede 1985, 117–18; citing Cyprian, *De zelo et livore* (*Jealousy and Envy*) 10.2–3.

true word so that we might be a kind of foretaste of what would become of everything he created" (1:18). Guided and enabled by God's wisdom, God's people orient themselves toward God and not toward what is "earthy, worldly, diabolic" (3:15). And this constitutes resistance.

Imperatives 4–5: Sinners, cleanse your hands! You double-minded, purify your hearts! (4:8bc). From the perspective of the LXX, *coming near to God* (4:8a) can suggest drawing near to God in worship and sacrifice,[89] so it is unsurprising that James moves directly from the imperative "Come near to God" to these parallel commands: Cleanse and purify.

Both terms participate in the conceptual metaphor MORALITY IS PURITY, according to which the abstract concept of moral uprightness is conceived in terms of the concrete experience of bodily cleanliness. (We came across this conceptual metaphor first in 1:19–27.) In fact, a growing literature in the neurosciences has demonstrated the psychosocial impact of bodily cleansing. As one research summary puts it: "The metaphoric notion of washing away one's sins seems to have generalized to a broader conceptualization of 'wiping the slate clean.' This allows people to remove unwanted residues of the past, from threats to a moral self-view to doubts about recent decisions and worries about bad luck. . . . In sum, physical cleansing removes not only physical contaminants but also moral taints and mental residues."[90] We find this association elsewhere in Scripture, as in Isaiah's juxtaposition of cleansing with moral uprightness: "Wash yourselves; make yourselves clean; remove the evil of your doings from before my eyes; cease to do evil, learn to do good; seek justice, rescue the oppressed, defend the orphan, plead for the widow" (Isa 1:16–17 NRSV).[91] Or recall Ananias's instructions for Paul in Acts, following Paul's visionary experience on the road to Damascus: "Why delay? Get up! Have yourself baptized and your sins washed away, as you call on his name!" (Acts 22:16 AT). Note that James refers both to *hands*, metonymic for a person's behaviors; and *heart*, the locus of human cognition in ancient psychology, including volition, thinking, feeling, and desire. James identifies these aspects of the human person by way of emphasizing the total person in his call for human transformation.

James introduces his instruction regarding purification by relabeling his readers and hearers. Repeatedly in his letter, he calls them "brothers and sisters,"[92] but most recently he identifies them as "adulterers" (4:4). Now they

---

89. In Exod 19:21–22, e.g., the Lord forbids the people from coming near to God but directs that "the priests who approach God be consecrated" (NETS). Cf., e.g., Lev 21:21, 23; Isa 29:13; Ezek 40:46.

90. Lee and Schwarz 2011, 309–10.

91. See, too, the interesting parallel in 1QS 3.9–10: "And when his flesh is sprinkled with purifying water and sanctified by cleansing water, it shall be made clean by the humble submission of his soul to all the precepts of God" (ET in Vermes 1997, 101).

92. See Jas 1:2, 16, 19; 2:1, 5, 14; 3:1, 10, 12; 4:11; 5:7, 9, 10, 12, 19 (all as AT).

are "sinners" and "double-minded." Apparently he continues to regard them as "in the family," so to speak, even if their idolatry (adultery), their failure to uphold the covenant with God (as "sinners"), and their wavering between allegiance to the world and allegiance to God (as "double-minded"; see on 1:7–8) signify their distance from God—or perhaps better, their moving away from God and in the direction of death (1:15). This way of putting things encourages the view that "in" and "out" concern the direction of one's life path. Indeed, the only other occurrence of *sinner* in this letter comes in its final verse: "Whoever turns a sinner back from a stray path will rescue the sinner from death" (5:20).

James's use of the language of cleansing and purity carries with it a strong bias away from friendship with or loyalty to the world. The prevailing world system, in this reckoning, is a pollutant, and humans are normally repelled by the putrid, the unclean, the contaminated. Moreover, James's language presses in the direction of community cohesion, as opposed to the embattled community he has depicted (4:1–2). This is because humans express a high correlation between shared moral commitments and close social networks.[93] A course reversal is needed. James thus calls for "a pure community (in its internal constitution and external boundary) in the midst of a polluting, antagonistic culture."[94]

Imperatives 6–9: Lament, grieve, and weep. Let your laughter be turned into grief and your joy into gloom (4:9). Jesus's words related in Luke's Sermon on the Plain may be in the background: "Happy are you who weep now, because you will laugh" (Luke 6:21 CEB). By implication, James's audience is finding happiness at the wrong time, in the wrong things. Since "happiness" is implicated (both in antiquity and in contemporary happiness studies) in growth, integrity, and well-being,[95] it is not found through living harmoniously with a world order that encourages self-promotion and violence, while ignoring or belittling the impoverished. Yet at least some in James's audience have sought happiness in just this way. For them, James mandates lament, sorrow, mourning—the very responses associated in Israel's Scriptures with the recognition of and turning away from one's sin (e.g., Ezra 10:1–6; Joel 2:12–14).

Additionally, we might recall from the Jesus tradition a parable in Luke 18 addressed "to certain people who had convinced themselves that they were righteous and who looked on everyone else with disgust." A Pharisee uses his prayer to promote himself before God by elevating himself above "thieves, rogues, adulterers" and even the tax collector standing nearby. For his part, though, the tax collector behaves as one in mourning, pleading for God's mercy. James's own instructions echo Jesus's conclusion: "I tell you, this man went

93. See above, on Jas 1:19–27.
94. Lockett 2008, 140.
95. See above, on 1:2–4.

down to his home justified rather than the other, for all who exalt themselves will be humbled, but all who humble themselves will be exalted" (Luke 18:9–14 AT; cf. Jas 4:6, 10).

Earlier in the letter, James tied happiness to the process of maturation in the face of life's trials (1:2–4) and identified the truly happy as "those who endure testing" and therefore who "receive the garland of life God has promised to those who love him" (1:12). Clearly, the people to whom James addresses this staccato list of commands—lament, grieve, weep—are not those growing into maturity. They worship at the altar of their own cravings and violently seek to indulge their own desires. For them, the appropriate response is grief.

Imperative 10: Humble yourselves before the Lord, and he will lift you up (4:10). Ironically, James addresses Christ-followers intent on lifting themselves up. They are sufficiently contaminated by a lifeworld prioritizing status and wealth that they allow their own cravings for this kind of recognition to run unhindered. Yet to be genuinely lifted up requires a tectonic shift in perception. On the one hand, God censures and exalts. High status is not the product of human craftiness. On the other hand, God defines what it means to be exalted in topsy-turvy ways. High status is not determined by earthbound, human norms. God regards as high in status those whom others regard as degraded, marginal, lowly; those who appear well-off, God regards as of low status (1:9–10). "Has God not chosen the poor according to worldly standards to be rich in terms of faith, and to be heirs of the kingdom he has promised to those who love him?" (2:5). Clearly, to "humble yourselves before the Lord" signifies adopting the Lord's perspective on such matters and therefore aligning oneself with those whom prevailing social conventions would shove to the fringes. We thus gain a sense of how radical, how thoroughgoing, James's call for transformation is.

4:11–12 Siblingship and the Shadow of Judgment

4:11 Do not vilify each other, brothers and sisters. Whoever vilifies a brother or sister or condemns a brother or sister vilifies the law. But if you condemn the law, you are not a doer of the law but a judge over it. 12 There is one lawgiver and judge, and this one is able to rescue and to destroy. But you who condemn your neighbor, who are you?

James closes this lengthy section (3:1–4:12) with the second half of a frame, partnered with 3:1–12, concentrated on speech ethics and divine judgment. As we might anticipate for the concluding segment of this larger section of the letter, James's closing words also sound the notes of the intervening material, especially his concern with rivalry and hubris (3:13–18) and his analysis of the problems of arrogance, intramural warring for advancing one's status at the expense of others, and idolatry (4:1–10). These final words thus tie together

James's instruction, though they also make clear a progression in the charge he brings against his readers and hearers. We can trace the sequence of his thought from arrogance to assuming the role of a judge, to vilifying and condemning each other, to contravening God's Instructions (or Torah), and finally to usurping God's own throne. In the end, we might say, the hubris on which James shines the light so brightly is more than a social and relational problem, though it is certainly also that. It is a theological problem. Their hubris in fact points to their assuming for themselves the status and roles of God. Indulging "your cravings" (4:3) leads to an indictment of adultery (4:4) precisely because it results in supplanting God with oneself. This progression is short-circuited, though, if these messianists follow James's simple counsel regarding a far-reaching transformation in speech habits: "Do not vilify each other" (4:11).

Given James's uncompromising rhetoric to this point, the fact that he addresses his audience as "brothers and sisters" must feel like the warmth of the sun's rays on a brisk morning. Labeled as adulterers, sinners, and double-minded (4:4, 8), they might wonder, along with us, whether they have been written out of the messianic community. To be sure, they are on a dangerous path, as James himself makes clear when he names God (and not his audience) as rescuer and destroyer (4:12; cf. 5:20). For now, though, James embraces his audience as his brothers and sisters, inviting them, again, to embrace a single-minded allegiance to God and to the Lord Jesus Christ (cf. 1:1). Identifying them as siblings, he implicates them in a kinship that runs deeper than friend-ship, a kinship identifying those whose lives are cojoined and interdependent, who are predisposed not to concern themselves with who is superior or inferior, who refuse to condemn each other, and who practice mercy and forgiveness in the face of conflict.[96]

"Vilify" translates a word that could have the more general sense of *speak against*, but here connotes the more serious practices of *defaming* or *maligning*.[97] This nuance is recommended by the preceding material on speech ethics and warmongering, together with James's concern with those who step on and over others in their pursuit of power and privilege (3:1–12; 4:1–4). James's concern with *judgment* also requires nuance. He seems clearly to have in mind the one who sits on the raised platform at the front of a great room or hall, the dais or bema, occupied by jurists tasked with determining and pronouncing verdicts.[98] James concerns himself, then, with people who elevate themselves over others as if they were themselves holding court as jurists and passing down judgments from the bench. Though verdicts can be positive or negative, my

---

96. See the extended discussion above, at 2:1.

97. *Katalaleō* (I defame/malign/vilify) corresponds to the noun form *katalalia* (slander/defamation); cf., e.g., Ps 101:5; Rom 1:30; 2 Cor 12:20; 1 Pet 2:1, 12; 3:16.

98. James is not concerned, then, with the exercise of critical thinking, e.g., or discernment.

translation focuses on the latter, "Whoever . . . *condemns* a brother or sister . . ." (4:11), since James pairs *judgment* with *vilify*. The sense might even be something like "Whoever curses a brother or sister," an option that gains ground from James's earlier lament that "we curse human beings made in God's likeness" (3:9). The significance of this earlier parallel is highlighted by the association James draws there between cursing human beings and by implication cursing God, and the association he now draws between condemning others within the messianic community and by implication condemning God's law. Those who thus condemn a brother or sister practice the favoritism that earns them the label of "evil-minded judges" (2:4); they nullify the law of neighbor love and present themselves as though they were the god who gives and executes Torah.

In this larger section, James has already concerned himself with divine approval and disapproval (3:1, 6), but this motif is now moved to the fore. God is able to rescue and destroy, a divine activity set within an end-time horizon. This reading is encouraged by material associated with Jesus that portrays God in just this way (e.g., Matt 10:28; Mark 8:35; Luke 12:4–5; 17:33). In this way, James anticipates the eschatological interests that will increasingly mark his teaching in the remainder of the letter.

The degree to which James's message here is nested within the letter as a whole and in Israel's faith is marked by an array of subtle echoes of Lev 19:11–18:

> You shall not steal; you shall not deal falsely; each of you shall not falsely accuse his neighbor. And you shall not swear by my name in an unjust matter, and you shall not profane the name of your God; it is I who am the Lord your God. You shall not act unjustly towards your neighbor, and you shall not plunder, and the wages of a day laborer shall not rest overnight with you until morning. You shall not speak badly of the deaf and put an obstacle before the blind, and you shall fear the Lord your God; it is I who am the Lord your God. You shall not do something unjust in judgment; you shall not accept the person of the poor or admire the person of a high official; with justice you shall judge your neighbor. You shall not go around in deceit among your nation; you shall not conspire against the blood of your neighbor; it is I who am the Lord your God. You shall not hate in your mind your kin; in reproof you shall reprove your neighbor, and you shall not assume guilt because of him. And your own hand shall not take vengeance, and you shall not be angry against the sons of your people, and you shall love your neighbor as yourself; it is I who am the Lord. (NETS)

Of course, we have already seen how James has worked with Lev 19, especially as this material has been interpreted by Jesus in relation to the Shema.[99] Thematically, we recognize many contact points between Lev 19 and James's

99. See above on Jas 2:5–7, 8–11, 18–19.

present concern with judgment. In terms of detail, James 4:11 is like Lev 19:17 in referring to "your brother and sister" (*ton adelphon sou*, "kin," NETS); Lev 19:16 rejects deceit and conspiratorial behavior (see Jas 4:11); James 2:8 cites Lev 19:18 as "the royal law found in Scripture: 'Love your neighbor as yourself'" and now refers to vilifying and condemning "the law" (Jas 4:11); and James 4:12 echoes the royal law when he moves from sibling language to "your neighbor."[100] Additionally, James's not-so-subtle reminder that "there is one lawgiver and judge" who can "rescue and . . . destroy" (4:12) echoes the litany we read in Lev 19: "It is I who am the LORD" (Lev 19:12, 14, 16, 18). For both James and Leviticus, then, behind the law stands the Lord who gave it. Closely related, James's declaration that "there is one lawgiver and judge" (Jas 4:12) recalls Israel's confession of God's singularity, the Shema (Deut 6:4–5; see Jas 2:19), along with God's singular capacities to give and take life: "See now that I, even I, am he; there is no god besides me. I kill and I make alive; I wound and I heal" (Deut 32:39 NRSV).

These examples of intertextuality, intricately woven into James's teaching, are clearly oriented around this purpose: recalling that God is god and his readers and hearers (you) are not, with its emphatic corollary that their (your) vocation is to follow God's Instructions (or Torah) and not to sit in judgment over it. James's language recalls his earlier emphasis on being doers of the word, not only listeners (1:22–25); it also recalls the epitome of God's Instructions (or Torah) he provides when he urges that belief in the one God, the God of Israel, is expressed above all in the royal law, the law of freedom: "Love your neighbor as yourself" (2:8, citing Lev 19:18; cf. Jas 1:25; 2:9, 12).

---

100. See L. Johnson 2004d, 128–29; Allison 2013, 633–34.

James 4:13–5:20
Life Aligned with the Lord's Purpose

James brings his letter to a close with a series of instructions that, first, illustrate and amplify the concerns he has raised and, second, map the way forward in terms of the commitments and practices he sanctions. The section as a whole is a reminder that the Jewish messianists he addresses are scattered outside their homeland (1:1). Metaphorically, they are in Babylon, not Jerusalem.[1] This means they must practice discernment as they negotiate the contours of faithful life in a world with Rome as its overlord and the culture center from which Roman ideals and habits radiate. Along with Jewish expatriates more generally, they would have participated in established patterns of Jewish resistance, especially as these were related to circumcision, diet, and Sabbath-keeping.[2] James presses further, though. Resistance also entails embracing and embodying the message of Jesus, who yoked Jewish faith in the one God (and the concomitant vocation to love the one Lord with all of oneself) together with what James calls the royal law: "Love your neighbor as yourself" (2:8, citing Lev 19:18).[3]

Accordingly, whatever else faithful life in a Rome-centered, Rome-fashioned world might look like, life patterns that detract from this singular, wholistic commitment to the one God and work against neighbor love are preemptively excluded. In this final section of the letter, then, James censures those who plan their lives without regard for the Lord's purpose (4:13–17) and pronounces prophetic judgment on those whose dependence on their own wealth and whose practices toward others counter faith in one God, the vocation to love God singularly, and the call to neighbor love (5:1–6). Such people are not engaged in "devotion that is pure and unsullied in God the Father's eyes," for they have failed "to come to the aid of orphans and widows in their trouble and suffering" and to keep themselves "from being contaminated by the world" (1:27). What of those who suffer at the hands of such people? James

---

1. James does not use the term *Babylon* as a cipher for Rome (as elsewhere in the NT: 1 Pet 5:13; Rev 14:8; 16:19; 17:5; 18:2, 10, 21). But he understands the Rome-patterned world similarly as a world order hostile toward God, God's ways, and God's people.

2. See above, on Jas 1:1.

3. See above, on Jas 2:18–19.

sets his pen, finally, to address these brothers and sisters directly, calling them to courageous endurance and prayer in anticipation of the Lord's restoration and justice (5:7–12, 13–20).

Although the motif of end-time approval and disapproval has dotted the landscape of James's letter thus far,[4] this final section is even more clearly set within the eschatological horizons of divine judgment. Thus we read that life is temporary (4:14), the affluent hoard their wealth for the last days (5:3), a day of slaughter is coming (5:5), messianists await the Lord's coming (5:7), the Lord's coming is near (5:8), messianists ought to speak so as not to be judged (5:9), the judge is at the door (5:9), oath-takers will be judged (5:12), and turning sinners from the wrong path will rescue them from death (5:20). On the one hand, James peppers this entire portion of the letter with references to *the Lord*—that is, with reminders of both the Lord's present activity and the Lord's future coming to set things right.[5] Irrespective of how things might at times seem, the Lord *is* involved in the unfolding of history. On the other hand, James engages in what literary theorists call *backshadowing*.[6] That is, James allows his vision of a future determined by the Lord to cast its shadow backward on the present, and this leads him to invite certain behaviors and to condemn others. In reality, these two emphases work together. The Lord *is* lord, now and in the future, and the Lord's good ends draw the Lord's people into them, shaping the character of and enabling faithful response in the present.

4:13–5:6 Putting the Arrogant and Wealthy on Alert

4:13 Pay attention,[a] you who say, "Today or tomorrow we will go to this or that city and spend a year there, trading and making money." 14 Whoever you are,[b] you do not know what will happen tomorrow, or what your life will be like. You are a mist that appears for a little while and then vanishes. 15 Instead of your saying,[c] "If the Lord wills, we will live and do this or that," 16 you now boast in your arrogance. All such boasting is evil.

17 Therefore, knowing the right thing to do and not doing it—this is a sin.

5:1 Pay attention,[d] you wealthy people. Weep and wail at the miseries coming upon you. 2 Your wealth has rotted. Moths have ruined your clothes. 3 Your gold and silver have become corroded. Their corrosion will be evidence against you. It will eat your flesh like fire. You have laid up treasure for the last days.

---

4. This is documented by Eng 2020, 96–190.

5. *Kyrios* is in Jas 4:15; 5:4, 7, 8, 10, 11 [2×], 14, 15. The Lord's work is implied in 5:18 NRSV, "The heaven gave rain."

6. Cf. Morson 1994, 234.

4 Listen!ᵉ The wages of the workers who harvest your fields—which you fraudulently held back—cry out, and the harvesters' cries have reached the ears of the Lord of heavenly armies.ᶠ 5 You live extravagantly and self-indulgently on the earth. You stuff your hearts for the day of slaughter. 6 You condemned and murdered the righteous one, who does not resist you.ᵍ

a. *Age nyn* might be translated more woodenly as "Come now" (NRSV). It serves as an interjection aimed at prompting attention so as to emphasize what follows.

b. *Hoitines*—indefinite subject of the verb *epistasthe* (you know). The pronoun is often left untranslated (e.g., CEB, NRSV), but its use here underscores James's reference in 4:13 to "whoever should say such and such."

c. The articular infinitive in the construction *anti tou legein hymas* has the present active infinitive of *legō*, so the more usual translation as an imperative, "you ought to say" (e.g., NRSV), is likely not the best rendering, even though the sense of James's words is not radically altered either way. See Moule 1959, 127–28.

d. See above, translation note a.

e. *Idou*, like *age nyn* (4:13; 5:1), prompts attention and emphasizes what follows.

f. *Sabaōth* is a Gk. transliteration of a Heb. term for *armies*. L&N §12.8: "pertaining to one who has overwhelming power—'Almighty, All Powerful, One who is powerful over all.'"

g. I have translated the phrase as declarative, though it is sometimes treated as an interrogative anticipating a positive answer, i.e.: "Does he not resist you?" See the comments, below.

Structurally, this portion of James's letter is held together by the repeated interjection, "Pay attention!" directed first to "you who say" and, second, to "you wealthy people" (4:13; 5:1). Although these two audiences, traveling merchants and those with propertied wealth involved in agribusiness, would not overlap significantly, they each provide case studies for grappling with what seems to be James's special concern with arrogance (cf. 4:1–10). In their presumptuousness, the traveling merchants whom James depicts consider themselves "masters of the universe."[7] They are wizards of commerce whose lack of humility allows them to think they can plan and carry out their lives as they please, quite apart from any consideration of God's work in the world. In their presumptuousness, the wealthy with vast landholdings reckon they can secure their own lives through their properties and possessions and, valuing others only for their utility, think they can exploit, even murder, those in their employ. James thus pictures people who cultivate ways of life fueled by earthbound, worldly, diabolic valuations of others (cf. 3:15), by a grossly exaggerated sense of their own importance and competencies, and by an ultradependence on their own ingenuity.

7. I borrow this phrase from Tom Wolfe's 1987 novel, *The Bonfire of the Vanities*.

In these two snippets, does James portray people within messianist communities or those outside the communities to whom he addresses the letter? Although their exclusion might be gratifying, for James the lines cannot be drawn so carefully. Deciding who is in or out is less clear when, like James, one thinks less in terms of people located inside a circle or outside, and instead considers whether one is on the right path and heading in the right direction (cf. 5:19–20). The life path that troubles James has its appeal both for the degraded poor and for the wealthy, after all. The one might crave the status, power, privilege, and self-mastery that wealth must surely bring; the other learns that wealth commands godlike devotion toward its evil ends and ends in condemnation.[8] Jesus is similarly remembered for calling his followers to watch out for "the yeast of the Pharisees" (that is, "the mismatch between their hearts and lives") and to watch out for the legal experts (who concern themselves with parading and extending their honor, while exploiting widows). Jesus alerts his followers because he recognizes that his own followers are not immune to similar proclivities (Luke 12:1 CEB; 20:45–47; cf. Mark 8:15; Matt 16:11–12).[9] Not for nothing does James, in both instances, begin his instruction with the exclamation "Pay attention!" Everyone must listen to his words and hear his warnings.

[4:13–14] "You who say" refers to merchants. These are not the commonplace shopkeepers we might envision, whose family dwells above the shop where goods are made and sold, nor those who display their wares daily in the local town center. James refers instead to merchants who travel Rome's network of roads and the seas in the service of commerce. These merchants were deeply implicated in a contradictory life. "The great earnings that brought much joy [also] took the merchant far from his origins. They took him closer to the social levels that traditionally held power, and they forced on him an agonizing shame."[10] On the one hand, dishonor accrued to the merchant on account of the merchant's outlander status in distant territories. Additionally, merchants were known for such stereotypical characteristics as cunning, trickery, and deceit. Indeed, "commerce involved an innate inclination to lie."[11] Theirs was a competitive profession, and they were known for their talents in manipulating situations and people to their own advantage. On the other hand, merchants were applauded on account of the courage they exemplified when undertaking the dangers of travel and acclaimed for bringing exotic, rare, and/or essential goods to their own townspeople. And some aspired and were promoted to the ranks

---

8. See further above, on 1:9–11; 2:5–7.

9. The parallel between James's warning and the warnings remembered of Jesus in the Gospels is not exact, since the Gospels have Jesus alerting his followers explicitly, and James targets "those who say" and "you wealthy people." This difference is mitigated, though, when we account for these disparate modes of writing: a narrative portrayal versus didactic prose.

10. Giardina 1993, 269. These summary comments draw on Giardina's helpful essay.

11. Giardina 1993, 254.

of city councils (and higher). With references to mercantile deceit, rivalry, self-promotion, and the like, even this brief sketch is enough to justify James's inclusion of merchants among those given to presumptuous life paths, though without casting aspersions on commercial activities wholesale.

Even more to the present point, though, is the specific relationship merchants had with time and space. Their learned business acumen and the inside knowledge they gained through extensive travel supported their practices of prognostication: What goods will be scarce (or plentiful), and where? Where will harvests be early or late, ample or disappointing? When and where will demand be high and supplies low? Merchants studied such signs in the service of commercial advantage, cleverly speculating on where to be and when to be there, to boost their prices and maximize their profits. This is precisely what James reports and censures: "Today or tomorrow," they say, "we will go to this or that city and spend a year there, trading and making money" (4:13).

The merchants whom James depicts are simply doing what merchants do, we might say. However, James's concern is that they do so as if they were masters of the universe. Calendars, itineraries, business dealings—everything is under "our" control. Perhaps we hear here a faint echo of words remembered of Jesus. In the days of Noah, people were "eating and drinking, and marrying and giving in marriage"; in the days of Lot, "they were eating and drinking, buying and selling, planting and building" (Luke 17:26–30 NRSV; cf. Matt 24:37–39)— that is, they were engaged in typical, day-to-day life. Yet catastrophe caught them unawares because they failed to factor God's agenda into their routines. Jesus draws the lesson: "Those who try to make their life secure will lose it, but those who lose their life will keep it" (Luke 17:33 NRSV; cf. Matt 10:39).

In effect, then, James depicts the future-casting and plan-making typical of those engaged in commerce only to undo it. How can you make plans for tomorrow when tomorrow is an unknown? How can you formulate a life plan when the character of your life is an unknown? Although it pertains to a wealthy landholder rather than a merchant, Jesus related a parable remarkably similar to the scene James depicts (Luke 12:16–21).[12] A well-to-do farmer experiences a bumper crop, decides to manipulate the market and secure his economic power by holding back his harvest in bigger barns, and he does so independently, without acknowledging how others might be affected by his plans. The parallels between his commercial scheming and that of James's merchants, beginning in each case with self-talk, are easy to trace. Most importantly, like James's merchants, this rich landholder sought to make his life secure without reference to God. In his case, God interjects: "You fool! This very night your life is being demanded of you. And the things you have prepared, whose will they be?" (Luke 12:20 NRSV). For James's merchants and Jesus's wealthy farmer,

---

12. On what follows, see Green 1997, 489–91.

pretentiousness leads to a false confidence that, through one's schemes and efforts, one can master and indeed secure one's future. With both sets of characters, words spoken expose inner dispositions, the heart, a reality otherwise very much at home in James's letter (e.g., 2:3, 16; 3:14–15).[13] In each case, Jesus and James use the prospect of life's end as an impetus for ethical formation.

Earlier, James spoke of the evanescence of life, its impermanence and fragility,[14] using the simile: "The wealthy . . . will fade away like wildflowers" (1:10–11). This image works for people in an arid climate who would recognize the sun's scorching heat baking the grass and withering its flowers. In that earlier text, James was countering the popular view, shared by the wealthy and impoverished alike, that the well-off might enjoy protection from life's perils and escape its limitations. Here he turns to a more universal metaphor: LIFE IS A MIST. Israel's Scriptures and Second Temple Jewish literature draw on this metaphor to conceptualize both life in general and the lives of the wicked.[15] "Therefore [idolaters] shall be like the morning mist or like the dew that goes away early, like chaff that swirls from the threshing floor or like smoke from a window" (Hos 13:3 NRSV; cf. Ps 37:20). "Our lives will be dispersed like a morning mist chased away by the sun and weighed down by the day's heat" (Wis 2:4 CEB). "We pass from the world like locusts, and our life is like a mist" (2 Esd 4:24 NRSV). In more prosaic terms, James's message calls to mind this proverb: "Do not boast about tomorrow, for you do not know what a day may bring" (Prov 27:1 NRSV). The metaphor LIFE IS A MIST is especially pertinent here, given how merchants play the long game, as it were, as though they could safeguard their investments and bolster their profits by managing the calendar. Should they not know better? After all, they live high-risk lives. They are not like those people of means who construct walls of protection from threats to health and wealth. In fact, John Chrysostom (347–407 CE) located merchants at the head of a list of those most familiar with life's dangerous ups and down, like soldiers and athletes.[16] Did they really need to be reminded of marauders on the open road, or of the sea pirates and sea storms that disrupt their voyages?[17] Apparently, in their delusions of mastery, they did.

13. L. Johnson 1995, 295.

14. Adewuya (2023, 79) compares a saying from the Yoruba people (of West Africa): *Aiye fele*, "Life is brittle."

15. Ecclesiastes repeatedly likens life to "morning mist," "steam," "a puff of air," or "vapor"— *hebel* in Heb., which the CEB translates as "perfectly pointless" in Eccl 1:2 (cf., though, the CEB marginal note); one might instead write, "A puff of air, nothing but a puff of air"; or, "a morning mist, nothing but a morning mist." Allison (2013, 657) notes that "the ephemeral nature of human existence or of evildoers" was commonly expressed in the Greco-Roman world.

16. *Patrologia Graeca* 47.309; cf. Giardina 1993, 258–59.

17. Cf. the catalog of hardships that Paul the traveler recounts: "Three times I was shipwrecked; for a night and a day I was adrift at sea; on frequent journeys, in danger from rivers, danger from bandits, . . . danger in the wilderness, danger at sea" (2 Cor 11:25–26 NRSV); and Luke's report of

[15–16] James now documents two ways of speaking, each with its source in the human heart. The first is the way *not* taken by these merchants. It attends to the Lord's will (4:15), demonstrating submission to and humility before the Lord (4:7, 10). What is more, it hammers home James's perspective concerning integrated human life. No part of life lies outside the Lord's purview, not even mercantile travel and business dealings. The second, the road chosen by James's merchants, brandishes words of confident independence and self-mastery (4:13) fed by hearts fixed on self-promotion, jealousy, rivalry, and hubris (cf. 3:14, 16; 4:1–4). This is practical atheism, ignoring God in daily life even while, perhaps, professing belief in God.[18] Borrowing James's own categories, the first puts on display friendship with God (since, after all, according to Greco-Roman moral philosophy, friends share a common mind, a common will) while the second, that of James's merchants, exposes friendship with the world (cf. 4:4).

An eye toward the will of the gods was a commonplace in the ancient Mediterranean, but attending to the Lord's will is deeply rooted, too, in Israel's faith[19]—and, perhaps more to the present point, in the Jesus tradition. Jesus taught his followers to pray that God's will would be done "on earth as it is in heaven" (Matt 6:10 NRSV), and Jesus himself put this prayer into practice while praying shortly before his arrest: "Your will be done" (Matt 26:42; cf. Luke 22:42: "not my will but yours be done," NRSV). This is more than a simple reminder of the Lord who superintends the cosmos. (If it were only a reference to divine sovereignty, one might account for James's concern by simply adding a postscript, "the Lord willing," to every plan made, without requiring one to interrogate the nature of those plans or question the way those plans are made.) In this setting, it performs more as a reminder that "friends of God" seek to discern, embrace, and serve God's purpose as they shape those plans. Commercial stratagems, then, are tamed as merchants aim to participate in the Lord's purpose to restore the cosmos in all of life, even in their business dealings. Importantly, the record suggests that merchants could practice what James assumes here, *and they could do so as merchants*. Like others involved in easily caricatured professions, some merchants could and did engage in

Paul's perilous sea journey (Acts 27). Unlike James's merchants, Paul says of himself (e.g., Rom 1:10; 1 Cor 4:19; 16:7), and Luke says of Paul, that he was attuned to the Lord's will in his travels (Acts 16:6–10; 18:21).

18. With this definition, I am following Borne 1961, 10. Cf. Davids 1982, 173: "These are people who shut God out of their commercial lives, although they may be pious enough in church or at home." Still worth contemplating is Carter's analysis (1993) of the way American law and politics narrow religious faith to one's so-called private life, with no public role.

19. Dibelius 1976, 233–34. Cf. Prov 19:21; Rom 1:10; 1 Cor 4:19; 16:7; Acts 16:6–10; 18:21; Heb 6:1–3.

commerce justly, for example, and even represented themselves as lovers of the poor, always eager to aid the impoverished.[20]

The contrast James draws between self-talk that humbly acknowledges and serves the Lord and the actual self-talk of the merchants he envisions is searing. He first marks this distinction with a Greek construction that might be translated as "in fact, however, as things really stand."[21] Then he uses language that could hardly be more unfavorable. Not only does he accuse these merchants of boasting, but he also declares that they boast in their arrogance. *Boasting* comprised problematic speech that might be appropriate in the Greco-Roman world only when done with heightened sensitivity and under special circumstances. Israel's Scriptures and Second Temple Jewish literature mandated that boasting be theocentric, never anthropocentric (cf. 1 Cor 1:31: "Let the one who boasts, boast in the Lord" [NRSV; citing Jer 9:24]).[22] James draws attention to this unacceptable behavior with neon lights by adding the term *arrogance*, using a Greek term that suggests *pretentious pride*, or *a puffed up* or *an inflated sense of superiority*.[23] Pressing even further, he adds the damning assessment: "All such boasting is evil." In this way, James associates these merchants' speech with earlier references to those who play favorites and so "become evil-minded judges" (2:4); to the fiery tongue, "a restless evil, full of deadly poison" (3:2–10); and indeed to those who, having befriended the world, have aligned themselves with the devil and set themselves up as God's enemies (4:4–10).

[17] At the midpoint of this section of the letter we find an aphorism: "Therefore, knowing the right thing to do and not doing it—this is a sin" (4:17). Note the shift from second-person communication with "you" (4:13–16) to third person as "anyone" (4:17)[24] and back to second person, "you" (5:1–6). The conjunction "therefore" suggests that James's proverb draws out the sense of the preceding paragraph (4:13–16), but it is worth reflecting, too, on how it captures what follows it (5:1–6). In fact, this saying functions like a hinge

20. Giardina 1993, 254, 264–66. We might be reminded of tax collectors and soldiers who came to John the Baptist in the wilderness and were told how to live conversionary lives *as tax collectors and soldiers* (Luke 3:7–14).

21. On *nyn de* in 4:16, cf. *CGL* 2:974: "expressing what is the case, opp[osite] what might have been."

22. See Watson 2016.

23. *Alazoneia*; see L&N §88.219. In the NT, the term is found only here and in 1 John 2:16: "All that is in the world—the desire of the flesh, the desire of the eyes, the pride in riches [*hē alazoneia tou biou*]—comes not from the Father but from the world" (NRSV). *Alazōn* (one who is pretentiously proud) is found twice, both times in vice lists: Rom 1:30; 2 Tim 3:2.

24. *Eidoti . . . poiounti*, "someone who knows, . . . someone who does" (I am reading these participles as substantival) + *autō estin*, "to him/her it is."

between these two subsections (4:13–16; 5:1–6).[25] Knowing what is right—whether regarding business plans, wealth, exploitation of others, or something else—and not doing it is a sin.

This may be a proverb, but it is hardly free-floating. James draws an immediate contrast with 4:14, "You do not know," and the resulting irony runs deep.

On the one hand,	On the other hand,
you act on the basis of what you do not know,	if you do not act on the basis of what you do know,
and thus engage in evil pomposity. (4:13–16)	this is sin. (4:17)

Setting these two claims side by side provides a stark reminder that, for James, *knowing* is not enough. You know "that the testing of your faithfulness produces endurance" (1:3), you know "that we teachers will be judged more stringently" (3:1), and you ought to know "that friendship with the world means enmity with God" (4:4), but such knowledge has not resulted in exemplary allegiance to the Lord.[26] The problem is twofold. First, James counsels not simply *knowledge* but also *practical wisdom*, with its paired interests in understanding well and doing well. This is the wisdom from above that provides the rich soil for human flourishing (1:8; 3:13–18), and it cannot be reduced to knowing merely at a formal level. (Indeed, for James, rather than prevent divine disapproval, knowledge may actually heighten it.)[27] Second, for James the human problem is not *lack of knowledge* but human craving, the human inclination that gives birth to sin (1:14–15). As important as *knowing* is for James, then, it is no substitute for the true word by which God give new birth, the wisdom from above that shows the way and enables the faithful journey along it.[28]

Additionally, James's proverb strongly echoes a key concern from the lengthy introduction to his letter. There, he insists that his readers and hearers be *doers* and not only *listeners* of the word (1:22–25; cf. 2:4–26). Not coincidentally, "active doers," those "genuinely happy in their doing," control their speech, give themselves to the aid of the needy, and keep themselves from

---

25. So also L. Johnson 1995, 298.

26. Bede 1985, 54: "Throughout the whole text of this Letter blessed James has shown that they to whom he wrote had the knowledge to do good things and at the same time they had so learned a right faith that they presumed to be able to become teachers even for others; but still they had not yet attained perfection of works or humility of mind or restraint of speech."

27. Wesley 1976, 867.

28. For "knowing" in James, see above, on 3:13.

being contaminated by a lifeworld out of step with the aims of God (1:25–27). These are the very issues James names in this later section of the letter, where he references those who speak wrongly (4:13–16) and the wealthy who hold tightly to their treasure while abusing laborers (5:1–6).

[5:1–6] James shifts his focus, using the same interjection we read in 4:13: "Pay attention!" (5:1). Previously, he concerned himself with traveling merchants, calling into question the speech habits with which these masters of the universe projected strategies for securing their commercial interests, without reference to the divine will (4:13–16). From "you who say," James now shifts to "you wealthy people" (5:1). The description that follows lets us easily discern that his attention has turned from one kind of wealth to another—from "new money" (traveling merchants), we might say, to "old money" (the landed nobility). Now he depicts households standing on the shoulders of prior generations noted for their increasingly vast landholdings. He thus targets those who occupied the Roman world's loftiest ranks.

Given the flow of James's letter thus far, this opening reference to "you wealthy people" heralds a serious disruption in the normal order of things. This is because the affluent have already been advised to consider the transient nature of life, notwithstanding the shields against ill health, aging, and death their wealth might purchase (1:10–11). Moreover, James has insisted that those faithful to the Lord Jesus Christ show no favoritism to the elite, adding to this his awareness of God's having chosen the poor (2:1–5). According to Roman conventions, those with landed wealth occupied the upper echelons of Roman society, with elevated prestige and political influence intertwined with land ownership. However, normal rules concerning who is up or down, in or out, are sidelined in God's upside-down, right-side-up economy. What James portrays, then, is the outcome of the clash between two visions of "the world," the one propagated by Rome and the other established by God. Carrying on from this recasting of the way the world works, James now develops in two movements the deficiencies of the wealthy. First, the affluent bank on wealth's capacity to guarantee life and the future, but wealth is itself momentary and, indeed, hazardous to life (5:1–3). Second, under the mastery of their privileged situation, the wealthy exploit and abuse their workers (5:4–6). Divine judgment is the outcome (5:1, 3, 4, 5).

As we will see, James's instruction in these two paragraphs (5:1–3, 4–6) is thoroughly grounded in Israel's Scriptures and the memory of Jesus's teaching. It is also at home in important strands of Second Temple Jewish thought. His censure of the wealthy parallels especially the section of 1 Enoch known as "The Epistle of Enoch" (including part of 1 En. 92 and 93.11–105.2, usually dated to the late first century BCE), with its heightened focus on socioeconomic justice. For example:

> Woe unto those who build oppression and injustice!
>> Who lay foundation for deceit.
> They shall soon be demolished;
>> and they shall have no peace.
> Woe unto those who build their houses with sin!
>> For they shall all be demolished from their foundations;
>> and they shall fall by the sword.
> Those who amass gold and silver;
>> they shall quickly be destroyed.
> Woe unto you rich people!
>> For you have put your trust in your wealth.
> You shall ooze out of your riches,
>> For you do not remember the Most High.
> In the days of your affluence,
>> you committed oppression,
> You have become ready for death,
>> and for the day of darkness and the day of great judgment.[29]

This is only one of many Enochian texts cast as woes on the rich and powerful who amass wealth and live extravagantly because of the work of others whom they trample underfoot. We will have occasion in what follows to refer to other writings as well. The point is not that James quotes these Second Temple texts or even anticipates that his readers and hearers will be able to identify the texts and traditions that have influenced him. Rather, correspondences like this suggest the degree to which James and his audience are breathing the air of contemporary Jewish criticism of wealth as a serious, damnable impediment to living out one's allegiance to the Lord. Jesus is remembered to have memorialized this sentiment in his simple declaration, "You cannot serve God and Mammon" (Matt 6:24 AT; Luke 16:13 AT), using the term *mamōnas* with the sense of *wealth personified*, as though it were a god. Within the database of what Jewish people, including these Jewish messianists, "know," we find such antipathy toward the power and privilege accompanying wealth. Clearly, even if James does not replicate the words of evaluation and judgment we find in these precursor materials, he has endorsed their sentiment as he creatively constructs his own criticism.

[1–3] Drawing on images of wealth, clothing befitting the monied and politically well-placed, and gold and silver, James fashions a collage that invites interpretation along at least three lines. First, it emphasizes the impermanence of wealth. This is especially striking since *landed wealth* comprises the most stable form of wealth—in the Roman world, typically held by firstborn sons

---

29. ET in Isaac 1983, 75. On the influence of this section of 1 Enoch on James, see DeSilva 2012, 122–26.

who inherited it from their fathers, who inherited it from their fathers, and so on. Second, it triggers somatic markers, intuitive responses that bias people for or against (in this case, most definitely against!) given stimuli. If the stuff of wealth is blanketed by rot, crumbling, and corrosion, and if that corrosion devours human flesh, would this not mark wealth as a danger zone, to be avoided? Third, ironically, thinking they have stored up treasures to secure their long lives, the wealthy now hear that their treasures both destroy life and open wide the door to divine judgment.

Importantly, James does not simply relegate these outcomes to the future. He uses verbs that identify what has *already* occurred, with their effects continuing in the present.[30] The idea that James thus portrays the present situation as the consequence of something accomplished in the past may seem odd, not least to those whom he addresses. They might respond: "What rot? What corrosion? Our wealth seems perfectly safe, our garments are clean and crisp, and our gold shines brightly in the noonday sun!" The point, of course, is that James writes from his vantage point while encouraging his addressees to exchange theirs for his. Everything turns on one's hermeneutical lens, the spectacles through which one views the accoutrements of this great treasure. Having donned their rose-colored glasses, the wealthy see only what life in the Roman world has taught them to see: the access and influence that accrues to those with grand landholdings. This is not James's perspective. He has framed his letter hermeneutically with reference to the Lord Jesus Christ (see above, on 1:1; 2:1). This interpretive commitment prioritizes the domain over which Jesus is Messiah, the household over which he is Lord, and indeed, the way Jesus expressed in word and deed his faith in God's aim and ability to overturn how human life is usually valued. It is as if James's christological lenses open keen-sighted eyes to a formerly foggy state of affairs so that they see how gripping one's wealth tightly counters Jesus's faith and does violence to those in need (cf. 2:1–4; 5:4–6). Additionally, James portrays the present against its eschatological horizons. If only you could see from *this* vantage point, James urges, then you would see what I see—not gold and silver and the finest apparel, but rot, ruin, corrosion, and acid-like burning. James does not seem hopeful that the wealthy he addresses will see things so clearly, but perhaps those who show favoritism toward the well-heeled social and political elites and those who long for the prestige and clout that comes with wealth—perhaps they will perceive what James perceives, and act accordingly.

We might puzzle over James's image of corroded, or rusted, silver or gold. Was he unaware that neither silver nor gold rusts (hence, their later inclusion

---

30. The verbs in question are all perfect indicative (on which, see von Siebenthal 2019, 329–31): *sesēpen* (has rotted), *sētobrōta gegonen* (have become moth-eaten / moths have ruined), *katiōtai* (have become corroded).

among the so-called noble gases)? Does he refer to rusting silver and gold in order to hint that these fortunes are fake? More likely, James's images are not to be read with an eye on chemical properties. After all, even if these metals were subject to rust, they still would not be able to "eat your flesh like fire" (5:3). James seems less concerned with metallurgy and more interested in highlighting the fleeting nature of wealth, wealth's vulnerability to ruin, and the capacity of wealth to disfigure and destroy those who accumulate it.

Strong images thus bolster James's message, but so do the ways his writing works with the Jesus tradition and with language reminiscent of Israel's Scriptures. In the Sermon on the Plain, Jesus matches his beatitudes point for point with corresponding woes: "How terrible for you who are rich. . . . How terrible for you who have plenty now. . . . How terrible for you who laugh now, because you will mourn and weep" (Luke 6:24–25 CEB). James's pronouncements are similar, both with regard to the alarming fate of the wealth and wealthy and with his appeal to "weep and wail." In the Sermon on the Mount, Jesus warns against storing up "treasures on earth, where moth and rust consume, . . . but store up for yourselves treasures in heaven, where neither moth nor rust consumes." He then adds, "For where your treasure is, there your heart will be also" (Matt 6:19–20 NRSV; cf. Luke 12:21, 33–34). Parallels with James's message are easy to discern, suggesting his indebtedness to Jesus's teaching, now imaginatively appropriated for this new context. With these words from the Jesus tradition in the background, note how James, with biting irony, introduces his belief that the affluent have not heeded Jesus's message. They have accumulated treasure, yes, but of the wrong sort. Their assets are earthbound, worldly, and so they are moth-eaten and ruined. Rather than outfitting them for life with God, their overflowing stockpile invites God's end-time judgment. If the moneyed ranks were to hear James well, they would recognize the calamity coming on them and respond with weeping and wailing. After all, Jesus and, before him, Israel's Scriptures associate howling in grief and pain with present and anticipated disaster—as in Isa 13:6: "Wail, for the day of the Lord is near and a destruction will come from God!" (NETS).[31] Jesus's words from the Sermon on the Mount provide little hope for such perception, however, since the hearts of the wealthy are wedded to a corruptible—indeed, a corrupt and corrupting—treasure.

[4–6] James introduces another interjection, "Listen!" though without shifting to a new addressee. He continues his prophetic denunciation of the wealthy (5:1), now sketching more of their abominable behaviors. He previously referred to their laying up treasure (5:3), and to this he adds that they fraudulently withhold wages, live extravagantly and self-indulgently, stuff their hearts, and

31. James has *klaiō* (I weep/wail) and *ololyzō* (I wail/howl). For the latter verb in the LXX, see, e.g., Isa 10:10; 14:31; 15:2.

condemn and murder the righteous (5:4–6). Weaving together these behaviors, this vile inventory suggests that, at least in part, the reason the wealthy can live so lavishly is from abusing their workers, even to the point of committing murder. It also suggests that they feel free to do so because they regard people like those in their employ with disdain, as if they were not actually "human beings made in God's likeness" (3:9).[32]

James's message gains much of its prophetic edge from its deep roots in the soil of Israel's Scriptures.

• Given the importance of Lev 19 for James's letter overall,[33] the words of Lev 19:13 are like a thunderclap: "You must not oppress your neighbors or rob them. Do not withhold a hired laborer's pay overnight" (CEB). In James's reckoning, the wealthy have obviously failed to keep Scripture's royal law: "Love your neighbor as yourself" (Jas 2:8; citing Lev 19:18). Elsewhere, the Lord of armies promises to be quick to come in judgment against "against those who cheat the day laborers out of their wages" (Mal 3:5 CEB; cf. Deut 24:14–15).

• The phrase I have translated as "Lord of armies" appears scores of times in Israel's Scriptures, above all in Isaiah. It is often translated as "Lord of hosts" (CEB: "Lord of heavenly forces"). A useful gloss would be "the Lord Almighty."[34] James's use of the phrase identifies the all-powerful God on the side of powerless, cheated harvesters, and so against those whose extraordinary wealth was to have won for them deference and influence.[35]

• According to the Gospels of Matthew and Luke, Jesus has it that inanimate objects, like stones, can participate in the drama of God's coming to bring salvation (Matt 3:9; Luke 3:8; 19:40). Israel's Scriptures, too, depict creation as responding to God with praise and joy (e.g., Ps 19). Inanimate objects might cry out for justice, too. Shortly after Abel's murder, God addresses Cain: "The voice of your brother's blood is crying out to me from the earth!" (Gen 4:10 NETS; cf. Heb 12:24; Hab 2:11). All of creation, even lifeless objects, participate in the divine drama, and this provides

---

32. This last suggestion is supported, too, by James's setting in parallel the examples of Abraham (surely an esteemed person of significant wealth) and Rahab (Abraham's opposite, in terms of the usual canons of status): both were shown to be righteous by their faithful actions (2:20–26). Note, too, James's appeal to Elijah, "a human being just like us" (5:17). Cf. Green 2020b, 347–49, 352.

33. See above, e.g., on 2:1, 8; 4:11–12; also L. Johnson 2004d; Lockett 2020.

34. See L&N §12.8. Mal 3:5 LXX (just cited) has "Lord Almighty," *kyrios pantokratōr*.

35. For the phrase in Israel's Scriptures, see Isa 2:12; 3:15; 5:9; et al.

context for hearing James's words: "The wages of the workers . . . cry out" (Jas 5:4).

• James's claim that those "cries have reached the ears of the Lord of armies" (5:4) leads us to additional, fertile parallels in Israel's Scriptures, such as the groaning of the Israelites under slavery, their crying out, God hearing their cries, and God remembering and acting on their behalf (Exod 2:23–25; 3:7–8). Deuteronomy summarizes: "The Egyptians did us ill and humbled us and imposed hard work on us, and we cried to the Lord, the God of our fathers, and the Lord listened to our voice and saw our humiliation and our toil and our oppression. And the Lord brought us out of Egypt" (Deut 26:5–10 NETS). Jesus is remembered for his promise: "Won't God provide justice to his chosen people who cry out to him day and night? Will he be slow to help them? I tell you, he will give them justice quickly" (Luke 18:7–8 CEB; recall James's declaration that God has chosen the poor, 2:5).

• James's indictment, "You stuff your hearts for the day of slaughter" (5:5), may seem macabre enough on its own terms, but it draws on scriptural antecedents as well. Isaiah describes God's impending, angry judgment "against all the nations, . . . to destroy them and to give them over for slaughter" (Isa 34:2 NETS; cf. 34:6), then later promises slaughter to those who have turned their backs on the Lord, who misheard the Lord's voice and set their will against the Lord's (Isa 65:1–16). Jeremiah writes of "a day of slaughter" for the impious who deluded themselves into thinking, "God will not see our ways" (Jer 12:3–4 NETS). Jeremiah asks the Lord to "purify them" in preparation for a day of slaughter, but James substitutes an image from the lifestyle typical of the affluent, for whom a feast would signal not a special occasion but, astonishingly, describe what would have been daily fare.[36] (Compare Jesus's description of "a rich man . . . who feasted sumptuously every day" [Luke 16:19 NRSV].) They may think they are living "extravagantly and self-indulgently," as James puts it (5:5), but, like livestock in a feedlot, they are in fact stuffing themselves in preparation for end-time judgment, "the day of slaughter."

James's word choices might send chills up the spines of the rich who know their Scriptures yet mistreat those on whose backs their wealth is maintained and increased (cf. 4:17!). Alternatively, the abused who are familiar with the

---

36. According to Hamel (1990, 33), to serve even ¾ pound of meat on the table each day, one must have the wealth necessary to support 30 workers for a year.

Scriptures may hear encouragement in these words and grow in their confidence that the Lord will come to set things right. James cites no scriptural texts here but clearly weaves scriptural language into his instruction. This indicates the world (the scriptural world, not the world of Roman convention) within which he wants to understand and portray God's work, the world within which his addressees, the wealthy, must take stock of their behaviors and consequent future.

Given James's reference to *hearts* in his image, "You stuff your hearts" (5:5), we should recall his integrated anthropology, in which one's cognitive life (or *heart*—that is commitments, emotions, thoughts, volition, etc.) is inseparable from the practices that feed and flow from it. Among the behaviors of the affluent that draw James's ire is, first, their cheating their workers. Although James does not identify these field hands as *day laborers*, for whom the loss of even one day's wage would put a family at risk, he nevertheless points in this general direction. Cheating those in one's employ can take more than one form, such as withholding wages partially or altogether, providing an unfair or an unlivable wage, or giving a wage disproportionate to the work involved or services rendered or the wealth garnered.[37] Rather than deploying their wealth in the service of those living on the edge, these wealthy do what the Roman world-system has taught them to do: expanding their influence through their practices of self-glorifying philanthropy, for example, or adding to their already-overflowing treasure trove.

Second, like Jesus's comparison of "a rich man who was dressed in purple and fine linen and who feasted sumptuously every day" and "a poor man . . . who longed to satisfy his hunger with what fell from the rich man's table" (Luke 16:19–21 NRSV), James contrasts the wealthy's exuberant lifestyle with their refusal to treat workers fairly (and in accord with God's Instructions, or Torah—see Lev 19:13; Deut 24:14–15; cf. Jas 2:8–13). James's earlier instruction against giving priority to the affluent and noble while dishonoring and neglecting the impoverished (Jas 2:1–17) thus reappears in a different form.

Third, he writes, "You condemned and murdered the righteous one, who does not resist you" (5:6).

Excursus: "The Righteous One"

Although I will urge that "the righteous one" is a collective singular designating those who practice single-minded allegiance to God and the Lord Jesus Christ, this charge against the wealthy bristles with possibilities, and the history of interpretation offers a range of options.[38] Is the "righteous one" to whom James refers *Jesus* (cf., e.g., Luke 23:47; Acts 3:14–15; 1 Pet 3:18)? Is it a reference to James himself (also known as

---

37. Cf. Adewuya 2023, 82–84; Tamez 1990, 16.
38. E.g., Gowler 2014, 264–77.

"James the Just" [i.e., "the Righteous One"]; see, e.g., Eusebius, *Church History* 2.1.2), written either by James in anticipation of his own death or added by a later editor? Is "righteous one" a collective noun that refers to a group of people, "the righteous," whom the wealthy have deprived of life?

Whoever the righteous one is, does this one (or someone else) resist the wealthy or not? This second point of ambiguity resides in the possibility that James's phrase could be read as a declarative statement, "The righteous one . . . does not resist you"; or as an interrogative, "Does he or she not resist you?" If this is an interrogative, who is the "he" or "she"? A reference to God, who resists the wealthy? A reference to "the righteous," already condemned and murdered (the verbs are in the aorist indicative, indicating completed actions), who now resist the wealthy (the verb is present indicative), presumably through their postmortem, heavenly intercession on behalf of those continuing to be abused by the wealthy in this life?[39]

Given the uncertainty arising from James's language and the concomitant range of options championed in the history of interpretation, we should admit the hesitation that accompanies any proposal for the best reading.

James's previous use of key terms may help us unpack this final phrase. Thus, he prepares for this reference to "the righteous one" by his prior use of the language of *righteousness* or *justice*.[40] James counsels his siblings to "be quick to listen, slow to speak, slow to anger . . . because a person's anger does not produce God's righteousness" (1:19–20). The righteous or just, like Abraham or Rahab, demonstrate their faith through their faithful behavior (2:20, 21, 23, 24, 25). Peacemakers peaceably sow the fruit of justice (3:18): they conform their commitments to Jesus's faith and embrace God's choice of the poor, with the result that their practices, including speech habits, demonstrate the double love of Jesus's message: love for God and love for neighbor. Finally, James will write of the effectiveness of the righteous person's prayer (5:16), a usage that similarly depends on how James has earlier parsed the language of righteousness or justice.[41] James's usage overall, therefore, points strongly in the direction of reading his phrase "the righteous one" as a singular collective. Accordingly, he is referring to a group of people who, on the one hand, conform to James's message and, on the other hand, could never be confused with the arrogant and wealthy about whom James writes. This reading finds support from the Jewish book Wisdom of Solomon (first century BCE), which likely influenced James on this matter. Hear the words of the ungodly as they take counsel with each other:

39. Cf. Rev 6:9–11 NRSV: "Sovereign Lord, holy and true, how long will it be before you judge and avenge our blood on the inhabitants of the earth?"

40. *Dikaioō*, "I consider just / I make just" (2:21, 24, 25), *dikaios*, "just" (5:6, 16), *dikaiosynē*, "justice / rectitude" (1:20; 2:23; 3:18); see MGS 529.

41. James uses two terms to signify *resistance*: *antitassō* in 4:6 ("God resists the proud") and 5:6 ("the righteous one . . . does not resist you"); *anthistēmi* in 4:7 ("Resist the devil"). Accordingly, we do not find James countenancing antagonism against other human beings.

Let us oppress the righteous poor man; let us not spare the widow or regard the gray hairs of the aged. But let our might be our law of right, for what is weak proves itself to be useless. Let us lie in wait for the righteous man, because he is inconvenient to us and opposes our actions; he reproaches us for sins against the law and accuses us of sins against our training. He professes to have knowledge of God and calls himself a child of the Lord. He became to us a reproof of our thoughts; the very sight of him is a burden to us, because his manner of life is unlike that of others, and his ways are strange. (Wis 2:10–15 NRSV)

Continuing, those speaking in Wis 2 plan the condemnation, torture, and killing of the righteous.

Alongside the scene James paints, in which the wealthy withhold wages from field-workers (5:4) and murder the righteous (5:6), we should set his concern with murder as a contradiction of Scripture's royal law of neighbor love (2:8–11), as well as his stunning reference to the practice of pronouncing a blessing over the hungry and naked while doing nothing to care for their needs (2:15–16). Could it be that James regards cheating those in one's employ and withholding hospitality to the impoverished as somehow tantamount to murder? Indeed! And James is not alone. Consider how James follows the path already taken in the Jewish book of Sirach (2nd century BCE): "The bread of the impoverished is life for the poor; whoever withholds it is a murderer. Whoever takes away the neighbor's living murders the neighbor. Whoever fraudulently holds back the wages of a hired worker commits murder" (Sir 34:25–27 [34:21–22 LXX] AT).

These righteous, James goes on to say, do not resist the powerful and affluent. Why not? Were we to account for the realities of the world within which James lives and writes, we would have to admit, first, that the world-system endorsed and enacted by the wealthy has robbed the righteous of the wherewithal to mount real efforts at resistance. Remember that James has in mind the Roman establishment, the landed and well-placed tasked with maintaining public order. As such, they are the ones who administer the courts (and who influence those who do: see above, on Jas 2:6). However, more is at stake than the gaping power differential opened up between the wealthy and these righteous, impoverished ones. The way of wisdom, James has taught, is not the way of warfare (4:1–10). The way of wisdom is not to make of ourselves judge and jury, but to recall that the Lord is both lawgiver and judge, rescuer and destroyer (4:11–12). The way of wisdom is to make peace peaceably (3:18). Accordingly, James emphasizes even more the substantial gulf separating the life patterns of the wealthy and those they defraud. The wealthy cheat, disdain, condemn, and murder. The righteous do not retaliate.[42]

---

42. Note how, to the wealthy whom James portrays, the way of the righteous would thus indeed seem strange, as those who speak in Wis 2:15 (cited above) recognize.

5:7–12 Patient Resolve until the Lord's Return

5:7 Be patient, therefore, brothers and sisters, until the coming of the Lord. Look! The farmer waits for the highly valued[a] fruit of the earth, waiting patiently for it until it receives the early and late rains. **8** You too must be patient and strengthen your hearts, for the coming of the Lord is near. **9** Do not complain against each other, brothers and sisters, so that you will not be judged. Look! The judge is standing at the door! **10** As an example of patience amid suffering,[b] brothers and sisters, take the prophets who spoke in the name of the Lord. **11** Consider how we regard as genuinely happy those who have practiced endurance. You have heard of Job's endurance, and you have seen what the Lord has accomplished, for the Lord is full of compassion and mercy. **12** Above all, my brothers and sisters, do not utter an oath[c]—neither by heaven nor by earth, nor by anything else. But let your "Yes" be yes and your "No" be no, so that you may not fall under judgment.

a. *Timios* is usually translated as *precious* (e.g., CEB, NRSV) or *valuable* (NIV), but, in contemporary English, the one too easily suggests *charming* or *dear*, while the other too easily suggests *expensive*. MGS suggests "honored, valued, distinguished" or "worthy, precious, dear" (2119).

b. *Tēs kakopatheias kai tēs makrothymias*—two nouns read as hendiadys.

c. *Omnyō* is often translated with the English term *swear*, but outside legal contexts in the USA, *swear* typically suggests *cussing* or otherwise *using profanity*. James refers to the ancient practice of calling on a deity to sanction someone who does not keep a promise or claims what is not true. See L&N §33.463.

James pivots away from castigating those masters of the universe who give voice to their business plans (4:13–16) and wealthy landowners who try to secure themselves in their affluence while exploiting those in need (5:1–6). Rather than pointing his finger at those who know the right thing to do and do not do it (4:17), he comes back to familial language: "[my] brothers and sisters" (5:7, 9, 10, 12). This is his preferred way of naming his audience, and he does so fifteen times in this letter, four in this small section alone.[43] After addressing the arrogant and wealthy again and again as "you," "you," "you" (4:13–5:6; cf. 4:1–10), James's reintroduction of the pronoun "we" (5:11) helps to emphasize this notable shift in tone.

How might we explain this dramatic change of direction in James's letter? Clearly, he moves from addressing those caught up in wealth-related sin and arrogance (which, for James, are intertwined) in order to speak more directly to the faithful, including those on the receiving end of systematic oppression,

43. See Jas 1:2, 16, 19; 2:1, 5, 14; 3:1, 10, 12; 4:11; 5:7, 9, 10, 12, 19 (all in AT).

the degraded who suffer at the hands of the wealthy. We should not overlook how James has just decimated certain responses to their situation that the impoverished might have considered. The lifeworld supported and propagated as the Roman way can be seductive—embraced by those who have ascended society's ranks on the back of its values and practices, and taken for granted by common folk, who applaud the fortunate few who prosper according to its measures; that lifestyle also looks alluring to the less fortunate and the needy, who wish they too could find success in just this way. For James, though, taking this path would comprise double-mindedness and worldly contamination (1:7–8, 27), a choice out of step with those who profess allegiance to the Lord Jesus Christ. God's people—not only, but certainly not least, the exploited, degraded poor—quite naturally inquire into the alternatives. If they are not to escape their circumstances, say, by paying homage to and buying into this world system—and so, with violence against others—what are they to do? How should they respond when they are trampled underfoot by those of the privileged strata? We might imagine their calling on the Lord with the words of Habakkuk:

> O LORD, how long shall I cry for help,
>   and you will not listen?
> Or cry to you "Violence!"
>   and you will not save?
> Why do you make me see wrongdoing
>   and look at trouble?
> Destruction and violence are before me;
>   strife and contention arise.
> So the law becomes slack
>   and justice never prevails.
> The wicked surround the righteous—
>   therefore judgment comes forth perverted. (Hab 1:2–4 NRSV)

How will James respond? He has already given a hint when he claimed that "the harvesters' cries have reached the ears of the Lord of heavenly armies" (Jas 5:4), since proper response depends, first, on the character and action of the Lord Almighty. Now James develops this thought more fully.

His answer is double-sided. On the one hand, *let the Lord be the Lord.* This is the Lord of heavenly armies who is coming soon to set things right (5:7, 8, 9). This is the compassionate and merciful Lord, whose aim will be accomplished (5:10–11). Accordingly, this is the Lord who is aligned with the degraded and impoverished in order both to bring justice against those who harass the impoverished and to come alongside the degraded with kindness. On the other hand, *respond with patience, strong hearts, and endurance, not least in your speech habits.* As James has already intimated, these two responses go hand in hand.[44] Taking matters into one's own hands—is this not grasping at the possibility of substituting oneself for the Lord (cf. 4:11–12)? How James proceeds is evident in these parallels:

A Brothers and sisters + patience + the Lord's coming (5:7a)
    B Example of patience: farmers + the Lord's coming (5:7b–8)
        C Speech habits + coming judgment (5:9)
A′ Brothers and sisters (5:10)
    B′ Examples of patience and endurance: prophets (speaking in the Lord's name) (5:10) and Job (for whom the Lord's aim was accomplished) (5:11)
        C′ Speech habits + coming judgment (5:12)

As in the previous section (4:13–5:6), so here too, James communicates his message through *backshadowing.* Emphasizing over and over the coming of the end, with its promise and threat of divine judgment, James qualifies present suffering as temporary (just as he has characterized the lives of the high and mighty as transient [1:10–11; 4:14]) and verifies that the Lord will certainly balance the scales of justice. God's purpose will not be frustrated but will be accomplished. James thus allows his vision of a future determined by the Lord to cast its shadow backward on the present; this leads him to call for certain behaviors (patience, encouragement, endurance) and to rule others out of court (complaining against each other, oath-taking). The Lord *is* lord, and the Lord's good ends draw the Lord's people into them, shaping the character of and enabling faithful response in the present.

The nature of the response James counsels is thus grounded in affirmations concerning the Lord, the Lord's justice, and the grand mural of the Lord's purposeful activity.[45] Note the conceptual resemblances:

- Christ-followers exercise patience in anticipation of the Lord's coming (5:7a, 8).
- Farmers exercise patience in anticipation of rain and fruit-bearing (5:7b).
- Christ-followers exercise patience in anticipation of the Lord's coming (5:9).
- Prophets fulfilled their prophetic vocation and are vindicated (5:10–11a).

44. R. Martin (1988, 191) helpfully refers to Ps 37, where one's comportment vis-à-vis the Lord is similarly associated with faithful and patient responses to the wicked.
45. Here I am drawing on and adapting material from Green 2020b, 350–51.

- We honor Job's endurance and witness how the Lord brought Job's story to its denouement in Job's restoration (5:11b).
- Christ-followers exercise patience in anticipation of judgment (5:12).

We might summarize by outlining the teleology James sets before us: suffering → endurance/persistence → restoration/vindication. The patience and endurance of which James speaks, then, are future oriented and grounded in certain strong affirmations about the Lord. So let the Lord be the Lord, rather than (through directing vicious words against each other) usurping the Lord's role as the one who rights wrongs. Like the prophets, continue to speak in the Lord's name. Like Job, cry out to God while refusing to participate in malicious speech and the words and ways of accusers.[46] And refuse oath-taking so as not to presume on the Lord, practicing instead an unbending integrity of speech.

[5:7–9] Importantly, James takes a path that differs markedly from the way of the arrogant and affluent (cf., e.g., 4:13–5:6). As masters of the universe, those merchants plot a future quite undeterred by the Lord's aims. James, though, frames his instruction now in relation to the Lord's household and the Lord's coming. For their part, those with landed wealth exploit their workers by treating them as not-quite-human—robbing them of agency, reducing them to the status of a cog in a machine controlled by the self-aggrandizing opulent. "They treated their workers as a means, allowing them to cultivate the land that would produce plentiful crops for the landowners, while the landowners kept both the crops and the wages."[47] Even if James's addressees include the messianists to whom he addresses the letter as a whole, he certainly includes the degraded and defrauded in his instruction. And, by way of contrast with their treatment by the privileged and propertied, James addresses these people directly, includes them within the family of Christ-followers, and identifies them as persons not only capable of response but also desirous of answering their oppressors and carving out faithful lives in ways congruent with their professed allegiance to the Lord Jesus Christ.

How should James's siblings respond amid their trying circumstances? We can summarize: James calls for patience (5:7a), uses an agrarian image to fill out the meaning of patience (5:7b), reiterates his call for patience (5:8a), includes strengthening one's heart in his definition of patience (5:8b), and points to the future coming of the Lord as the chief motivation for present patience (5:8c). Exercising patience, James goes on to say, leaves no room for complaining against other Christ-followers (5:9).

---

46. Cf. Job 27.
47. Scacewater 2017, 236.

With his reference to "brothers and sisters," James reminds his readers and hearers of their shared status within the household of the Lord Jesus Christ (cf. 1:1; 2:1). This is important for at least three reasons. First, his sibling language counters all hints of structured hierarchy and every inclination toward haughtiness and disdain, preferring instead status symmetry, mutual belonging, and oneness. In a sense, he draws a thick "X" over the dispositions and community-oriented behaviors he has critiqued in the body of his letter thus far (2:1–5:6; cf., e.g., 3:14–16): favoritism, bitter rivalry, devious self-promotion, falsifying the truth, and the like. Second, he activates a household schema (a schema further triggered by the repeated references to *the Lord* in this subsection of the letter) that spotlights patterns of thinking, feeling, believing, and behaving characteristic of and appropriate to *this* household, the household over which Jesus Christ is lord. (This is manifestly *not* the household of Rome. Roman sensibilities and rules are not and cannot be assumed. Sibling talk is in this important sense counterworldly.) Third, kinship language projects onto relationships a desired outcome while at the same time cultivating those relationships in the direction of that ideal. Naming his audience as "brothers and sisters," then, James establishes a base from which he can launch his instructions regarding appropriate response to this current life situation.

Patience may not be the best translation of the term James repeatedly uses: "Be patient" (5:7), "waiting patiently" (5:7), "be patient" (5:8), "as an example of patience" (5:10). This is because *patience* can signify do-nothing-ism, passivity, resignation, deference. However, it can also be used to communicate a sense much more at home in the present context: *withstand, persist, persevere*.[48] Our understanding of patience is shaped in part by James's example of the farmer. This is not the wealthy landowner of whom he has just spoken (5:1–6). The farmers to whom he now refers are those who find their homes and daily lives on single-family farms. Those with an agrarian background know that, when such farmers wait patiently for the rains,[49] their patience is directed to what they *cannot* control (such as the coming of the rains) while they direct their considerable industry toward what they *can* control (working the soil, tending to livestock, etc.). By way of analogy, the patience James countenances "is a question of doing everything possible not to despair in spite of the desperate situation, relying on the future that will put an end to the suffering."[50] Our understanding of patience is also shaped by James's pairing it with his directive to "strengthen your hearts," that is, to mounting courage or resolve amid

---

48. *Makrothymeō*—5:7 [2×], 8; *makrothymia*, 5:10. Cf. MGS 1272.

49. As the CEB makes clear, James's reference to "the early and late rains" refers to "the rain in the fall and spring" (5:7).

50. Tamez 1990, 46.

trying circumstances.[51] Patience does not include—or, we might say, is contravened by—complaints against each other.[52] James underscores this last point by reminding his audience again of their shared siblingship: "Do not complain against each other, *brothers and sisters*" (5:9). As we noted earlier, ideally in the Greco-Roman world, siblings avoid conflict by refusing to judge each other and overcome conflict through practices of mercy, compassion, and forgiveness toward each other (see above, on 2:1). Additionally, James has observed that vilifying a brother or sister abrogates God's Instructions (or Torah)[53] and is tantamount to replacing the Lord-as-Judge with oneself-as-judge (4:11–12). The point is obvious: a community that finds itself struggling with external influence, "being contaminated by the world" (1:27), needs to tighten its bonds, not damage them through complaining against each other.

The end time, and especially the coming of divine judgment, stretches over this entire subsection like an umbrella: "until the coming of the Lord," "the coming of the Lord is near," "so that you will not be judged. Look! The judge is standing at the door!" (5:7, 8, 9). James does not simply emphasize the end time, but the end time as the coming of the Lord to set things right. He thus moves the temporary nature of present suffering to center stage, assures his audience that the scales of justice will indeed be balanced, leaves open the possibility that this can happen at any moment, and clarifies that the disruptive work of making things right belongs to the Lord (and not to Christ-followers). (Drawing insight from James's farmer-analogy, patience apparently includes continuing work in preparation for the harvest while waiting for the Lord to bring vindication. After all, the Lord is the one who will "rescue and destroy" [4:12].) James does not clarify whether "Lord" signifies Jesus or the Father in this cotext. He has referred to both with this term. Such ambiguity supports the notion that Jesus and the Father share in the one divine identity and that Jesus participates integrally in the work anticipated of God in Israel's Scriptures. Comparison with other NT literature recommends a decision in favor of James's reference to Jesus's (second) coming.[54]

[10–12] James presses further into the situation he envisages and the response for which he calls. First, he provides an example of patience, yes, but now refers

---

51. *Kardia* refers to the *heart*, the seat of courage, the source of cognitive strength.

52. James 5:8–9 pairs as opposites the soundalike verbs *stērizō* and *stenazō*: *strengthen* (your hearts), and (do not) *complain* (against each other).

Baker (1995, 180) observes that *stenazō* often refers to *groaning*, but here "encompasses a wide assortment of verbal wrongs, including gossip, slander, mockery, cursing, angry speech, perjury, and probably also speech that reflects partiality."

53. Recall that James epitomizes God's Instructions with what he terms "the royal law": "Love your neighbor as yourself" (2:8, citing Lev 19:18).

54. E.g., Acts 1:9–11; 1 Cor 15:23–28; Heb 9:28. And note that James pictures the judge "standing at the door (or gate)" (Jas 5:9), which parallels references to Christ in Matt 24:32–33; Mark 13:29; Rev 3:20. Cf. K.-W. Niebuhr 2020, 185; Bauckham 2021, 95–96; Baker 2002, 53–55.

to "patience amid suffering" (5:10). Second, he yokes patience with *endurance* (5:11 [2×]). For James, endurance signifies a courageous fidelity that emerges through stubborn trust in God,[55] and this contributes to our understanding of patience (in 5:7–9) as *persistence*—which should never be confused with passivity. All this is set within James's continued emphasis on siblingship, living as "brothers and sisters" (5:10) in a household shared by those to whom he writes. He thus underscores the intracommunal nature of his instruction and the nonhierarchical mutuality they share (see above, on 5:7–9).

This is one of only two places in the letter where James refers explicitly to *suffering*,[56] though he has just referred to the distress experienced by defrauded workers and the righteous (5:4–6). Moreover, he opens the letter by characterizing the life situation of his brothers and sisters in terms of the agitation messianists encounter because of their identification with the Lord Jesus Christ (1:1–3). It is not that they go out in search of harassment or suffering (nor is it that suffering is a universal, essential condition of the faithful). Rather, their allegiance to the Lord results in counterworldly lives that attract opposition precisely because they fail to conform to life patterns taken for granted in a world that has Rome as its overlord.

Take as an example the prophets, James urges. They "spoke in the name of the Lord" even when it was not convenient to do so, even when doing so invited opposition and even death. Indeed, the suffering and death of the prophets is axiomatic.[57] Thus we read in a detailed description in Hebrews:

> Others were tortured, refusing to accept release, in order to obtain a better resurrection. Others suffered mocking and flogging and even chains and imprisonment. They were stoned to death, they were sawn in two, they were killed by the sword; they went about in skins of sheep and goats, destitute, persecuted, tormented—of whom the world was not worthy. They wandered in deserts and mountains, and in caves and holes in the ground. (Heb 11:35–38 NRSV)

The phrasing "the prophets who spoke in the name of the Lord" recalls prophetic activity in Israel's Scriptures,[58] but also helps to fill out the nature of "patience amid suffering." Such patience does not signal an end to speaking, but its continuation. (Again, the idea of patience as passivity or resignation is

---

55. See above, on 1:2–4.

56. In 5:10 James uses the noun *kakopatheia* (suffering pain/hardship), and in 5:13 he uses the related verb *kakopatheō* (I suffer pain/hardship). *Homiopathēs*, in 5:17, refers to "similar feelings" or, better, "same nature," and not to suffering per se.

57. See, e.g., Heb 11:32–39; 1 Kgs 18:13; 19:10, 14; 2 Kgs 9:7; Neh 9:26 CEB, "They killed your prophets who had warned them so that they might return to you"; Matt 23:30, 34, 37; Luke 11:47–51; 13:34; Acts 7:52.

58. See, e.g., Deut 18:22.

set aside, now by this image of prophets unwearyingly raising their voices: "Thus says the Lord!")

James's directive is also reminiscent of Jesus's words in the Sermon on the Mount:

> Happy are people whose lives are harassed because they are righteous, because the kingdom of heaven is theirs.

> Happy are you when people insult you and harass you and speak all kinds of bad and false things about you, all because of me. Be full of joy and be glad, because you have a great reward in heaven. In the same way, people harassed the prophets who came before you. (Matt 5:10–12 CEB; cf. Luke 6:22–23)

James, like Jesus, refers to the prophets for inspiration amid suffering, countering any presumption that suffering disqualifies one as outside of the orbit of divine approval. James, like Jesus, also refers to happiness and, in doing so, recalls the introduction to this letter.

Jas 5:10–11	Jas 1:2–3
"As an example of patience <u>amid suffering</u>, *brothers and sisters*, . . . consider how we regard as *genuinely happy* those who have practiced *endurance*."	"My *brothers and sisters*, consider <u>the various trials you encounter</u> as occasions for the *greatest happiness*, knowing that <u>the testing of your faithfulness</u> produces *endurance*."

True, *happiness* will suggest to some such responses as *glib merriment* or *cheeriness*. A more robust sense of the term would reflect Greco-Roman usage, however. Happiness connotes a way of life characterized by growth and integrity. It refers to human flourishing.[59] In James, as in Ps 1 ("Happy are those . . .") and Jesus's Sermon on the Mount/Plain, happiness is a verdict pronounced over lives lived before God, not a momentary condition based on the occasional experience of a windfall. Happy lives may be absent the resources and recognition associated with power and privilege, they may attract harassment from those who have not aligned themselves with the Lord Jesus Christ, yet they are affirmed and celebrated in God's economy. And, for James, that vision of faithful life (amid suffering) is marked by *endurance*, what one interpreter recognizes as an "unyielding, defiant perseverance in the face of aggressive misfortune."[60] The road to human wholeness and thriving is paved with endurance.

59. See above, on 1:2–4.
60. Radl 1993, 3:405. See above, on 1:2–4.

From the prophets as models of patience, James now turns to Job as exemplar of endurance.[61] Singling out Job in this context may be surprising, given how James has just taken on the wealthy—that is, those who cheat their workers, whose wealth has rotted, who stuff their hearts for the day of slaughter, and so on (5:1–6). After all, the book of Job portrays Job as megawealthy: "He had seven sons and three daughters, and owned seven thousand sheep, three thousand camels, five hundred pairs of oxen, five hundred female donkeys, and a vast number of servants, so that he was greater than all the people of the east" (Job 1:2–3 CEB). This is a reminder, first, that James's instruction in this subsection (beginning with 5:7) is not narrowly directed toward the swindled workers he has just described (5:4–6), but more generally to the "brothers and sisters" to whom he has addressed the entire letter (5:7, 9, 10, 12). Second, together with James's earlier reference to exemplary Abraham (2:21–24), this allusion to Job reminds us that James is not using *wealth* or *wealthy* as essentialist terms.[62] In his presentation, concepts like *wealthy* cannot be equated simply with owning or controlling the means of production, for example, or having this or that level of personal worth. For James, those of relative prosperity might have significant resources (referring, say, to society's top 10 or 15 percent), but they would also be characterized by such life patterns as favoritism, disparagement and exploitation of the impoverished, use of the courts against the indigent, insulting the Lord's name, planning one's business pursuits without reference to God's will, and lavish lifestyles (2:2–7; 4:13–5:6). Apparently, there are ways to make use of one's resources that have less to do with the exercise of parading and extending one's power and privilege, and more to do with neighbor love, such as the redistribution of resources on behalf of those in need (2:14–17). Recall, too, that the book of Job identifies Job as wealthy *and* upright: "That man was honest, a person of absolute integrity; he feared God and avoided evil" (Job 1:1 CEB). Accordingly, James can present one wealthy person as exemplary for the way he models faith-in-action (Abraham) and another for his endurance amid severe trials (Job).

With its steady translation of James's varied vocabulary with the English term *patience*,[63] the AV has done us no favors, exegetically or pastorally.

---

61. For this material related to Job, I am indebted to Green 2020b, 349–51.

62. An essentialist reading would have it that the term *wealth* has a set, intrinsic meaning—as though the meaning attached to significant economic holdings is something other than a social construction, and as though persons with those assets are necessarily characterized by such and such approved (or disapproved), stereotypical properties: "That is just the way they are." See above, on 1:9–11.

63. *Makrothymeō* (I demonstrate patience), 5:7 [2×], 8; *makrothymia* (patience), 5:10; *hypomonē* (endurance), 5:11. Given its habit of using the translation "patience" for these terms elsewhere in James, it is strange that the AV translates a verbal form (substantival participle) of *hypomenō* (I

This is because the AV apparently attributes to Job what the book of Job does not: patience. Regrettably, this has led to the problematic idiom "the patience of Job" and the problematic counsel to those mired in troubling, stressful circumstances that they should simply accept their dire situations with quiet acquiescence.

The scriptural book of Job, read as a whole, does not portray Job as a model of virtuous calm amid suffering, and this has led some to seek the background for James's interests in the Testament of Job (first century BCE or CE).[64] Here, Job gathers his children in order to reflect on his life, counsel his heirs, and settle his affairs. God's messenger, he recounts, revealed to Job that his battle against idolatry would attract Satan's ire: "He will bring you many plagues, he will take away for himself your goods, he will carry off your children. But if you are patient, I will make your name renowned in all generations of the earth till the consummation of the age" (T. Job 4.5–6). Job draws out the lesson for his children, "You also must be patient in everything that happens to you. For patience is better than anything" (27.7).[65] This storyteller sounds like the prototype of patience to whom James refers, and it may be that Jame was aware of the tradition represented by the Testament of Job.

In actuality, though, his depiction of Job makes good sense of the Job of Israel's Scriptures—once we remember that James's term *hypomenō* is closer to our English word *endurance* than to the passive, silent waiting we moderns might associate with the term *patience*.[66] In some ways, the book of Job presents its central character like James's farmer awaiting the fall and spring rains—in his case, though, protesting, searching for insight into God's character and purpose, *and* waiting in trust for God's vindication (cf., e.g., Job 13:15–18). James extends his interest in Job to include "what the Lord has accomplished, for the Lord is full of compassion and mercy" (5:11), alluding to the book's epilogue, wherein "the LORD doubled all Job's earlier possessions," blessing "Job's latter days more than his former ones" (42:10, 12 CEB). Job's story, then, exemplifies for James the movement from trials to endurance to vindication.[67]

As it turns out, the scriptural story of Job—reflection on which James triggers by referring to Job's endurance and "what the Lord has accomplished"—reverberates with words from the Jesus tradition about suffering and happiness,

---

endure) in 5:11a as "endure": "Behold, we count them happy which [who] *endure*. Ye have heard of the *patience* of Job, and have seen the end of the Lord; that the Lord is very pitiful, and of tender mercy" (emphasis added).

64. Cf., e.g., the discussion in Gray 2004.

65. Spittler 1983, 841, 851.

66. Seitz 1993.

67. Luke uses different terminology, but he too provides an example of faithfulness that tracks well with the response of persistence or endurance to which James refers: Jesus tells of the widow seeking justice, who takes her case to the judge repeatedly and finally receives justice (Luke 18:1–8).

models the response to trials that James urges, and anticipates the accomplishment of God's purpose. We can also see how Job's story might prompt empathy and attraction, even identification with Job, among the Christ-followers to whom James addresses his letter. This is both because his struggles are like theirs and because of James's expectation that the compassionate, merciful Lord, so obviously at work in Job's circumstances, will also bring about a good end in theirs.

In the immediately preceding paragraph (Jas 5:7–9), James illustrated what patience looks like, then gave an example of its opposite, drawing on his larger interest in speech habits: Patience is contradicted by complaining against each other. He follows the same logic here: exemplifying endurance, then contrasting it with wrongheaded speech habits: "Do not utter an oath" (5:12). In antiquity the kind of oath-taking to which James refers ("neither by heaven," etc.) signified more than making a pledge or promise. Oath-taking identified or called on God or the gods as witness(es).[68] An oath thus had an intrinsically religious association. Moreover, swearing an oath implicated the deity by identifying divine sanctions against the oath-taker in cases of perjury.[69] Set against this backdrop, oath-takers begin to resemble the masters of the universe about whom James has written, who imagine that their lives— especially their calendars, itineraries, and business dealings—are under their own control (4:13–16). Oath-takers take this a further step by assuming that their pledges place demands on the Lord to act in such and such a way. On this point, James's prohibition looks very much like Jesus's: "But I say to you: Do not swear at all, either by heaven, for it is the throne of God, or by the earth, for it is his footstool, or by Jerusalem, for it is the city of the great King. And do not swear by your head, for you cannot make one hair white or black. Let your word be 'Yes, Yes' or 'No, No'; anything more than this comes from the evil one" (Matt 5:34–37 NRSV; cf. 23:16–22). For both the Sermon on the Mount and James, oath-taking appears contrary to appropriate reverence for the Lord, for it looks like an attempt to obligate the Lord to certify the veracity of merely human speech. Such arrogance stands in tension with James's directives: "Therefore, submit to God" and "Humble yourselves before the Lord" (Jas 4:7, 10).

Furthermore, oath-taking rises to the level of necessity only among those not recognized for the integrity of their speech. Again, James's ban resembles Jesus's: "Do not swear at all. . . . Let your word be 'Yes, Yes' or 'No, No'; anything more than this comes from the evil one" (Matt 5:34–37). Reflecting on this Jesus material, James (like the Sermon on the Mount) rejects the notion

68. In Israel's Scriptures, see, e.g., Gen 31:50; Jer 42:5–6.
69. Cf. Milkason 1996; Thiselton 2009.

that some situations or pledges command greater reliability or truthfulness than others. Allegiance to the Lord Jesus requires routine truth-telling.[70]

5:13–20 Final Instructions

5:13 Are any among you suffering hardship? They should pray. Are any in good spirits? They should sing songs of praise. 14 Are any among you sick? They should summon the elders of the community,[a] and the elders should pray over[b] them, anointing them with oil in the name of the Lord. 15 Trusting prayer[c] will heal the sick, and the Lord will raise them up.[d] And if they have committed sins, they will be forgiven. 16 Therefore, confess your sins to each other, and pray on behalf of each other so that you [in Southern idiom, y'all][e] may be healed.

The prayer of a righteous person is powerful in what it can achieve. 17 Elijah was a human being just like us. He earnestly prayed[f] that it would not rain, and it did not rain on the land for three and a half years. 18 He prayed again, heaven gave rain, and the earth produced its fruit.

19 My brothers and sisters, if any of you strays from the truth and someone turns them back, 20 recognize that whoever turns sinners back from a stray path will rescue them[g] from death and will cover innumerable sins.

a. *Ekklēsia* is often translated as *church* (e.g., CEB, NIV, NRSV), but *community* or *assembly* more accurately reflects the situation in the first century (esp. the situation envisioned by James), when Christ-followers have not broken off into a separate faith called "Christianity." I prefer *community* over, say, *assembly* because the former term suggests more strongly the presence of shared commitments and lives.

b. James uses the preposition *epi* (signifying spatial deixis *on top of* or *over*). As the comments will show, James sketches this situation using a verticality schema, with *down* correlated with inactivity, illness, or disorder; and with *up* correlated with renewed health. Praying "over" someone suggests that the person is disabled or confined to a bed by disease.

c. *Hē euchē tēs pisteōs* can be woodenly translated as "prayer of faith" (as in AV and NRSV), but this does not clarify the relationship of *prayer* with *faith*: Does prayer come from faith? Is the prayer itself faithful? Etc. My translation is guided by the reference to praying in faith in 1:5–8 (see above), where *pistis* has the sense of *confidence* or *trust* (or *entrustment*).

d. See translation note b, above. The Lord's raising the sick is tantamount to the Lord's restoring them to health (as in the CEB).

e. *Iathēte*—the form is second-person plural.

70. The history of interpretation has struggled with Matthew's and James's bans on oath-taking, not least in light of the oath-related practices in Israel's Scriptures (including God's own swearing of oaths: e.g., Isa 45:22–23; Amos 6:8) and in Paul (e.g., 2 Cor 1:23; Gal 1:20). See the brief discussion in Kotva 2011.

f. *Proseuchē prosēuxato*: this use of a dative of manner intensifies the action of the verb (von Siebenthal 2019, 260–61).

g. *Psychēn autou*: I have translated *psychē* with reference to its usual sense of *life*; cf. L&N 9.20: "a person as a living being."

Although the document penned by James opens like a letter, its finale does not remind us much of other letters we find in the NT or more generally. Moreover, it is not easy to provide a single heading for the somewhat disparate material we find here. Adopting a bird's-eye view of the whole, we might say that James concludes his letter with practical wisdom that emphasizes human flourishing in relation to God. Accordingly, irrespective of the situation (Suffering hardship? In good spirits? Sick or disabled?), turn to the Lord (5:13–18). Participate with the Lord in the healing of the sick and disabled, aware of the effectiveness of prayer (5:14–18). And keep watch over each other through mutual confession and prayer, and by guiding and accompanying each other on the true path (5:15–16, 19–20). This final section of the letter centers on the health of the messianic community and the brothers and sisters comprising it.

[5:13] Throughout his letter, James has encouraged practical wisdom—that is, wise habits of discernment and practice that are a gift from God and therefore enabled by God. As he comes to the end of his letter, he writes concerning responses appropriate to persons and persons-in-community as they experience life in one of three ways: suffering, in good spirits, and sick or disabled. He wants his readers and hearers to put practical wisdom into play as they evaluate their life situations, participate in their communities, and reflect on their patterns of thinking, feeling, believing, and behaving.

Those suffering hardship should pray. This is one of only two places in the letter where James refers explicitly to *suffering*.[71] He has nonetheless called attention to the distress and anguish experienced by defrauded workers and the righteous (5:4–6). Furthermore, in the opening of his letter he recognizes the less-than-tranquil circumstances his brothers and sisters experience as they inhabit the Jewish diaspora of the Roman world (1:1–3). Evidence from the first century encourages our recognition of both anti-Jewish attitudes among, and anti-Jewish actions by, non-Jewish neighbors as well as patterns of Jewish resistance—or perhaps better, Jewish efforts at maintaining Jewish distinctiveness in diasporic settings where Jews were in the minority.[72] Allegiance to the Lord leads to counterworldly lives that attract opposition because they fail to conform to life patterns expected of all in a Rome-centered, Rome-patterned world.

---

71. Here in 5:13 he uses the verb *kakopatheō* (I suffer pain/hardship). In 5:10 is the related noun *kakopatheia* (suffer pain/hardship).

72. See, e.g., Schäfer 1997; L. Feldman 1993; Berthelot 2021. Also see above, on 1:1, 2–3.

James's instruction here reminds us in a second way of his opening reference to "the various trials" his brothers and sisters encounter. There, in that earlier context, he advises, "Ask God" (1:5–6; cf. 4:2–3), just as now he directs, "They should pray" (5:13). As before, so now he frames the life-world within which his readers and hearers are to make sense of and move forward with their lives. Rather than turning to self-help problem-solving or to brainstorming potential counterstrikes, James's audience is urged to open themselves to "God and the Lord Jesus Christ" (1:1). When viewed as scenes within the expansive, textured mural of the Lord's work in the world (and in light of the promise of the Lord's balancing the scales at his coming), how might these episodes of "suffering hardship" best be understood? God's wisdom, after all, turns conventional perspectives and practices upside down, right side up, and this work of repairing frames of reference has been central to James's message. Thus, in the introduction to his letter, James sketches a chain of effects that gives hardships fresh meaning: trials → endurance → maturity (all set under the larger umbrella of "the greatest happiness" [1:2–4]). Moreover, James's directive to pray amid hardship should prompt his siblings to remember that "there is one lawgiver and judge, and this one is able to rescue and to destroy" (4:12); and to revisit his message that present-day circumstances call for patience, strong hearts, and endurance while waiting for the Lord's coming to set things right. The Lord Almighty is coming. Courageous endurance, not retaliation or other human machinations, is needed (5:7–12).

Those in good spirits should sing songs of praise. It may not be too much to suggest that those who populate this second category, those *in good spirits*, are those who have already heeded James's counsel to occupants of the first group, those *suffering hardship*. This would parallel his earlier message that those encountering trials ought to regard them as "occasions for the greatest happiness" (1:2).[73] A comparison with Acts 27:22 helps to clarify what James's language envisions. In Luke's account of Paul's voyage to Rome, the ship encounters a winter storm that leaves the crew unnerved, hungry, and desperate (Acts 27:14–22). Paul addresses them: "I urge you now to recover your composure" (27:22 AT). Accordingly, the term James (5:13) and Luke (in Acts 27:22) share suggests planting one's feet firmly on the ground (or deck) again, finding one's equilibrium, returning to calm.[74] A comparison between James

---

73. The points of contact with 1:2–4 would be more conceptual than linguistic, and the reference to being *in good spirits* may not rise to the level of the *life of happiness* to which James earlier alluded. The term James uses here, *euthymeō* (I am in good spirits / regain my composure / am serene), is found only here in the letter. Recall that *happiness* in ancient moral philosophy is not so much a "feeling" as a set of "inclinations and behaviors associated with human flourishing" (quoted from above, on 1:2–4).

74. *TLNT* 2:114–17 (cf. *CGL* 1:618: "in good spirits"). Spicq argues against the common attempt to translate *euthymeō* with reference to *courage* (*TLNT* 2:114).

here and Luke's account of the sea journey might push still further, to include not only contentedness amid trying circumstances but also the motivation for recovering one's composure rather than sinking into despair. In Acts 27, the promise of (and Paul's faith in) God's intervention is the basis of Paul's call to his shipmates to regain their composure (27:23–26). James can think of balance and composure because the Lord's coming to set things right is on the near horizon (5:7–12).

In wider Greek usage, James's term for *singing songs of praise* refers to fingers plucking the strings of a musical instrument. Over time, though, and particularly in Israel's Scriptures, it signifies *making music* more generally as well as *singing*, either with an instrument or a cappella.[75] The term appears repeatedly in the Psalms (45×), most often with God or the Lord or "you" or "your [the Lord's] name" as its indirect object: "Let all the earth worship you and sing to you; let them sing praises to your name" (Ps 66:4; 65:4 LXX, AT). James mimics this usage, but he uses shorthand, with the result that he provides little indication of the content of the praise songs he imagines. If we turn to the psalter for inspiration, though, we find a stable form: words of praise plus reasons for praise (e.g., Pss 8, 33, 47, 100, 135, 136). And if we review James's letter, we find several reasons why praise is due. For example:

- God "gives to everyone without a second thought, without reservation" (1:5).
- The Father of Lights "chose to give us birth by means of his true word" (1:18).
- God has "chosen the poor . . . to be heirs of the kingdom he has promised to those who love him" (2:5).
- The Lord will lift up those who humble themselves (4:10).
- The Lord "is able to rescue and to destroy" (4:12).
- "The harvesters' cries have reached the ears of the Lord of heavenly armies" (5:4).
- "The coming of the Lord is near" (5:8).
- "The Lord is full of compassion and mercy" (5:11).

Accordingly, those in good spirits do not turn to singing as a form of escaping or denying their difficult circumstances. Instead, they sing on account of the Lord's gracious and magnanimous character, the Lord's just promise, and the Lord's good ends. This means that, for them, human understanding must be

---

75. MGS 2395–96. *Making music* is suggested in those instances where *psallō* (I pluck a musical instrument / sing) is paired with *adō* (I sing)—e.g., Ps 68:4, 32 (67:5, 33 LXX), though it is also possible to read the pair as an example of hendiadys.

and is shaped by allegiance to the Lord Jesus Christ and by its entailments for trusting in the Lord, who has chosen the poor, who has heard the cries of the oppressed, and who will, at any moment, come to set things right.

[14–16a] James begins this final section of the letter (5:13–20) by outlining responses appropriate to persons and persons-in-community as they experience life in one of three ways: suffering, composed (in good spirits), and sick or disabled. As we turn to the third of these, the question immediately arises whether or how it is related to the first two (5:13). James's counsel to the suffering and to those who are in good spirits makes good sense in relation to the foregoing material, concerned as it is with hardship, anguish, and responses fitting for those who have declared their allegiance to the Lord Jesus Christ. What of the third? In fact, James's concern with those who are sick meshes well with these other matters, though how this is so requires some development.

First, and most obviously, this larger subsection is peppered with the language of prayer.

Reference	English Translation	Greek Term
5:13, 14, 17, 18	I pray, I ask God for	*proseuchomai*
5:15	Words directed to God, prayer	*euchē*
5:16	I speak to or ask of God	*euchomai*
5:16	An urgent request or prayer	*deēsis*

This is consistent with the heightened emphasis James's letter as a whole places on *theology* as the basis for his instruction to his audience. That is, what he has to say about patience and endurance is predicated on what he has to say about the work of the Lord Almighty. Prayer, he now intimates, points his brothers and sisters beyond themselves and so to their need for and dependence on the Lord to bring personal and relational health. In fact, it looks as though James, having introduced prayer in the context of suffering and sickness (5:13–14), found himself needing to develop this motif much further (5:15–18), especially regarding prayer's efficacy.

Second, we should account for the range of terms with which James refers in this larger section to the recovery of health, since these provide strong hints of how deeply embedded in James's letter this concern with healing is:

- *sōzō*—"I save," "I heal" (5:15, 20): Although this term signified rescue from all kinds of misfortune, by far its most common usage in the Greco-Roman world was medical. It is often used in this way, too, in the Synoptic Gospels and Acts.[76] And this is how James uses the term when he declares, "Trusting prayer will heal the sick" (5:15). James shows the elasticity of the term when he then writes of *rescuing* the wayward from death (5:20).

• *egeirō*—"I raise up" (5:15): James's language participates in the universal metaphor UP IS MORE, with its corollary DOWN IS LESS. Up is better, up is healthy, up is good. Down is inferior, down is weakness, down is bad.[77] That is, we conceptualize abstract notions like "better" or "bad" by means of embodied experiences. As children, we watch the rise and fall of fluids or other substances and so learn to associate *up* and *down* with these value judgments. For example, we say, "She is down with a fever," and we tend to picture those with visible disabilities, and the sick more generally, in just this way. We look down at (and on) them. They are beneath us, bedridden or bent over or in a wheelchair. And so on. Accordingly, the elders, once summoned, are to pray *over* the sick or disabled, who are thus represented spatially as *down*. The phrase "the Lord will raise them up," then, signifies renewed health.[78]

• *iaomai*—"I restore," "I heal" (5:16): Although this is one of the terms we might anticipate in any discussion of sickness and healing, its use here implies wider connotations. Restoration is promised to "y'all," not just to an individual or to one person at a time. (In 5:14–15, my translation refers to sick people [pl.] who are healed rather than individuals [sg.] in order to avoid the use of a singular pronoun, which would imply that James refers only to the healing of a male; James does write of individuals, however.) Moreover, restoration is promised in the context of mutual confession of sin. This speaks to the communal context of healing and,

---

76. *TLNT* 3:346–47. See, e.g., Matt 9:21–22; Mark 3:4; 5:23, 34; 6:56; Luke 8:36, 48, 50; Acts 4:9.

77. Note, however, that the data sometimes works at cross-purposes with the up-down conceptual metaphor. Sometimes, up is bad. We use up-related words in English to express a reversal of common usage: uppity, high and mighty, highfalutin, stuck-up. Note how, elsewhere, James instructs his readers and hearers to submit to God (DOWN) and to humble themselves before the Lord (DOWN), who will lift them up (UP) (4:7, 10). It is true that UP IS MORE and DOWN IS LESS, but not if one craves upness—that is, not if one craves elevated honor, chases after the heightened social status that permits one to abuse subordinates, places others under burdens of perpetual obligation, or grabs for the sort of power realized in lording it over others.

78. Hence, the CEB translates: "the Lord will restore them to health" (5:15). On the up-down metaphor, see, e.g., Luke 4:39; 5:18–19, 24–25; 13:11–13; Acts 3:1–10.

more particularly, to the confession of sin and its forgiveness as a basis for the restoration of a community torn apart by the sorts of violent attitudes and practices James has documented throughout his letter (e.g., 3:1–4:10).

Third, note the terms James uses to identify the sick—those who are frail or needy, the sick or disabled especially, who may even be on the verge of death (5:14);[79] and the sick or desperately ill (5:15)[80]—together with the association of persons having these conditions with the community (5:14), with prayer (5:14, 15, 16), and with confession and forgiveness of sins (5:15–16). Why is this important?

Imagine that James has drawn two circles. Here, he draws a circle comprising those who are sick or disabled. Earlier, he drew a circle that includes those who are demeaned and impoverished (e.g., 1:9, 27; 2:1–7, 14–16). In fact, however, these are not two distinct circles but one—or, at least, these two circles overlap considerably. Although cultural exchange across the Greco-Roman world promoted advances in the medical sciences (including anatomical research, the rise of pharmacology, and notable developments in surgical techniques and instruments), these health-care innovations were available mostly in urban centers, and even there they were restricted almost entirely to the urban elite.[81] Rural medicine and peasant health care continued more generally to feature snake charmers, herbalists, and other folk healers. It was as if some 85 percent of the population lived in a parallel universe, light-years removed from city-based, household physicians and their medicaments. Only people of some means (perhaps the top 10–15 percent of the population) could afford the advice and care of a trained physician, leaving town-and-country folk vulnerable to manipulation by quacks, who took what little money they had but provided little by way of actual help.[82] Accordingly, the impoverished might find themselves forever on the downward slope toward sickness, and the sick and disabled would find themselves increasingly indigent—and forgotten. These realities underscore the real-world consequences when the wealthy elite are given the spotlight at the expense of the impoverished (2:1–4) and when the poor are met with cheery words of blessing devoid of actual assistance (2:14–16). In short, when James begins to speak of the

---

79. *Astheneō* (I am sick/disabled); see, e.g., Matt 10:8; 25:36; Mark 6:56; Luke 4:40; John 5:3; 11:1–3; Acts 9:37; 20:35. See L&N 23.144; Albl 2017, 430–31; Albl 2022, 125.

80. *Kamnō* (I am sick / distressed / sick beyond hope); cf. L&N 23.142; BDAG 506–7.

81. Nutton 2004, 140–66.

82. Mark 5:26 CEB is illustrative: "She had suffered a lot under the care of many doctors, and had spent everything she had without getting any better. In fact, she had gotten worse."

sick and disabled, he is not really introducing a new category of people. Instead, he is filling out the nature of his earlier interest in the degraded poor.[83]

Excursus: Sickness and Health

When reading material on healing and health in James, we ought to remind ourselves of how our own experiences with and definitions of sickness can skew our understanding.[84] (The same can be said of our engagement with other biblical texts and with texts from cultures unlike our own.) Medical anthropologists have found that different societies construct sickness (including its definition, its nature, and its cause) and healing (recovery) in different ways. One useful classification of sickness introduces three categories:[85]

1. *Disease accounts* focus on the body of the individual as the source of sickness. Patients are treated as individuals, with the site of disease sought in the structure and function of bodily organs. Biomedical interventions serve as the primary mode of therapy.
2. *Illness accounts* focus on patients as embodied persons nested in their families or communities. The cause and treatment of sicknesses thus require attention to people in their social environments, with recovery of health measured in the interrelation of biology and relationality.
3. *Disorder accounts* focus not only on the patient's body and relational networks, but also on the cosmic order of things. Sharply put, the universe is out of whack; the work of gods or evil powers has disordered life.

Of course, actual accounts of sickness and recovery sometimes blur the lines between these categories.

People in the West tend to think of sickness in terms of *disease accounts*, so Western health-care systems are largely concerned with biomedical diagnoses and therapies focused on individual bodies and the symptoms they present. However, the biblical materials—along with many cultures outside the West—typically concern themselves with *illness* and *disorder accounts*. This is certainly the case with James, whose interests track well with the definition of *illness accounts*. His discussion reveals his interest in the health of individuals-in-community, in the community's health, in the potential relationship of sin and health, in the way community turmoil influences health, and in the expectation that the Lord will restore health.

83. This point is well made by Albl 2017, 431–33. My reading of this section of James more generally has also been informed by Warrington 2004. For an overview of approaches to this material, see Bowden 2014.
84. With these ruminations on healing, health, and health-care systems, I am dependent on Green 2013. See also Albl 2002.
85. Hahn 1995.

The priority James places on the Lord's intervention is very much at home in Second Temple Judaism. Reaching back into Israel's Scriptures, only rarely do physicians appear and, when they do, they are usually seen as negative alternatives to Yahweh (e.g., 2 Chr 16:12; Jer 8:22–9:6), offering worthless advice (Job 13:4). Israel's faith also rejected magic in favor of divine intervention and care (e.g., Lev 19:26–28; Deut 18:10–14; Ezek 13:17–18). The resulting scriptural emphasis on the Lord-as-Healer continues in the Second Temple period, but we also find some fresh developments.[86] In the literature of this era, we encounter a range of possible causes of illness: God, who causes illness in the service of his own purpose (e.g., to discipline or punish), divine intermediaries (e.g., angels or his Word), evil spirits (e.g., demons or fallen angels), astrological phenomena, natural factors, and sin. This literature also articulates a variety of therapies that could lead to recovery: faith and/or prayer, virtuous living (esp. effective for avoiding illness), exorcism, physicians (whether professional physicians or practitioners of folk medicine), and magical or quasi-magical means (e.g., amulets or magic bands). This variety is important for the way it calls into question those blanket statements we often hear about "what ancient Jews thought." Instead, we see references to an array of interrelated causes and cures (cosmological, spiritual, psychological, moral, physical, relational, etc., as well as combinations of these) that easily map on to the different ways a society articulates and practices its understanding of healing and health. When turning to a document like James, then, we must proceed on the basis of careful reading rather than on our presumptions.

Also of interest is the way divine action and human action were held in tandem in Second Temple Jewish materials related to health and healing. Writing in the second century BCE, for example, Ben Sira shows how wide the door has been opened to the work of physicians:

> Honor doctors for their services,
> since indeed the Lord created them.
> Healing comes from the Most High,
> and the king will reward them.
> The skill of doctors will make them eminent,
> and they will be admired in the presence of the great.
> The Lord created medicines out of the earth,
> and a sensible person won't ignore them.
> Wasn't water made sweet by means of wood
> so that the Lord's strength might be known?
> And he endowed human beings with skill
> so that he would be glorified through his marvelous deeds.
> With those medicines,
> the doctor cures and takes away pain.
> Those who prepare ointments will make a compound out of them,
> and their work will never be finished,
> and well-being spreads over the whole world from them.

86. See Hogan 1992.

> My child, when you are sick, don't look around elsewhere,
>> but pray to the Lord, and he will heal you.
> Stay far from error,
>> direct your hands rightly,
>> and cleanse your heart from all sin.
> Offer a sweet-smelling sacrifice and a memorial of fine flour,
>> and pour an offering of oil, using what you can afford.
> And give doctors a place, because the Lord created them also,
>> and don't let them leave you, because you indeed need them.
> There's a time when success
>> is in their hands as well.
> They will also ask the Lord
>> so that he might grant them rest.
>> and healing in order to preserve life.
> May those who sin against their creator
>> fall into the hands of a doctor. (Sir 38:1–15 CEB)

Among the many observations we might make of this passage, two are especially notable. First, with respect to healing and health, Sirach coordinates divine sovereignty with his endorsement of medical practitioners (e.g., Sir 38:1–4, 6–8, 12–13). Second, Ben Sira navigates among different causes of disease and, therefore, different remedies. For example, observe how he advises his audience to turn first to the Lord and then to "give doctors a place," to "cleanse your heart from all sin," as well as to submit to physicians, who themselves will offer prayers as well as their therapies (38:9, 12–14). The point is not that one turns to the doctor if prayer fails (or vice versa). The Lord stands behind the healing irrespective of the medical intervention envisaged. Nor is the point that one must address, say, both spiritual and physical needs (as though these were so easily separable), for this suggests a duality more at home in the contemporary West than in Ben Sira (or in James). When life is an integrated whole, healing and health must be approached in an integrated and wholistic way.

From an ethnomedical perspective, James is not working with a modern, Western approach to health focused narrowly on human biology—not in his definition of sickness, not in his assessment of the cause of sickness, not in his location of the site of sickness, and not in his understanding of the nature of recovery. (Nor does he identify the devil or the devil's underlings as agents of sickness and destroyers of health.) He works, rather, with an understanding of threats to health as *illness accounts* that might present themselves in a variety of ways among persons-in-communities and within communities.

James has little to say directly about the etiology of illness, but what he does say is important. First, his initial reference to sin comes in a conditional clause, "if they have committed sins . . ." (5:15); apparently, then, James does not assume that people who are sick or disabled are implicated in an autobiographical narrative of sin, even if he leaves open the possibility that sinful practices can be contributing factors. Second, in this letter he concerns himself with the health of the communities to which he writes, communities suffering from internal wars and fighting (e.g., 4:1–4); this leads to his directive: "Therefore, confess your sins to each other and pray on behalf of each other so that you [y'all] may be healed" (5:16a). Third, once we have associated illness and disability with the impoverished and demeaned (see above), we recognize the significant degree to which Rome's economic structures and Rome's conventions concerning status, privilege, influence, and favoritism together promote ill health for everyone other than the elite. Put sharply, then, James does not name biological agents or physical mishaps or even bad luck as causes of illness. Instead, his medical handbook features worldly systems that cast poisonous shadows over these messianists and have even infected messianist communities. In short, the relationship between sin and illness is not straightforward. The health of the messianic community is certainly harmed by the relational sins that appear again and again on the landscape of James's writing (e.g., 3:13–16: bitter rivalry, devious self-promotion, gloating, falsifying the truth, disorder, and every contemptible deed). Roman economic realities and the Roman world system have a deleterious effect on the long-term health of individuals and communities. But James is not invested in the view that an individual necessarily suffers illness as a penalty for his or her sins.

A brief inquiry into an account of healing in Jesus's ministry might shed light on important aspects of James's teaching. A few details differ, but the Synoptic Gospels each tell of some people who brought to Jesus a man who was paralyzed, lying on a stretcher. On seeing *their* faith, Jesus speaks to the man who was paralyzed: "Child, your sins are forgiven." After an interchange with some legal experts concerning the propriety of his response, Jesus speaks to the man a second time: "Stand up, take your mat and go to your home" (Mark 2:1–12 NRSV; cf. Matt 9:1–8; Luke 5:17–26). We find no hint that this man was paralyzed on account of his sin, nor that being forgiven of his (unspecified) sins was a prerequisite to his being enabled to walk. On this point, the Gospel accounts track well with James's presentation. We can identify other telling points of comparison. In the Gospel accounts, the evangelists draw attention to the friends' faith, just as James refers to the trusting prayer of the community's elders (Jas 5:15). And the Gospel accounts represent the man's recovery of health multidimensionally: he is forgiven, he walks, and he is returned to his family. Likewise, James refers to healing in its various aspects: the gathering of the community through its elders, forgiveness, and recovery of health (5:14–15).

The scene James paints is like these Gospel accounts in a further way, namely, by referring to the active presence of Jesus. This is obvious in the encounter of Jesus with the man who was paralyzed, but it is also assumed in James's instruction. The elders pray and anoint the sick "in the name of the Lord"; their prayer is qualified as "trusting prayer" (5:15), signifying both unwavering allegiance to the Lord's purpose and unwavering entrustment of the sick to the Lord's openhanded graciousness (see above, on 1:5–8). The Lord is responsible to "raise them up"; and the passive verb, "they will be forgiven," assumes that "the Lord" is the one doing the forgiving (5:14–15). Incredibly, those who, earlier in the letter, "do not hold the faith of our glorious Lord Jesus Christ" on account of their favoritism (2:1) are now called to exercise confident faith in God's purpose and power to bring recovery of health and, indeed, to trust that this power is available now in the name of the Lord Jesus.[87]

What James portrays, then, is an unbalanced synergy. On the one hand, Christ-followers have a role to play in the healing of the sick. The sick person summons the elders, not professional healers or holders of a special office but informal leaders of messianic communities, likely called "elders" because of their seniority in the faith.[88] They exercise trusting faith as they pray, and they represent the larger messianic community within which the sick find renewed health. The elders pray, anointing with oil—that is, olive oil, used perhaps because of its widely recognized medicinal role, though more surely because it signified placing the sick person in the Lord's hands and calling on the Lord to draw near with healing power.[89] James envisions, as it were, a community of healing. On the other hand, James leaves no doubt that recovery of health, in its many aspects, is the Lord's doing.

[16b–18] James uses a proverb to signal a transition: "The prayer of a righteous person is powerful in what it can achieve." We can almost hear his readers and hearers as they respond to his instruction regarding the sick: *Does prayer actually make a difference?* After all, are these not the people to whom James directed his indictment: "You ask and do not receive because you ask with bad intentions, namely, to indulge your cravings" (4:3)? Had he not warned them that double-minded people, like some to whom he addresses his letter, "must never expect they will receive anything from the Lord" (1:7–8)? For good reason, we might have the impression that these messianists sometimes pray, but often to no avail. Accordingly, James provides this proverb regarding the efficacy of prayer (5:16b), then introduces Elijah as a model person of prayer, a "righteous person" whose prayers are "powerful" in their effect (5:17–18).

Clearly, the force of James's aphorism turns on his reference to "a righteous person," for this qualifies whether a prayer is effective. James's use of the

---

87. Cf. Acts 3:16 NRSV: "And by faith in his name, his name itself has made this man strong, whom you see and know; and the faith that is through Jesus has given him this perfect health in the presence of all of you." Similarly, cf. Baker 2002, 56.

88. See Campbell 1994; Campbell (1993) provides a précis.

89. See Mark 6:13; Luke 10:34; Lev 14:12, 16; Ps 23:5; Job 29:2–6; Eccl 9:7–9; Sir 38:8, 11; Allison 2013, 759–62; Matthews 2009; Albl 2002, 137–38.

terminology of righteous (or just) earlier in the letter informs us here.[90] James instructs his brothers and sisters to "be quick to listen, slow to speak, slow to anger, . . . because a person's anger does not produce God's righteousness" (1:19–20). Like Abraham or Rahab, the righteous or just put their faith on display through their deeds (2:20, 21, 23, 24, 25). Peacemakers peaceably sow the fruit of justice (3:18)—that is, they align themselves with Jesus's faith and embrace God's choice of the poor. Consequently, their practices demonstrate love of God and love of neighbor. The righteous find that they are targeted for abuse by society's privileged, but they do not retaliate (5:6). In short, "a righteous person" is one with a single-minded allegiance to God and the Lord Jesus Christ, who therefore adopts patterns of believing, thinking, feeling, and behaving that grow out of and embody the faith of the Lord Jesus. The righteous could never be confused with the arrogant and wealthy about whom James writes. Their prayers would never be fueled by bad intentions but would be aligned with the Lord's purpose.

James immediately rejects any notion that, when he refers to *the righteous*, he is speaking of superheroes, as though his claim regarding the effectiveness of prayer were relevant only to specially endowed Christ-followers. He does not speak of next-level righteousness, but refers to the baseline for all Christ-followers. His model, after all, is Elijah, "a human being just like us" (5:17). The prophet is introduced as an exemplary person of prayer, a righteous person whose prayers are powerful in their effect.[91]

According to 1 Kings, Elijah was clearly remembered as someone who prayed with conviction and whose prayers were effective. This is evident in the story of Elijah and the widow of Zarephath (1 Kgs 17:8–24), in which he prays for Yahweh to restore the widow's son to life and "the LORD listened to Elijah's voice and gave the boy his life back" (17:20–22); and in the story of the contest with Baal's prophets (ch. 18), in which he prays for God to reveal "that you, LORD, are the real God" (18:37), after which "the LORD's fire fell" and "all the people saw this and fell on their faces," exclaiming, "The LORD is the real God!" (18:36–39 CEB). Given these powerful occasions of prayer, it is all the more fascinating that, according to 1 Kings, Yahweh chose to allow rainfall in the third year of the drought quite apart from any mention of Elijah's prayerful request that Yahweh might send rain (18:1). This detail underscores the reality that the withholding and sending of rain is Yahweh's doing (cf. Jas 5:7; Amos 4:7), not the outworking of some extraordinary power on Elijah's part. This accent on praying for God to act also recalls James's earlier claim that God responds to prayer with openhandedness: God "gives to everyone without a second thought, without reservation" (Jas 1:5).

---

90. See above, on 5:6.
91. I am borrowing from Green 2020b, 351–52.

Of the stories that might be told of Elijah, why this interest in drought and rainfall? The immediate context concerns prayer for the sick (5:13–16), but this follows immediately on James's advice that those who suffer ought to pray (5:13). Only a few sentences earlier, James imagines farmers who wait patiently for rainfall as an analogy for the patience of those who suffer in anticipation of the Lord's coming to bring justice. That is, among the choices from the biblical tradition from which James might draw, he selects this one about prayer for God to bring drought (judgment) and rain (life), thus adding to the bridge he is constructing from his audience's experiences to those of Elijah.

Even so, the primary building blocks for this bridge come from James's introduction of Elijah as "a person just like us." Effective prayer is clearly not dependent on the extraordinary nature of the one doing the praying. Concerns with human status are irrelevant. If Elijah can pray earnestly, so can everyone else—and so *should* everyone else. God is not moved by games of favoritism. Indeed, our author bypasses those stories and traditions that depict Elijah's astonishing deeds, drawing attention instead to that part of the story where we find an Elijah possessed of life struggles common to all human beings: "subject to suffering as we are because of the frailty of both mind and body," Bede observes. "For he showed that he was frail in body by asking for food from the widow of Zarephath; he made it clear that he was also subject to suffering in mind when, after he had restored water to the earth and killed the prophets and priests of idols, he fled to the desert."[92] He is a mere mortal, "just like us."

Of course, the opposite case could be made, too. If Elijah is "just like us," it follows that we are like him. From this vantage point, emphasis might fall less on Elijah's frailties and more on his capacities as God's servant, and therefore on the capacities we share with him. Either way, the emphasis falls on God's (not human) performance, and concerns with status and belonging (up, down, in, out) are made immaterial. Recalling the creation story again (see above, on 1:2–18; 3:5b–10—esp. 3:9, with its reference to "human beings made in God's likeness"), James underscores his view that the human family is privileged as bearers of God's image, with no one more privileged than the next.

James deploys Elijah as a means of encouragement to his audience, to be sure, but also encourages imitation of Elijah. This is not easy, given the biblical traditions of Elijah's exploits and his elevated status.[93] Accordingly, James urges empathy, attraction, and identification with the prophet in his introductory character reference: "Elijah was a human being just like us."

[19–20] James concludes his letter with a final reminder that he regards his readers and hearers as his siblings: "My brothers and sisters."[94] Once again,

92. Bede 1985, 63.
93. See, e.g., Mal 4:5–6; Sir 48:1–14; 2 Esd 7:106–11.
94. See Jas 1:2, 16, 19; 2:1, 5, 14; 3:1, 10, 12; 4:11; 5:7, 9, 10, 12, 19 (all AT).

then, he has chosen an address form that prompts belonging and mutuality, hopefully drawing his audience into the family portrait he wants to paint. In *this* household, we might hear him saying, we share such and such commitments: from his introduction (1:2–27), endurance amid trials, humbly welcoming the implanted word, caring for orphans and widows in their difficulties; more recently (5:7–18), patience and endurance, truthful speech, mutual confession of sins, and praying for each other.

Although his direct address sets this final, one-sentence paragraph apart from the preceding, James has certainly prepared his audience for his conclusion. On the one hand, those who know the traditions about Elijah will recall expectation of his involvement in the end-time restoration of God's people. The Lord is "sending to you Elijah the Tishbite before the great and celebrated day of the LORD comes, who will restore the heart of parents to the children and the heart of people to their neighbors" (Mal 4:5–6; 3:22–23 LXX, AT). Glorious Elijah is "ready for the designated times, to calm anger before it turns to wrath, to turn the heart of a father to his son, and to restore the tribes of Jacob" (Sir 48:10 CEB). John the Baptist "will turn many of the people of Israel to the Lord their God. With the spirit and power of Elijah he will go before him, to turn the hearts of parents to their children and the disobedient to the wisdom of the righteous, to make ready a people prepared for the Lord" (Luke 1:16–17 NRSV). The linguistic match among these texts is close though not exact,[95] but the tradition bears strong witness to Elijah's role in turning or restoring people to the Lord. In the shadow of the Lord's coming (5:5, 7, 8, 9), having just urged his readers and hearers to imitate Elijah, James now presents to them the Elijah-like task of encouraging those who have strayed to turn back to the way of truth. Supporting this connection of James's conclusion to what immediately precedes, too, is the continuing motif of forgiveness of sin (5:15–16, 20).

On the other hand, we might recognize a giant *inclusio* that holds together the beginning and end of James's letter. He begins by addressing "the twelve tribes who are in the diaspora" (1:1), intertwining an eschatological image of the restoration of God's people with an image of God's people exiled, making their homes and lives in the diaspora. Integral to this portrait is the temporal nature of the diaspora, according to which they are depicted as a journeying people, but also a recognition of the socioreligious threat confronting diasporic people challenged with the ever-present possibility and threat of assimilation and defection. Will they maintain their identity? Will they stay the course? Perhaps it should not surprise us, then, when James concludes his letter by making

---

95. James twice (5:19, 20) uses *epistrephō* (I turn / turn back). Mal 3:23 LXX (4:6 NRSV) has *apokathistēmi* (I cause to go back / restore). Sirach 18:13 has *epistrephō* (I turn / turn back); 48:10, *kathistēmi* (I restore). In Luke 1:16–17, Luke uses *epistrephō* (I turn / turn back) twice.

plain the image of a journey and the actuality of some losing their way, not just as a remote possibility.

Additionally, these closing comments comport well with James's overall interest in inter-relationality. Although he expends significant energy on addressing such challenges as poverty and wealth, for example, or speech habits, even these emphases serve his larger concern with nurturing the faithful life of the messianist communities to which he addresses this letter. Accordingly, his final words stress restoration to the community and, indeed, to God.

James invokes the conceptual metaphor LIFE IS A JOURNEY, an image schema that calls to mind a range of journey-related features—a road, a traveler, an itinerary, fellow travelers, a mode of transportation, obstacles encountered, starting point, destination, and so on.[96] The metaphor LIFE IS A JOURNEY maps potential ingredients of the embodied experience of travel onto more abstract notions concerned with life patterns. Some examples come to mind: a *traveler* is a *person living a life*, a *destination* is a *life purpose*, a *road* is a *means of achieving a life purpose*, and *obstacles* are *impediments to achieving a life purpose*. James's final sentence is lengthy, but even so it is not complex enough to develop the metaphor LIFE IS A JOURNEY fully. If we allow some of his earlier instruction to fill in a little background, though, we nonetheless find that this image schema serves as a valuable rubric for assessing what he has written.

Journey → Life Patterns of James's Brothers and Sisters

Note how James's language choices prompt images of the journey as a way of portraying the life of faith. He uses the term *path*; twice he mentions *deviating* from the path; and he refers twice to *turning* or *turning back*.[97] These last two language choices, deviating and turning back, are especially interesting for the way they track what happens when religious followers migrate from their community's central beliefs and practices (whether with a deliberate decision or, as might be more typical, through a succession of unselfconscious microdecisions that, when tallied together, eventuate in departure) and when those who have drifted from their community's central beliefs and practices return to them (that is, when they repent). In each case, movement *away from* or *back toward* continue the journey metaphor.

Destination → Divine Approval (or Disapproval)

In some ways, our grasp of the (final) destination of this journey depends a great deal on the entire letter, with its persistent interest in end-time judgment

---

96. Lakoff and Turner 1989, 3–6.

97. *Hodos* (way/path); *planaō* (I go astray / wander); *planēs* (wandering/straying/error); *epistrephō* (I turn / turn around).

and the certainty of the Lord's coming to set things right.[98] Even so, at the letter's close, James writes of "rescuing them from death." In this case (as in 1:15), *death* is more than the cessation of life in this world (DEATH AS THE END OF LIFE'S JOURNEY) but, as one often sees in Israel's Scriptures,[99] DEATH AS SEPARATION (from God, especially). This speaks to the prospect of end-time judgment, divine disapproval in particular. It also recalls that earlier chain of effects: cravings → temptation → sin → death (1:14–15). Other images help to fill out the picture, such as James's emphasis on divine approval: "They will receive the garland of life God has promised to those who love him" (1:12).

James holds out hope for those for whom death is the destination, that they will return to the way of truth and be forgiven.[100] This is the sense of the phrase he uses to characterize the repentant: their innumerable sins will be covered.[101]

Road → Way of Truth

Forks in the Road → Stray Paths

The letter's conclusion recalls its introduction, where James set out two "ways" (see the chart "Two Ways in James 1:2–27"). One is the way of human flourishing, maturity, and integrity; this comprises the road to an afterlife with God. The other is the way of useless devotion, bitter rivalry, and devious self-promotion; this comprises the road to death. The setting for both is the same: messianists distant from their homeland are experiencing trials as they work out what it means to live lives of allegiance to the Lord Jesus Christ in a world

98. E.g., Jas 1:12, 18; 2:12–13; 3:1, 6; 5:1–12.

99. E.g., Pss 6:5; 30:9; Isa 38:10–11.

100. Theoretically, the syntax of 5:20 leaves open the possibilities that (1) the one who restores the wanderer is rescued from death *and* has his or her sins covered; (2) the one who restores the wanderer has sins covered while the wanderer is rescued from death; (3) the wanderer has sins covered while the rescuer is rescued from death; or (4) the wanderer is rescued from death *and* has sins covered. The question turns on the antecedent of the second *autou* ("his," though in my translation "them"). Something like reading (2) or (3) would make sense if one is thinking of a background to the idea in the Lord's directive to Ezekiel, making Ezekiel responsible to deliver a warning to the wicked: "But if you do warn the righteous not to sin, and they don't sin, they will be declared righteous. Their lives will be preserved because they heeded the warning, and you will save your life" (Ezek 3:21 CEB; cf. 3:17–21; 33:7–9). More likely, though, *psychēn autou* refers back to *hodou autou*, supporting option (4); for further discussion, see Davids 1982, 200–201; McKnight 2011, 458–59.

101. This phrase is often traced back to Prov 10:12, where it matches the Heb. text (as with the NRSV: "Love covers all offenses") far better than the Greek (as with NETS: "Friendship covers all who are not fond of strife"). Most plausibly, the phrase comes to James and other writers (cf. 1 Pet 4:8; 1 Clem. 49.5; 2 Clem. 16.4) as an axiom rather than as a deliberate citation of Prov 10:12. See Pss 32:1–2 and 85:2 (85:3 LXX), where *sins covered over* parallels *lawless behavior forgiven*.

where Roman conventions act like a contagion, seeking to despoil relationships of all kinds. How messianists respond to those trials will lead them down different paths. One way, sourced by God's true word, by which messianists have been birthed (1:18), bears this name: Truth. The other, sourced in human craving and double-mindedness, bears this name: Death. These are not parallel routes. Rather, the one diverges from the main path and leads away from it.

The road to divine approval is the way of truth; the road to divine disapproval is the way that strays from the truth. This *truth* is not for James primarily a matter of right doctrine. Practical theologian that he is, though, he recognizes that the practical wisdom for which he calls embeds a range of theological commitments concerning the nature of the Lord and the Lord's work within the practices he encourages. For example, acts of favoritism counter the faith of the Lord Jesus Christ (2:1), God's choice of the poor contradicts the behaviors of those who dishonor the poor (2:5–7), and faithful endurance is possible because the Lord is the judge whose coming is near (5:7–12). He first calls attention to what is true when he writes of God's "true word, . . . the implanted word that has the power to save you" (1:18, 21). This is the practical wisdom that God gives, comprising the capacity to embody patterns of perception and performance in sync, or aligned, with God's ways. James's interest in what is true comes to the surface, too, when he writes of Christ-followers who falsify the truth (3:14). Clearly, James is targeting those whose patterns of thinking, believing, feeling, and behaving display their having strayed from the True Way.

Traveler → A Brother or Sister

Companion → Guide

James refers to travelers as "brothers and sisters." Obviously, he is not focused on Christ-followers one at a time. This is a family trip.

Without naming any specific individuals, he goes on to write of two kinds of traveler: "if any of you . . . someone . . . whoever." Both belong to the messianic community, but one "strays from the truth" and is a "sinner." Elsewhere in the letter, "sinners" appear in the company of "adulterers," enemies of God, and the double-minded (4:4–8). Their idolatry (making them "adulterers"), their failure to uphold the covenant with God (as "sinners"), and their wavering between allegiance to the world and allegiance to God (as "double-minded"; see on 1:7–8) signify their moving away from God and in the direction of death (1:15). The word "sin(s)" appears earlier in the letter as part of the life cycle of craving and death (1:15). And James explicitly identifies some practices as sinful, namely, setting aside God's Instructions (or Torah; 2:9–11), favoritism (2:9), and "knowing the right thing to do and not doing it" (4:17). Undoubtedly, though, the whole range of problematic behaviors he discusses would fall under the heading of *sin*, even if the primary sins that capture his attention center on those that counter the royal law of neighbor love (2:8).

The other traveler is one who "turns them back" to the True Way. They are fellow travelers, but one has come to a "Y" in the road and taken the wrong fork, while the other jumps into service as a guide. (And who knows whether the one who has strayed and the one who shoulders the mantle of guide today will reverse their roles tomorrow?)[102] Given the importance of Lev 19 to James's thought overall, and especially his summation of God's Instructions (or Torah) in Scripture's royal law, "Love your neighbor as yourself" (2:8; citing Lev 19:18), it is easy to imagine James reflecting on this role of guide in light of the notion that, as neighbors (fellow travelers) are responsible for each other, so they should reprimand each other (Lev 19:17; cf. Ps 51:13).

Of course, James counts himself among these travelers. He shares sibling relations with those whom he addresses throughout the letter. It is perhaps not too much to suggest that the abrupt ending of his letter shows how, with this letter, he himself attempts to turn back those who stray from the truth, to rescue them from death and to cover innumerable sins.

102. I raise this hypothetical question in order to distance my understanding of 5:19–20 from any notion that James envisages some messianists as designated sentinels or guards. He refers to "someone . . . whoever." These are brothers and sisters noted for their mutuality (see above, on 2:1), and no one has the special role or office of watchdog over the others.

INDEX OF SCRIPTURE
AND OTHER ANCIENT SOURCES

INDEX OF SUBJECTS AND AUTHORS